Kurdish Identity, Islamism, and Ottomanism

Kurdish Societies, Politics, and International Relations

Series Editor: Bahar Baser, Coventry University

This series strives to produce high quality academic work on Kurdish society and politics, and the international relations of Kurdish organizations and governments (Kurdistan Region of Iraq) both regionally and globally. The books in this series explore themes of contemporary relevance as well as presenting historical trajectories of the Kurdish populations. The series contributes to the rapidly growing literature on this topic with books that are original and make substantial empirical and theoretical contribution. The series' main focus are the Kurds and the social, cultural and political environment in which Kurdish issues play out. The subjects that we are interested in include but are not limited to: the history of the Kurds, Kurdish politics and policies within Iraq, Iran, Turkey, and Syria, as well as Kurdish politics and their impact on the international relations of the Middle East. This series also publishes books on the policies of the USA, Europe, and other countries towards Kurdish movements and territories, and interdisciplinary research on Kurdish societies, religions, social movements, and the Kurdish diaspora. Lastly, our aim is to contribute to the academic literature on Kurdish culture, arts, cinema and literature. This series speaks to audiences outside academia, and is not limited to area-studies topics. All books in this series will be peer-reviewed and demonstrate academic quality and rigor.

Titles Published

Kurdish Identity, Islamism, and Ottomanism

The Making of a Nation in Kurdish Journalistic Discourse (1898–1914)

Deniz Ekici

LEXINGTON BOOKS
Lanham • Boulder • New York • London

Published by Lexington Books
An imprint of The Rowman & Littlefield Publishing Group, Inc.
4501 Forbes Boulevard, Suite 200, Lanham, Maryland 20706
www.rowman.com

6 Tinworth Street, London SE11 5AL, United Kingdom

British Library Cataloguing in Publication Information Available

Library of Congress Control Number: 2020952454

ISBN: 9781793612595 (cloth)
ISBN: 9781793612618 (pbk)
ISBN: 9781793612601 (electronic)

To Xelîl Xeyalî and other contributors of the early Kurdish periodicals

Contents

List of Figures and Tables

FIGURES

TABLES

List of Abbreviations

AKP	Adalet ve Kalkınma Partisi (Justice and Development Party)
CDA	Critical Discourse Analysis
CUP	Committee of Union and Progress
KTC	Kurdistan Teali Cemiyeti (The Society for the Rise of Kurdistan)
KTTC	Kürd Teavün ve Terakki Cemiyeti (The Kurdish Society for Mutual Aid and Progress)
KTTG	Kürd Teavün ve Terakki Gazetesi (The Kurdish Gazette for Mutual Aid and Progress)
M.M. Bedir Khan	Miqdad Midhat Bedir Khan
PKK	Partiya Karkerên Kurdistan (Kurdistan Workers' Party)
SFL	Systemic Functional Linguistics
TIC	Teşkilat-i Içtimaiye Cemiyeti (The Society of Social Organization)

Acknowledgments

I would like to express my sincere appreciation to all those who afforded me the opportunity to complete this book over the past several years. First and foremost, I would like to offer my deepest gratitude and appreciation to Professor Christine Robins (formerly Allison), who continually and persuasively conveyed a spirit of adventure regarding research and scholarship. Without her excellent guidance, constant help, and encouragement, this work would not have been possible.

I am eternally indebted to my wonderful friend Michael Chyet for his suggestions and constructive criticism of the manuscript that improved the quality of this work. I am grateful to Professor Jaffer Sheyholislami, who provided me with astute comments and suggestions on the applicability of the CDA approach to the early Kurdish periodicals covered in this book. I would like to extend my very great appreciation to Michiel Leezenberg for his useful critiques. I would also like to thank my colleagues at Middle Tennessee State University, who during my tenure as a visiting lecturer, provided me with a suitable teaching schedule to facilitate the completion of this research. I am particularly indebted to Professors Allen Hibbard, who has been a fantastic friend, mentor, and colleague; Joan McRae, Mohammad Albakry, Sanjay Asthana, Clare Bratten, Ronald A. Messier, and Kari Neely. Moreover, I would like to express my gratitude to Professor Ilan Pappe, M. Emin Bozarslan, Tahir Baykusak, and Malmisanij for all their assistance and help.

Last but not least, my heartfelt thanks to my caring and loving family and my dearest friends Servet Tosun and Natsumi Ajiki for their encouragement and constant support. It was a great comfort and relief to know that they were always there for me.

Translation and Transliteration

The original languages used in the primary sources for this study are Kurdish (Kurmanji and Sorani) and Ottoman Turkish. The excerpts taken from the primary sources were translated to English by the present author, who has remained as faithful to the source texts as possible to allow for a meticulous and accurate close textual analysis of their rhetorical devices. The present author relied on M. Emin Bozarslan's and Koma Xebatên Kurdolojiyê's (Kurdology Study Group) system for the transliteration of the excerpts from their original Arabic script to the Latin alphabet.

As far as the spellings of proper nouns are concerned, if they have an established anglicized form, they will appear in the text as such, for instance, "Ahmad Khani" and "Mosul." However, they may appear as "Ehmedê Xanî" and "Musul" when they are in a transliterated Kurdish or Ottoman Turkish text taken from this study's primary sources. Below I have included the pronunciation key for the Kurdish and Ottoman Turkish alphabets to make it easier for readers to pronounce the original Kurdish and Ottoman Turkish correctly.

PRONUNCIATION KEY FOR THE KURDISH ALPHABET

The Kurmanji alphabet consists of thirty-one letters with eight vowels and twenty-three consonants.

Vowels

Table 0.1   Vowels

A,a	as in *car*
E,e	as in *pen*
Ê,ê	as in *fake*
I,i	as in *dim*
Î,î	as in *seek*
O,o	as in *boat*
U,u	as in *wing*
Û,û	as in *cool*

Consonants

Table 0.2   Consonants

B,b	as in *book*
C,c	as in *jam*
Ç,ç	as in *cheap*
D,d	as in *door*
F,f	as in *far*
G,g	as in *bargain*
H,h	as in a *head*
J,j	as in *leisure*
K,k	as in *kettle*
L,l	as in *lock*
M,m	as in *morning*
N,n	as in *net*
P,p	as in *poll*
Q,q	like Arabic ق *(qaf)*
R,r	r as *room*
S,s	as in *sad*
Ş,ş	as in *shake*
T,t	as in *telephone*
V,v	as in *victory*
W,w	as in *wide*
X,x	like German *ch*
Y,y	as in *yes*
Z,z	as in *zebra*

Chapter 1

Religion, Nationalism, and Power

INTRODUCTORY REMARKS

The late Ottoman period (1789–1918) constitutes one of the most critical eras in the Ottoman Middle East, marking the decline of the empire and the rise of competing national identities among various Ottoman communities. The emergence of new identities, coupled with numerous local and global factors, culminated in the formation of nationalist narratives and movements that eventually led to the breakup of the empire. This formative era, particularly the historical period around World War I, presented Kurdish intellectuals with an opportunity to construct a Kurdish national identity discourse, claim the status of nationhood, and perhaps set up their own nation-state in the ensuing years.

The Kurdish nobility lost its traditional power during the first half of the nineteenth century when the last semi-independent Kurdish emirates disappeared as a result of *Tanzimat* centralization policies. In the absence of powerful tribal confederacies in the form of emirates, the Kurdish tribes remained fragmented and dispersed. In this power vacuum, which led to a period of anarchy in Kurdistan, the Ottoman state neither allowed for the emergence of another strong Kurdish principality nor the formation of a new polity. Nevertheless, in the late nineteenth and early twentieth centuries, a group of nationally oriented Kurdish intellectuals, who had received European-style education and been exposed to European ideas, began to envisage a new Kurdish society based on European concepts of ethno-national identity and political autonomy. As the material expression of this nationalist endeavor, starting from 1898, this Kurdish intellectual elite, some members of the Kurdish nobility, launched several publication initiatives, including newspaper publication. This undertaking was an attempt to forge

1

a Kurdish nationalist narrative against the backdrop of the hegemonic discourses of Pan-Islamism/Ummahism and Ottomanism, on the one hand, and Kurdish parochial loyalties on the other. Several such periodicals opened a communicative space to negotiate, construct, and disseminate a novel discourse on Kurdish identity. Thus, not surprisingly, the formation of Kurdish nationalism as a concept and a political project began around the same time as the inception of the first nationally oriented Kurdish organizations and their publication activities in the late nineteenth and early twentieth centuries.

However, despite the various theoretical accounts in the historical commentary on the emergence of Kurdish nationalism, little has been said, particularly in Western scholarship, about the Kurdish intellectual elite's[1] publication work during the last decades of Ottoman rule. This has been the case despite the fact that journal publication constituted the driving force behind the formation of Kurdish nationalism in its early period. For the most part, an exhaustive content analysis of the Kurdish journals has been neglected or overlooked. With few exceptions, when the Kurdish press has been analyzed, it has been considered as a component of Kurdish political associations or subsumed under the general narrative of Kurdish nationalism and thus has not received the attention it deserves.

There are a few outstanding works, however, that have focused specifically on Kurdish journals. The most comprehensive of such account is Janet Klein's unpublished MA thesis "Claiming the Nation: The Origins and Nature of Kurdish Nationalist Discourse, a Study of the Kurdish Press in the Ottoman Empire." As the title suggests, the study provides an intricate analysis of the first Kurdish journals during the late Ottoman period. She examines how Kurdish intellectuals made use of Kurdish history, language, and literature in the production and dissemination of a unique Kurdish identity. Relying mostly on articles that appeared in Ottoman Turkish and giving space to a few Kurdish articles, Klein reproduces a number of passages taken from Kurdish journals and provides an in-depth analysis. The study concludes that Kurdish journalistic discourse from the late Ottoman Empire represents the "proto-nationalist" stage in Kurdish history as it could not go beyond producing forms of "Kurdism" "tinted with varying shades of meaning" in each journal. Martin Strohmeier's *Crucial Images in the Presentation of a Kurdish National Identity: Heroes and Patriots, Traitors and Foes* covers the late Ottoman period from 1700 to 1938 with a particular focus on the first Kurdish journals of the late Ottoman period. Similar to Klein's work, Strohmeier provides passages from the corpora of the Kurdish journals and analyzes them. He relies *entirely* on articles written in Ottoman Turkish, leaving out Kurdish texts altogether. Strohmeier asserts that because their demands could not go beyond linguistic and cultural reforms within the

Ottoman political framework, "it would be anachronistic to speak of Kurdish nationalism before World War I."[2]

From a different perspective, the works of two Kurdish scholars stand out as particularly important. M. Emin Bozarslan, who gathered and republished the collections of the journals *Kurdistan, Kürd Teavün ve Terakki Gazetesi,* and *Jîn,* presents a thoroughly researched account of Kurdish journals in the introductory sections of each collection and supplies invaluable analyses of the journals' contents. Besides, Malmîsanij (Mehmet Tayfun) has published several books on the intellectual activities of the Kurdish intelligentsia of the late Ottoman period and the biographies of those involved. Malmîsanij's descriptive and narrative works are wonderful resources for studying the Kurds of the late Ottoman period. Djene Bajalan has written extensively on the Kurdish intellectuals of the late Ottoman period and the development of Kurdish identity in the pre-World War I period. His argument primarily revolves around the question of whether Kurdish intellectuals were Kurdish or Ottoman nationalists, and the author concludes in favor of the second option.[3]

Further, there are several other MA theses on early Kurdish nationalism. Notably Gülseren Duman's *The Formation of the Kurdish Movements 1908–1914: Exploring the Footprints of Kurdish Nationalism,*[4] concerns itself with the gradual evolution of Kurdish identity in pre-World War I Kurdish journals. Duman, in her analysis, utilizes Hroch's three chronological stages in the formation of a nation. She concludes that the discourse of pre-World War I Kurdish journals corresponds to a stage between phase A and B in the form of "Kurdism," rather than "Kurdish nationalism." Finally, it is worth mentioning Hakan Özoğlu's *Kurdish Notables and the Ottoman State,* which also focuses on the activities of the Kurdish nobility during the late Ottoman period. Based on primary sources, including some Turkish articles in Kurdish journals, he analyzes the social, political, and historical forces behind the evolution of Kurdish politics. Özoğlu, much like Strohmeier and the others, situates the emergence of Kurdish nationalism in the post–World War I period, arguing that Kurdish associations and their periodicals did not go beyond cultural clubs and publishing as they stopped short of making political demands.[5]

These works represent interesting lines of research and they have contributed significantly to our knowledge and understanding of the inception and evolution of Kurdish national identity in the late Ottoman period. However, most existing scholarship—mainly Western scholarship—on early Kurdish journals remains inconclusive on some vital points for several reasons. First of all, the general literature on Kurdish journals relies almost entirely—in some studies exclusively—on a few articles that appeared in Ottoman Turkish, thus leaving out more nationalist Kurdish language articles from their studies. Second, they do not approach this material with a textual analysis from the perspective of a corpus linguistic methodology. Third, they analyze these early Kurdish journals in isolation from their spatio-temporal setting and the historical circumstances in which they were published. Fourth, these inadequacies are exacerbated by limitations in the theoretical concepts utilized to explain Kurdish nationalism; and fifth, their misconstruction of the nexus between religion, that is, Pan-Islamism, Ottomanism, and nationalism has contributed to misreading Kurdish nationalism. To sum up, the scarcity or total exclusion of the articles in Kurdish, lack of close textual analysis, oversight of relevant historical circumstances, theoretical limitations, and obstruction of the connection between religion and nationalism together constitute the underlying misconceptions in the relevant scholarship produced on Kurdish journalistic discourse. Consequently, a major common assumption prevailing in most existing literature on pre-World War I Kurdish intellectuals and their journalistic discourse is that they cannot be labeled Kurdish nationalists for two reasons. First, they genuinely endorsed and promoted Pan-Islamism and Ottoman nationalism instead of Kurdish ethnic nationalism. Second, as the publications of cultural clubs, they allegedly eschewed political demands and instead concerned themselves with basic ethno-cultural issues to articulate forms of "Kurdism" rather than "Kurdish nationalism."

Therefore, this book proposes to explore the construction of Kurdish nationalism in Kurdish journalistic discourse from the late Ottoman Empire by interrogating these underlying misconceptions. Contrary to the prevailing view in the literature, which portrays the corpora of the Kurdish press of the period as primarily Pan-Islamist or Ottomanist cultural publications, this book argues, based on empirical findings, that the Kurdish press of the late Ottoman period served as a communicative space in which Kurdish intellectuals negotiated, imagined, and disseminated an unmistakable form of Kurdish nationalism. Hegemonic Ottomanist and Pan-Islamist political thought were used in pragmatic ways in the service of burgeoning Kurdish nationalism, but were rejected altogether when they were no longer useful to fostering Kurdish nationalism.

The primary data sources for this book are the Kurdish journals published during the last decades of Ottoman rule. Some journals published during this period include *Kurdistan*[6] (1898–1902), *Şark ve Kurdistan* (East and Kurdistan) (1908), *Kürd Teavün ve Terakki Gazetesi* (The Kurdish Gazette for Mutual Aid and Progress, henceforth *KTTG*) (1908–1909),[7] *Yekbûn* (Unity) (1913), *Rojî Kurd/Hetawî Kurd* (Kurdish Sun) (1913–1914),[8] *Bangî Kurd* (Kurdish Voice or Kurdish Call) (1914), and *Jîn* (Life) (1918–1919).[9] To limit the data to a manageable sample, this study selected the three most prominent Kurdish journals as the primary sources for analysis in a comparative perspective. These are, in chronological order, the first *Kurdistan*,[10] *KTTG*, and *Rojî Kurd*. The significance of these three journals lies in the fact that the nationalist narratives developed in each corresponded to different stages and divergent forms of Kurdish nationalisms during three distinctive historical periods in the decades leading up to World War I. This periodization is based on the distinctive social, political, and cultural contexts for each historical period, marked by particular political paradigms, momentous events, and the general circumstances for both Kurds and the Ottoman Empire.

The Kurdish nationalist narrative within each of these historical periods seems to a certain extent to be steady, coherent, and even homogeneous. The first journal, *Kurdistan*, appeared between 1898 and 1902 as the very first clandestinely disseminated Kurdish journal to articulate the sociocultural and political demands of the Kurds from a nationalist perspective. This period was marked by the authoritarian regime of Sultan Abdulhamid II and his hegemonic Turkish brand of Pan-Islamist ideology. Consonant with state-sponsored Islamic Ottoman nationalism, for practical purposes, *Kurdistan*'s nationalist narrative incorporated notions of Pan-Islamism and Ottomanism from a Kurdish perspective, which will be discussed in detail. *KTTG*, on the other hand, was the first legally disseminated Kurdish journal, which came out shortly after the pseudo-liberal 1908 Young Turks Revolution, which brought the Committee of Union and Progress (henceforth CUP) to power. Noteworthily, *KTTG*, as the mouthpiece of its parent organization *Kürd Teavün ve Terakki Cemiyeti* or the Kurdish Society for Mutual Aid and Progress (henceforth *KTTC*),[11] articulated and negotiated the terms of Kurdish nationalism with the Young Turks and the Committee of Union and Progress through the seemingly fervent and secularist Ottomanist standpoint espoused by the CUP. And finally, during the historical period from the early 1910s to the beginning of World War I, *Kurd Talebe-Hêvî Cemiyeti*, or the Kurdish Students-Hope Society, started publishing *Rojî Kurd/Hetawî Kurd*, which coincided with the empire's humiliating defeats and extensive loss of territories due to the Italo-Ottoman and the First Balkan Wars (1912–1914). These setbacks led to another paradigmatic shift in which Ottoman politics came to be dominated by an increasingly heavy-handed CUP regime and its chauvinist Turkish nationalist ideology. Due to the new social, political, and ideological circumstances, which left little room for the utilization of Ottomanist rhetoric, *Rojî Kurd*—later on *Hetawî Kurd*—adopted a distinctive Kurdish nationalist discourse in which it articulated a more refined Kurdish national identity in the context of Islamic modernity. To sum up, the nationalist narratives developed in each of the three journals investigated in this book reflect different stages and divergent forms of Kurdish nationalisms that correspond to three distinctive historical contexts in the decades leading up to World War I. This book reproduces a great number of excerpts taken from the corpora of the Kurdish journals to refute these misconceptions by citing textual evidence.

Faced with intertwined meta-narratives such as Turkish Pan-Islamism, Ottomanism, Islamic modernity, as well as Turkish nationalism, during the final decades of Ottoman rule, the Kurdish intellectual elite attempted to produce an alternative discourse utilizing the printing press and other available discursive and nondiscursive resources. The printing press provided the Kurdish intellectual elite with the means to construct and disseminate their own nationalist discourse in the form of a counter-discourse or a *heretical discourse* vis-à-vis the hegemonic meta-narratives of Turkish Pan-Islamism, Ottomanism, and later Turkish nationalism. Therefore, the power-resistance relationship in the case of the Kurds, as a subaltern group, found its interpretation in this heretical, counter-identity discourse in the Kurdish newspapers under consideration.

CONTEXTUALIZING KURDISH NATIONALISM

Although in the course of its development as an object of philosophical and scholarly inquiry, many scholars have analyzed the "nation" as a concept, it is still one of the most problematic and tendentious political terms in academic scholarship as it lacks a generally accepted definition.[12] Although it is challenging to reify it as substantial and enduring collectivities,[13] this study suggests the following working definition: a nation is an imagined political community of people formed on the basis of a real or putative common culture, which may include common religion, language, and customs, common homeland, common political past (history), shared beliefs and mutual commitment.[14] Another major source of disagreement revolves around the order of causality between the concepts of nation and nationalism and which comes first. Broadly speaking, adopting an evolutionary narrative of historical continuity, perennialists believe in the existence of nations in the premodern period, positing that nationalism is merely an ideological tool and political movement produced by modernity for the realization of the historical rights of a nation. Although *new* nations were deliberately created due to the spread of nationalism after the French Revolution, some nations predated modernity.[15] The proponents of the constructivist/modernist paradigm, on the other hand, assert that both the concept of a nation and the ideology of nationalism are relatively new phenomena, products of modernity formed in the wake of the French Revolution. As such, both nation and nationalism are socially constructed modern phenomena produced or invented by the ideology of nationalism in the service of nationalist politics, with nationalism being the *prima causa* of the nation.

In contemporary historical argument, scholarly works have presented diverse theoretical accounts in an attempt to explain the origins and the emergence of

Kurdish nationalism. Some scholars from a modernist perspective subscribe to the view that Kurdish nationalism, as a modern phenomenon, emerged in the late nineteenth and early twentieth centuries, which corresponded to the social, political, and cultural developments of the late Ottoman period. Others, from a perennialist point of view, locate the origins of Kurdish nationalism in much earlier periods. Scholars such as Hamid Bozarslan, Abbas Vali, and Celîlê Celîl, among others, accept the modernist view, while Amir Hassanpour, Ferhad Shakely, and Jamal Nebez subscribe to the perennialist interpretation.

The theoretical assumption of this book, in line with the constructivist/modernist paradigm, is based on the view that nations are relatively recent phenomena concurrent with modernity and that nationalism is the *prima cause* of the nation. Accordingly, nationalism as a product of modernity, which emerged in the late eighteenth century, is essentially a conscious and organized ethno-cultural ideology and movement around a collective identity to attain or maintain autonomy on behalf of a community perceived to be a nation. Nevertheless, this work does not assume that national identities are entirely *inventions* or *fabrications* of modernity or social engineering from out of thin air. Instead, borrowing concepts from the ethno-symbolist approach, it suggests that although national identities are discursive social constructs, the selection and "reinterpretation of pre-existing cultural motives" and traditions—real or conceived—significantly contribute to the formation of national identities.[16] Consequently, a view of nationalism that benefits from the insights of modernist as well as ethno-symbolist theories allows for a more fruitful and compelling analysis of the issue at hand.

From an instrumentalist point of view,[17] even though the political and intellectual elite presents nationalism as the political expression of the nation, nationalism is strictly a political movement in the service of the elite, pursuing or exercising state power and justifying such power by using the rhetoric of "national cause." In other words, nationalism is an invention of the elite for generating mass support in their attempts to secure or maintain political power and prestige.[18] Consequently, any type of nationalism depends on the nature of power relations between the state, dominant elites, and nondominant elites. This instrumentalist approach to nationalism is a useful conceptual framework to explain the incentives for the Kurdish nationalist elite to promote Kurdish nationalism. As I will discuss in more detail later, the descendants of the Kurdish nobility who, after the centralization policies during the *Tanzimat* period, were excluded from the Ottoman power structure, saw in nationalism an opportunity to reclaim their former political power. To this end, they attempted to inculcate a sense of nationalism among the Kurdish masses and present themselves as the leaders of a nation in the making because, in the age of nationalism, authority was seen as legitimate only if it arose from the nation.[19]

The use of nationalism as the rational impetus for power was most obvious in the discourse of the journals *Kurdistan and KTTG*. Both journals clearly showed how the Kurdish elite constructed and reconstructed various forms of Kurdish nationalism following their own conditions of existence, that is, their personal and/or familial concerns, the nature of their relations with the state and the commoners, the ideological fluctuations in the empire, as well as the changing local and global power dynamics. In other words, the political aspirations of the Kurdish elite and the political future they envisioned were conditioned by historical circumstances, which in turn determined the form and expression of Kurdish nationalism in the Kurdish journals under consideration.

Kurdish Nationalism against the Backdrop of Ottomanism and Pan-Islamism

A major debate in the field of nationalism revolves around the nexus between religion and nationalism as to whether nationalism is intrinsically secular or religious or whether nationalism replaced religion as a result of the decline of the latter.[20] It is important to note at the outset that this book does not claim that the historical conditions which contributed to the development of nationalism in the Ottoman Empire were identical to those in Europe; nor does it claim that nationalism was a distinctively secular phenomenon that *replaced* religion, a fundamental misconception in studies on nationalism that has obscured the link between religion and nationalism. That being said, the historical developments in the Ottoman Empire suggest parallels with the advent of nationalism in Europe and its interaction with religion, albeit following its own unique patterns. In the Ottoman East, nationalism did not arise from the decline of or as an antithesis to religion; rather, the two concepts were closely intertwined. If anything, religion played a central role in the formation of nationalist narratives, as was evident in the nationalization of Islam by both the ruling majority nationalism of the Ottoman Turks as well as by the emerging minority nationalisms of non-Turkish subjects of the empire.

Ottoman Sultans and reform-oriented Ottoman statesmen became increasingly aware of the need to modernize and rejuvenate the decaying Ottoman imperial system in the face of the interventionist policies of the European colonialist powers, on the one hand, and the rise of ethnic nationalist tendencies among non-Turkish subjects of the empire, on the other. Modernization, as an imitation of Western sociopolitical culture, resulted in the declaration of what is known as the *Tanzimat Proclamation* (The Reorganization). In line with European notions of progress, *Tanzimat* introduced a series of reforms ranging from the military, economic, social, and political spheres to the formation of a new state-society connection based on new modes of political legitimacy and loyalty around the notion of *Ittihad-ı Anasır* (or Unity of the Elements).[21] In pursuit of this goal, the *Imperial Edict of Gülhane* (1839) and *the Imperial Reform Edict* (1856) proclaimed that all Ottoman subjects, regardless of their ethnicity or religious affiliation, would enjoy safety of life and honor as well as political and religious liberty and equality as *Ottoman citizens.* The two edicts introduced the notion of *citizen*, or *Osmanlı* (Ottoman man), and *Osmanlılık* (Ottomanness) as a brand of Ottoman *official nationalism*, which culminated in the 1869 Ottoman law of nationality. *Osmanlılık*, as the Ottoman version of civic nationalism, meant to integrate non-Muslim groups into the Ottoman citizenry systematically by granting them civil rights and equality, which was expected to inspire universal loyalty to the Imperial State.[22] The empire also embarked on a civilizing mission to cultivate peripheral provinces and their people and turn them into "useful" Ottomans.

Nevertheless, the notion of *Osmanlılık* as an integrative ideology proved to have a minimal appeal among Ottoman "citizenry," Muslims and non-Muslims alike, largely due to the state's concealed ethnic nationalist tendencies. Islamic and Turkish nationalist elements *tolerated* the existence of non-Turkish and non-Muslim subjects but never considered them as equals. If anything, the Tanzimat modernization efforts reduced non-Turks—e.g., Arabs, Armenians, Kurds, and Bulgarians—to the position of unreformed premodern subjects, while it elevated Ottoman Turks to the only civilized and "fundamental element" [unsur-u asli] of the Ottoman political system, which justified the latter's rule over the rest.[23] What is more, the increasing wealth and status of Christians, which became more visible by the 1860s, created resentment among the Ottoman Turkish elite, who felt that the new political setting was threatening the basis of the status quo in which the Ottoman Turks prevailed.[24] Reflecting the attitude of the Ottoman statesmen and intellectual elite toward the declaration of reforms, Cevdet Paşa wrote: "This is a day of tears and mourning for the Muslim brethren."[25] "Muslim brethren" meant none other than the dominant Turkish element of the Muslim empire. As a result, contrary to expectations, the Tanzimat notion of *Osmanlılık* failed to realize its goals, but instead created a breeding ground for ethnic nationalism among non-Turkish Ottoman subjects. It eventually ushered in the rise of nationalist movements, first among non-Muslims and later among non-Turkish Muslim constituencies.[26]

The Ottoman Turkish political elite's dissatisfaction crystallized in the formation of the *Young Ottoman* movement (1865) led by middle-ranking Ottoman bureaucrats and intellectuals. Despite considerable variation in their outlook on politics and society, these Ottoman modernizers vehemently opposed the imitation and wholesale adoption of Western/Christian thought and values. Although they were sympathetic to Western political institutions, they felt that their own cultural values could be used as a foundation for the modernization and progress of the empire; they proposed Turkish Pan-Islamism, an Islamic modernist synthesis led by Turkish nationalism.

However, Pan-Islamism only found its true manifestation during the reign of Sultan Abdulhamid II, who ascended to the throne with the advent of the first Ottoman constitutional period in late 1876. As a means of survival against the rising European colonialism and ethno-nationalist currents among Ottoman subjects, Sultan Abdulhamid II promoted what is known as Pan-Islamism or Islamic Ottomanism as an integrative ideology by fashioning a strong link between Islam and the Ottoman identity dominated by Turkish nationalism. Following his seemingly Pan-Islamist policy, Sultan Abdulhamid II, more than any previous Ottoman sultan, made extensive use of his title as the Islamic Caliph—which had hitherto usually remained dormant. In this way, he appealed to Muslim solidarity inside and outside the empire's borders to rally them around his anti-Christian/anti-Western sentiments and struggle against European domination.[27] His Turkish brand of Pan-Islamism depended on religious antagonism between Muslims and non-Muslims as a survival tactic in the face of European colonialism. His administration attempted to standardize Islamic belief through state-led religious homogenization, intermixing state and religious institutions, and associating loyalty to the Turko-Ottoman state with loyalty to Islam. The Sultan's Pan-Islamist policy, as the binary of the more encompassing *secular* nationalism of the *Tanzimat* period, did, in fact, reflect the new reality in which the empire was more Muslim both in terms of population and territory. The steady retreat of the Ottoman Empire from Europe resulted in the changing religious composition of the empire. With the loss of territories and the migration of Muslims from the Balkans and Russia into the empire, the proportion of Muslims to Christians within the empire had markedly increased. Thus, Sultan Abdulhamid II promoted the Turkish brand of Pan-Islamism or Turkish Islam as an integrative factor, a hegemonic tool, and "a colonizing instrument" to impose his authority as the protector of the Islamic *ummah* over the empire's Muslim elements. Eventually, the Hamidian policy of the nationalization or Turkification of religion resulted in the growth of nationalist sentiments among non-Turkish Muslims.[28]

Thus, I argue that as far as the nexus between nationalism and religion is concerned, nationalist tendencies among non-Turkish Muslims of the empire did not arise as a result of the decline of Islam per se, but rather the decline in the popularity of the Turkish brand of Pan-Islamism or Turkish brand of Ummahism. This decline gave rise to nationalist ideologies and movements among non-Turkish Muslims, such as Kurds and Arabs. Multiple factors contributed to this outcome: first, the rise of state-sponsored Turkish ethnic nationalism as the new hegemonic colonial identity that was imposed on non-Turkish Muslims; second, the standardization of Islamic belief through a state-led religious homogenization program, intermixing state and religious institutions to associate loyalty to the Turko-Ottoman state with loyalty to Islam; third, the waning power of Arabic as the sacred language of Islam and the imposition of Turkish as the official language of the state and education system; fourth, the weakening of the Ottoman dynastic realm against European colonialism; fifth, "Ottoman Orientalism" as a particular form of Turkish Islamic modernity that alienated non-Turkish Muslims.

Consequently, in the Ottoman context, it was not Islam or Islamic identity per se, but rather a particular type of Islam, that is, Turkish Islam—falsely presented as Pan-Islamism—that was declining among non-Turkish Muslims in favor of bourgeoning ethno-national identities as the new fundamental social units. Put it differently, Turkish Islam exacerbated ethno-nationalist tendencies among non-Turkish communities of the empire, who, much like the Ottoman Turks, adopted the nationalization of religion as a critical discursive strategy and practice to advance their respective nationalist programs. As far as the Kurds are concerned, the hegemonic power of Islam among Ottoman Muslims, coupled with the extensive use of Pan-Islamism by the Ottoman establishment as a strategy of manipulation, compelled Kurdish intellectuals to adopt a dense religious (Islamic) intertextuality as a convenient instrument through which they justified their Kurdish nationalist ideas. In any case, because the empire did not tolerate any ethnic nationalist tendencies among its non-Turkish subjects, the non-Turkish nationalist elite, including the Kurdish nationalist elite, had to subscribe to Sultan Abdulhamid II's Pan-Islamist political thought and ideals as a way to justify their demands and carve out a discursive space to promote their respective national interests.

As far as Ottomanism is concerned, after the 1908 Constitutional Revolution, the Young Turks of the CUP imagined a new state-society connection based on the notion of a more secular and inclusive form of *Osmanlılık* to embrace both Muslim and non-Muslim elements of the empire, similar to Tanzimat Ottomanism. However, their version of Ottomanism was also unable to achieve its goals because, like their predecessors, they did not truly believe in the egalitarian ideal of Ottomanism. For them, it was synonymous with Turkish racial identity and dominance. The Young Turks' Ottomanism further alienated both non-Turkish and non-Muslim elements of the empire. Nevertheless, during the initial but short-lived pseudo-liberal period following the 1908 Young Turk Revolution, all non-Turkish ethnic communities of the empire, including Kurdish nationalists, particularly those around the *KTTG*, incorporated this new type of Ottomanism into their discourses to avoid the wrath of the Young Turks, who were suspicious and intolerant of any kind of nationalist tendencies. As we shall see, this seemingly liberal Ottomanist policy opened a niche for non-Turkish nationalists to promote their own nationalist programs without provoking

Turkish nationalists' wrath. What is more, they also utilized Ottomanism as a discursive tool to prevent the rising Turkish nationalism from turning into an oppressive chauvinist state ideology. Since this pragmatist approach to Ottomanism and Pan-Islamism has been overlooked or analyzed in isolation from its historical circumstances, some students of Kurdish history have taken it at face value and labeled the Kurdish nationalists of the period as Pan-Islamists or Ottoman nationalists or both. However, as will become more evident in this book's analysis, both Pan-Islamism and Ottomanism were discursive tools at the disposal of non-Turkish nationalist intellectuals to promote their nationalist narratives even while seeming to comply with the meta-narratives of the historical period.

THE KURDS: AN OVERVIEW

Little is known about Kurdish history before the Islamic conquest in the seventh century. Nevertheless, the origins of the Kurds have been traced by many scholars back to Iranian-speaking tribes who migrated from Central Asia toward the western parts of the Iranian plateau, Eastern Anatolia and Mesopotamia at the turn of the second and first millennia BCE. It is believed, on the basis of geographical, linguistic, and historical evidence, that Kurds are the descendants of the Median tribes, who, together with the Persians, established the empire of the Medes (728–550 BCE) that stretched from Asia Minor to Central Asia.[29]

Kurdish, which belongs to the Indo-Iranian branch of the Indo-European languages, does not constitute a unified standard language. The speech varieties spoken by people self-identifying as Kurds can be classified into five major groups, namely: Northern Kurdish, Central Kurdish, Southern Kurdish, Zazakî/Kirmanckî, and Goranî.[30] These major groups, in their turn, are further divided into several subdivisions. As the speech varieties employed in Kurdish journals were limited to Kurmanji (Northern Kurdish) and Sorani (Central Kurdish), the focus of this study will be on these two major varieties of Kurdish. As far as the geographic distribution of Kurdish speech varieties is concerned, Kurmanji is spoken by Kurds in the Turkish and Syrian parts of Kurdistan; Kurds in the former Soviet Union; a third of the Kurdish population in Iraqi Kurdistan; and a sizable population in Iranian Kurdistan. Sorani, on the other hand, is spoken by Kurds who reside in the southern part of Iraqi Kurdistan and the central parts of Iranian Kurdistan. Although reliable statistical information is lacking, approximately 75 percent of all Kurds speak the Kurmanji dialect.[31] The Kurdish speech varieties are not necessarily mutually intelligible. The speakers of different dialects often have difficulty understanding one another due to differences at basic grammatical, structural, as well as lexical levels. Nevertheless, these difficulties can be mitigated if the speaker of one variety was exposed to another variety due to close contact over a considerable period of time.

During the last decades of the Ottoman Empire, Kurdish-speaking communities retained their ancient tribal organization under hereditary chieftains who were invested with Ottoman titles in return for military service. A Kurdish tribe was a sociopolitical and usually territorial unit based on real or imagined descent and kinship. Nonurban Kurds primarily remained a tribal society and were politically and militarily dominated by nomadic or seminomadic tribesmen led by tribal chieftains. Tribal loyalties often led to inter-tribal blood feuds and complex conflicts, sometimes over scarce resources including grazing land and cattle, and other times over military and political dominance. Conflicts between various tribal and sectarian groups, among other things, prevented the Kurds from taking collective action toward forming a state in the modern sense. Nevertheless, throughout their history, Kurdish tribes organized themselves around tribal confederacies where the tribes bound together in a pact to form larger political units such as emirates or principalities.[32]

As far as intra-tribe social structure and stratification are concerned, the hereditary tribal chieftains dominated over landless settled peasants or serfs who were not tribally organized. The intra-tribe hierarchy, assigned by the degree of power of the tribal chieftain, played a pivotal role in the formation of certain norms that determined social distance, interactions, and relationships between tribesmen and peasantry. So far as the ethnic perception of tribesmen is concerned, Bruinessen[33] has observed that the ethnic or religious roots of the tribes or peasantry were not central in inter- or intra-tribal relations: while non-Kurdish or non-Muslim tribesmen were treated as equals, non-tribal groups, be they Muslim or Christian, were referred to as *re'aya* (subjects), *Feleh*/File (for Christian peasants), and Kurmanc/*Kurmanj* (for Muslim peasants in Northern Kurdistan). Tribesmen referred to themselves as *aşire/Ashura* (tribe) or *Kurd* as opposed to *Kurmanj*. From these naming practices, it is apparent that the Kurdish tribesmen considered themselves to be the *real* Kurds while they labeled the cultivators or the non-tribal Kurdish peasantry with caste terms such as *Kurmanj*.[34] Interestingly, as will become obvious in the analytical chapters of this study, a discernible semantic shift occurred in the use of the term *Kurmanj* in the discourse of the early Kurdish journals when the journals referred to all Kurds as *Kurmanj* regardless of their social status. Moreover, as a powerful discursive act, they used the terms *Kurmanj* and *Kurd* interchangeably, transforming the meaning of the word *Kurmanj* from a mere peasantry into an ethno-national group that encompassed all strata of what they perceived to be the Kurdish national community.[35]

CRITICAL DISCOURSE ANALYSIS AS
AN IDEAL FRAMEWORK TO STUDY THE
KURDISH JOURNALISTIC CORPORA

This book adopts the Critical Discourse Analysis (CDA) approach for close textual analysis of the Kurdish journals to investigate the ideological function of language in the formation of Kurdish nationalism. It methodically and analytically conducts an exhaustive close textual examination of discourse samples from the corpora of three Kurdish journals "to unmask ideologically permeated and often obscured structures of power, political control, and dominance, as well as strategies of discriminatory inclusion and exclusion in language use."[36] CDA, as a multidisciplinary branch of linguistics, is a type of research mainly concerned with investigating the nexus between language, power, and ideology to give new insights into the use of language in the exercise of power, in the production, maintenance, or challenging of social and political domination, and the construction of national identities. To that end, the book adopts two major CDA approaches, namely Fairclough's *three-dimensional analytical framework* and Wodak et al.'s *discourse-historical approach*.[37]

Drawing on Halliday's trinity of *metafunctions*, that is, *ideational, interpersonal*, and *textual metafunctions*,[38] Fairclough developed what he calls a *multifunctional* view of the text in his CDA methodology. Fairclough's three-dimensional analytical framework is instrumental in revealing the systematic links that connect a text's metafunctions, which consist of textual analysis, discourse practices, and sociocultural practices. For Fairclough, the significance of *textual analysis* is that meanings are essentially realized in forms, and differences in meaning entail differences in form. Likewise, where forms differ, there also will be some differences in meaning. Thus, a text can be best defined as a semantic unit: a unit not of grammar and form, but of meaning, in which lexical and grammatical resources produce meanings via "complex sets of choices."[39] In other words, in a CDA semiotic interpretation, a text is viewed as a specific and unique realization of a discourse in that its language use is a deliberate structuring practice to produce particular ideologies in line with particular purposes.[40] The *discourse practice* dimension in Fairclough's CDA framework corresponds to the *interpretation* stage of critical discourse analysis. CDA assumes there is a dialectical relationship between a particular discursive practice and a social structure. Discourse and discursive practice are socially constitutive and socially constituted and, therefore, contribute to either the reproduction and maintenance of the social status quo or to challenging and transforming it.[41]

The third dimension in Fairclough's framework is discourse as a *sociocultural practice*. For CDA, language is a *social act*. As such, the meaning of an utterance does not only depend on *lexicogrammatical choices* but also on the particular nonlinguistic circumstances or extra-textual contexts of the situation, for example, social and historical circumstances, within which a text occurs.[42] In this sense, language use or discourse is a "context-bound social practice," and a complete analysis of language can be possible only when it is analyzed against the backdrop of its historical circumstances. Given the fact that social conditions regulate the speakers' and writers' choices, as well as audiences' interpretations, an utterance is both the *result* of and the *representative* of social conditions. As pragmatics suggests, to understand the meaning of the choices made is to understand the meaning of the social environment in which they were made and vice versa.[43] Then, it is fair to argue that in different historical moments, discourses produce objects of knowledge fundamentally different from one another.[44] "Historicization of the discourses" as such means things were meaningful or true only *within a specific historical context*.[45] Consequently, with socio-diagnostic critique, analysts have to make full use of their contextual knowledge to situate a text in the broader frame of social, economic, and political circumstances to make sense of it. This is because every text is conditioned by some noticeable aspects of historical circumstances, which a text either tries to reproduce, maintain, or challenge.[46] Thus, thanks to its sociocultural dimension, CDA goes beyond a purely textual analysis to study the "invisible meaning" of a text. It not only deduces context from the text, but it also predicts the meaning of the text from its historical context.

The Discourse-Historical Approach, as a branch of CDA developed by Wodak and other members of the Viennese School of CDA, is an analytical tool for studying "a large quantity of available knowledge about the historical and cultural sources as well as the background of social and political fields in which discursive 'events' are embedded."[47] Following Wodak et al., this work identifies the following set of semantic areas for a content analysis of the Kurdish journals: the discursive construction of a common political present and future; common language; common history and political past; common culture; common territory/homeland; and the discursive construction of identities and relations between the Kurdish elite and commoners. As will become apparent in the analytical sections of this book, this set of semantic areas not only allows for a systematic content analysis of the journals, but also reveals the diachronic changes in the Kurdish journals' discursive practices. Tracking such changes is extremely helpful when analyzing and conceptualizing the constant discursive shifts in the corpora of the early Kurdish journals. It is beyond the scope of this book to textually analyze each journal's corpus sequence by sequence in its entirety. Instead, articles or parts of articles that most clearly demonstrate discursive elements and strategies—and for that reason are the most significant for the analysis of Kurdish nationalism—were chosen for a discourse analytical approach. These include articles with such recurrent themes as a common political present and future, national history, homeland, language, literature, and national culture in the context of Kurdish national identity narratives.

NOTES

1. The term "elite" is understood as "people with attributes that qualify them to be ranked higher and accorded more prestige and respect than ordinary people. These attributes include being politically or administratively powerful, being rich or propertied, having a title or high official rank, being well-educated . . . and so forth." Whitmeyer, Joseph. "Elites and Popular Nationalism," *British Journal of Sociology*, Vol. 53, No. 3, (December 2003): 322.

2. Strohmeier, Martin. *Crucial Images in the Presentation of a Kurdish National Identity: Heroes and Patriots, Traitors and Foes.* (Laden: Brill, 2003), 54.

3. Djene Rhys, Bajalan. "Kurds for the Empire 'The Young Kurds' 1898-1914" (MA thesis, Istanbul Bilgi University, 2009); Djene Rhys, Bajalan. *Jön Kürtler: Birinci Dünya Savaşı'ndan Önce Kürt Hareketi (1898-1914)* [Young Kurds: Kurdish Movement before World War I (1898-1914], Istanbul: Avesta Yayınları 2010.; Djene Rhys, Bajalan."Kurdish Responses to Imperial Decline: The Kurdish Movement and the End of Ottoman Rule in the Balkans 1878-1913", *Kurdish Studies* 7: 1 (2019), 51-71.

4. Duman, Gülseren. "The Formation of the Kurdish Movement(s) 1908–1914: Exploring the Footprints of Kurdish Nationalism," Master's Thesis, (Istanbul: Boğaziçi University, 2010).

5. Özoğlu, Hakan. *Kurdish Notables and the Ottoman State: Evolving Identities, Competing Loyalties, and Shifting Boundaries.* (Albany: State University of New York Press, 2004).

6. The journal *Kurdistan* appeared three times between 1898 and 1919. The one analyzed in this book appeared for the first time between 1898 and 1902. *See*, Bozarslan, M. Emin. *Kurdistan (1898–1902).* (Uppsala: Weşanxana Deng, 1991). It should be noted that the 10th, 12th, 17th, 18th and 19th issues of the journal *Kurdistan* are missing from Bozarslan's collection, while the 2010 of *Kurdistan* by Kamal Fuad is missing only the 19th issue. *See*, Fuad, Kamal. *Kurdistan (1898–1902).* (Tehran: Bedirxan, 2006).

7. *See*, Bozarslan, M. Emin. *Kürd Teavün ve Terakkî Gazetesi [The Kurdish Gazette for Mutual Aid and Progress] (1908–1909).* (Uppsala: Weşanxana Deng, 1998).

8. Due to state pressure *Rojî Kurd* to change its name to *Hetawî Kurd* after its 4th issue. *See*, Koma Xebatên Kurdolojiyê [Kurdology Study Group]. *Di Sedsaliya Wê De Rojî Kurd 1913 [Rojî Kurd (Kurdish Sun) on Its 100th Anniversary 1913].* (Istanbul: Istanbul Kurdish Institute Publication, 2013).

9. *Jîn* (1918–1919) was the organ of the *Kurdistan Teali Cemîyetî* or *the Society for the Rise of Kurdistan. See*, Bozarslan, M. Emin. *Jîn - Kovara Kurdî-Tirkî [Life Kurdish-Turkish Journal]: 1918–1919.* (Uppsala: Weşanxana Deng, 1985).

10. *Kurdistan* resumed publication under the editorship of Sureyya Bedir Khan between 1908 and 1909. Ten years later, in 1919, it surfaced again, this time under the editorship of Muhammed Mîhrî Hilav. In addition, another journal, also called *Kurdistan*, was published by German missionaries in the Kurdish city of Mahabad in East Kurdistan during the period preceding World War I, *see*, Malmîsanij, Memehed. *Yüzyılımızın Başlarında Kürt Milliyetçiliği ve Abdullah Cevdet [Kurdish Nationalism and Dr. Abdullah Cevdet at the Turn of the Century]*. (Uppsala: Jîna Nû Yayınları, 1986); Elaeddin Seccadi. *Mêjui Edebi Kurd*, cited in Celîl, *Kürt Aydınlanması [The Kurdish Enlightenment]*. (Istanbul: Avesta Yayınları, 2000), 94–95.

11. *KTTC* was the first legally established Kurdish organization.

12. Smith, Anthony. *Nationalism: Theory, Ideology, History*. (Cambridge & Malden: Polity Press, 2003).

13. Brubaker, Rogers. *Nationalism Reframed: Nationhood and the National Question in the New Europe*. (Cambridge: Cambridge University Press, 1996), 21.

14. Smith, *Nationalism: Theory, Ideology, History*; Hobsbawm, Eric John. "Introduction: Inventing Traditions," in *The Invention of Tradition*, edited by Eric John Hobsbawm and Terence Ranger. (Cambridge: Cambridge University Press, 1983), 1–14; Gellner, Ernest. *Nations and Nationalism*. (London: Weidenfeld & Nicolson, 1994); Anderson, Benedict. *Imagined Communities: Reflections on the Origins and Spread of Nationalism*. (London: Verso, 2006).

15. Vali, Abbas. "Introduction: Nationalism and the Question of Origins," in *Essays on the Origins of Kurdish Nationalism*, edited by Abbas Vali. (California: Mazda Publishers, Inc., 2003), 1–13; Smith, Anthony. *The Ethnic Revival in the Modern World*. (Cambridge: Cambridge University Press, 1981); Smith, *Nationalism: Theory, Ideology, History*; Seton-Watson, Hugh. *Nations and States: An Inquiry into the Origins of Nations and the Politics of Nationalism*. (London: Methuen & Co. Ltd., 1977); Hastings, Adrian. *The Construction of Nationhood Ethnicity, Religion and Nationalism*. (Cambridge: Cambridge University Press, 1997).

16. Smith, *Nationalism: Theory*; *The Ethnic Revival*.

17. Breuilly, John. "Reflections on Nationalism," in *Nationalism in Europe: From 1815 to the Present*, edited by Stuart Woolf. (London: Routledge, 1996), 137–154.

18. Brass, Paul R. "Elite Groups, Symbol Manipulation and Ethnic Identity among the Muslim of South Asia," in *Political Identity in South Asia*, edited by David Taylor and Malcolm Yapp. (London: Curzon Press, 1979), 35–68.

19. Silopî, Zinar. *Doza Kurdistan: Kürt Milletinin 60 Seneden Beri Esaretten Kurtuluş Savaşı [The Kurdish Cause: Sixty Years of Kurdish Nation's War of Liberation from Bondage]*. (Diyarbekir: Weşanên Bîr, 2007), 28; Klein, Janet. "Claiming the Nation: The Origins and Nature of Kurdish Nationalist Discourse, A Study of the Kurdish Press in the Ottoman Empire," Master's Thesis, (Princeton University, 1996), 8–9; Janet, Klein. "Kurdish Nationalists and Non-nationalist Kurds: Rethinking Minority Nationalism and the Dissolution of the Ottoman Empire, 1908–1909," *Journal of the Association for the Study of Ethnicity and Nationalism*, Vol. 13, No. 1, (January 2007): 135–153, 149; Özoğlu, *Kurdish Notables and the Ottoman State*, 383.

20. Brubaker, Rogers. "Religion and Nationalism: Four Approaches," *Nations and Nationalism*, Vol. 18, No. 1, (November 2012): 2–20; Anderson, *Imagined Communities*.

21. Mardin, Şerif. *The Genesis of Young Ottoman Thought*. (New York: Syracuse University Press, 2000); Deringil, Selim. "They Live in a State of Nomadism and Savagery," *Comparative Studies in Society and History*, Vol. 45, No. 2, (April 2003): 311–342.

22. Zürcher, Eric J. *The Young Turk Legacy and Nation Building: From the Ottoman Empire to Ataturk's Turkey*. (London: I.B. Tauris, 2010); Azarian, Reza. "Nationalism in Turkey: Response to a Historical Necessity," *International Journal of Humanities and Social Science*, Vol. 1, No. 12, (September 2011): 72–82; Firro, Kais. M. *Metamorphosis of the Nation (al-Umma): The Rise of Arabism and Minorities in Syria and Lebanon, 1850–1940*. (Eastbourne: Sussex Academic Press, 2009).

23. Deringil, *They Live in a State of Nomadism*; Makdisi, Ussama. "Ottoman Orientalism," *The American Historical Review*, Vol. 107, No. 3, (June 2002): 768–796.

24. Islahat Fermanı was dictated to the Ottoman government by Stratford Canning, the British ambassador to Istanbul, *see*, Zeine, N. Zeine. *The Emergence of Arab Nationalism: With a Background Study of Arab-Turkish Relations in the Near East* (2nd ed.). (Beirut: Khayats, 1966), 82; Kendal. "The Kurds under the Ottoman Empire," in *A People without A Country: The Kurds & Kurdistan*, edited by Gerard Chailand. (London: Zed, 1980), 11–13, 11.

25. Cited in Şerif, *The Genesis of Young Ottoman Thought*, 18.

26. Kedourie, Elie. *Nationalism* (4th ed.). (Oxford: Blackwell, 1994); Göçek, *Rise of Bourgeoisie*; Akçam, Taner. *From Empire to the Republic: Turkish Nationalism and the Armenian Genocide*. (London: Zed Books, 2004); Türesay, Özgür. "The Ottoman Empire Seen through the Lens of Postcolonial Studies: A Recent Historiographical Turn," *Revue d'historie modern et contemporaine*. Translated by Cadenza Academic Translation, No. 60–2, (2013/2): 127–145; Zürcher. *The Young Turk Legacy*.

27. Only Selim III had used the title of caliph in a similar manner during the Russo-Ottoman war, *see*, Gelvin, James L. *The Modern Middle East: A History*. (New York: Oxford University Press, 2005), 136; Azarian, *Nationalism in Turkey*, 79.

28. Jabar, Faleh A. "Arab Nationalism Versus Kurdish Nationalism: Reflections on Structural Parallels and Discontinuities," in *The Kurds Nationalism and Politics*, edited by Faleh A. Jabar and Hosham Dawod. (London: Saqi, 2006), 277–306, 289–292; Gelvin, *The Modern Middle East*, 134; Zürcher, Eric J. *Turkey: A Modern History* (3rd ed.). (London & New York: I.B. Tauris, 2004), 79; Lapidus, Ira M. "Between Universalism and Particularism: The Historical Bases of Muslim Communal, National, and Global Identities," *Global Networks*, Vol. 1, No. 1, (December 2001): 37–55, 46.

29. Blau, Joyce. "Kurdish Written Literature," in *Kurdish Culture and Identity*, edited by Philip Kreyenbroek and Christine Allison. (London: Zed Book Ltd, 1996), 20–28, 20; Jwaideh, Wadie. *The Kurdish National Movement: Its Origins and Development*. (New York: Syracuse University Press, 2006), 37.

30. Haig, Geoffrey and Opengin, Ergin. "Introduction to Special Issue-Kurdish: A Critical Research Overview," *Kurdish Studies*, Vol. 2/2, (October 2014): 99–122, 110.

31. Blau, *Kurdish Written Literature*; Chyet, Michael. "Foreword," in *Amir Hassanpour, Nationalism and Language in Kurdistan 1918–1985*, xix–xxi. (San Francisco: Mellon Press, 1992).

32. van Bruinessen, Martin. *Agha, Shaikh and State: On the Social and Political Structure of Kurdistan*. (London: Zed Books, 1992); van Bruinessen, Martin. "Kurdish Society, Ethnicity, Nationalism and Refugee Problems," in *The Kurds: A Contemporary Overview*, edited by Philip Kreyenbroek and Stefan Sperl. (London: Routledge, 1992), 26–53; Özoğlu, *Kurdish Notables and the Ottoman State*.

33. van Bruinessen, Martin. "Kurdish Paths to Natio," in *The Kurds: Nationalism and Politics*, edited by Falah A. Jabar and D. Hosham Dawood. (London: Saqi, 2006), 21–48, 26.

34. Ibid.

35. Explaining the advent of Arab nationalism, Gelvin similarly argues that "[b]efore the 19th century, the term Arab did not have the same meaning among Arabic speakers the way it has today. Instead, the word was commonly used as a term of contempt by town-dwellers when referring to 'savage' Bedouins." Only in the nineteenth century did the Arab intellectuals begin using the term "Arab" to refer to their distinctive linguistic and cultural community, *see*, Gelvin, *The Modern Middle East*, 202. The word "Turk," in a similar way, acquired its current meaning only during the late Ottoman period. Because in earlier periods it denoted Anatolian peasants, calling an Istanbulian gentleman a Turk was considered an insult, *see*, Lewis, Bernard. *The Emergence of Modern Turkey* (2nd ed.). (New York: Oxford University Press, 1968); Zeine, *The Emergence of Arab Nationalism*; Makdisi, *Ottoman Orientalism*.

36. Wodak, Ruth. de Cillia, Rudolf, Reisigl, Martin and Liebhart, Karin. *The Discursive Construction of National Identity*. Translated by Angelica Hirsch and Richard Mitten. (Edinburgh: Edinburgh University Press, 1999), 8.

37. Fairclough, Norman. *Critical Discourse Analysis: The Critical Study of Language*. (London: Longman, 1995); Fairclough, Norman. *Media Discourse*. (London: Hodder Education, 1995); Fairclough, Norman. *Discourse and Social Change*. (Cambridge: Polity Press, 1992); Fairclough, Norman. *Language and Power*. (London & New York: Longman, 1989); Wodak et al. *The Discursive Construction of National Identity*; van Dijk, Teun A. "Principles of Critical Discourse Analysis," in *Discourse Theory and Practice: A Reader*, edited by Margaret Wetherell, Stephanie Taylor and Simeon J. Yates. (London: Sage Publications, 2002), 300–318.

38. Halliday's SFL, in turn, draws on Saussurian linguistics and the theory of semiotic systems. *See*, Halliday, Michael Alexander Kirkwood. *An Introduction to Functional Grammar*. (London: Edward Arnold, 1985).

39. Fairclough, *Media Discourse*, 57.

40. Wodak, Ruth. "What CDA Is About—a Summary of Its History, Important Concepts and Its Development," in *Methods of Critical Discourse Analysis*, edited by Ruth Wodak and Michael Meyer. (London: Sage Publications, 2002), 1–13; Fairclough, *Media Discourse*.

41. Hodge, Robert and Kress, Gunter. *Social Semiotics*. (New York: Cornell University Press, 1988).

42. Fairclough, *Media Discourse*; Wodak, Ruth. "The Discourse-Historical Approach," in *Methods of Critical Discourse Analysis*, edited by Ruth Wodak and Michael Meyer. (London: Sage Publications, 2002), 63–94; Halliday, *An Introduction to Functional Grammar*; Sheyholislami, Jaffer. *Kurdish Identity, Discourse, and New Media*. (New York: Palgrave, 2011).

43. Kress, Kress, Gunther. "From Saussure to Critical Sociolinguistics: The Turn Towards a Social View of Language," in *Discourse Theory and Practice: A Reader*, edited by Margaret Wetherell, Stephanie Taylor and Simeon J. Yates. (London: Sage Publications, 2002), 29–39, 34–35.

44. Foucault, Michael. "Nietzsche, Genealogy, History," in *Language, Counter-Memory, Practice: Selected Essays and Interviews by Michael Foucault*. (New York: Cornell University Press, 1977), 139–164.

45. Foucault, Michael. *Archaeology of Knowledge and the Discourse on Language*. Translated by A. M. Sheridan Smith. (London: Routledge, 2002).

46. Fairclough, *Media Discourse*, 57; Sheyholislami, *Kurdish Identity, Discourse, and New Media*, 156; Wodak, *The Discourse-Historical Approach*, 65; Wodak, et al., *The Discursive Construction of National Identity*, 7–8.

47. Wodak, *The Discourse-Historical Approach*; Wodak et al., *The Discursive Construction of National Identity*.

Chapter 2

The Journal *Kurdistan*

Kurdish Nationalism and Pseudo-Pan-Islamism

THE OTTOMAN POLITICAL LANDSCAPE
IN THE NINETEENTH CENTURY AND
OTTOMAN-KURDISH RELATIONS

To set the scene in which the journal *Kurdistan* appeared, this section outlines some of the most momentous events that shaped this historical period, along with an analysis of the sociocultural, ideological, and political context. To this end, I discuss historical circumstances under the despotic rule of Sultan Abdulhamid II, during whose reign *Kurdistan* first started publication. Next, I present a brief account of the journal's ownership, followed by short biographies of its editors, discussions of their politics, and an analysis of the social, political, and economic conditions for their journalistic activities. This section concludes by establishing semantic macro-areas for a content analysis of numerous discourse samples drawn from the complete corpus of *Kurdistan.*

Within the framework of the Tanzimat reforms, the Ottoman state, particularly under the reigns of Sultan Mahmut II (1808–1839), Sultan Abdulmecid I (1839–1861), and Sultan Abdulaziz (1861–1876), tightened its central control in the periphery to increase its coercive capabilities and hence directly extract additional taxes. This policy led to the gradual destruction of the semi-autonomous principalities in the empire—including the Balkans, Arabia, and Kurdistan—which created resentment among the members of the formerly autonomous dynasties who had enjoyed their privileges since the early sixteenth century. In Kurdistan, this bitterness culminated in a series of Kurdish revolts throughout the nineteenth century, which were violently suppressed. As a result, by the time Sultan Abdulhamid II ascended the throne, the Kurdish emirates had lost their traditional power and eventually disappeared.[1] Remarkably, even after the destruction of the Kurdish principalities, the Kurdish aristocratic stratum continued to play its leading role in Kurdish society and politics. In fact, it was the sons of these aristocratic families that became pioneers of Kurdish nationalism, and they spearheaded the first Kurdish nationalist organizations and publications in the final decades of Ottoman rule explored in this book.

Following the end of the Kurdish principalities, the Kurdish nobility was exiled to various imperial centers, notably the capital Istanbul. At the turn of the twentieth century, however, their descendants began to seek ways to reclaim their former power.[2] Efforts by Miqdad Midhat Bedir Khan (henceforth M. M. Bedir Khan) and Abdurrahman Bedir Khan, the sons of Bedir Khan Beg, the former emir of the Botan Emirate, represented an initial attempt by Kurdish elites to reclaim their former status. The Bedir Khan Brothers found nationalist ideology particularly appealing and the only realistic means to regain their family's former political prestige and power.[3] In support of this goal, they began to seek a place for themselves within the Ottoman political world as national leaders of the Kurds. Their Kurdish nationalist narrative first found expression in the journal *Kurdistan*, published on April 22, 1898 (figure 2.1). Their privileged access to newspaper publication equipped the Bedir Khan Brothers with a powerful and persuasive ideological tool through which they negotiated, produced, and disseminated a new discourse on Kurds and Kurdish nationalism.

The First Ottoman Constitutional Period started on December 23, 1876. Earlier that year, leading members of the Young Ottomans carried out a coup d'état that deposed Sultan Abdulaziz on May 30, 1876, and replaced him first with Sultan Murat V and then with Sultan Abdulhamid II, who accepted the Young Ottoman's conditions, including adopting the constitution written by Midhat Paşa. However, this victory was short-lived, as Sultan Abdulhamid II suspended the constitution on February 14, 1878, and thereafter ruled the empire as an absolute monarch. To justify his actions, the Sultan cited the threat of European colonialism (a.k.a. the "Christian threat"), the rising nationalist ideologies and movements across the empire, the defeat in the 1877–1878 Russo-Ottoman War, and the growing influence of European liberal currents. Seeing nationalism as a disruptive force, Sultan Abdulhamid II strictly banned discussion of all political matters as well as ethno-nationalist activities by non-Turkish groups, in other words, by Kurds, Arabs, Armenians, Albanians, and so forth.[4]

Despite these efforts, one of the palpable weaknesses of the Hamidian administration was its failure to instill loyalty in the new generations of Ottoman bureaucrats, officers, and intelligentsia, products of the Sultan's own educational institutions. This new breed of Ottoman intellectuals formed the Committee of Union and Progress (CUP), the first organized opposition group, in 1889. Influenced by Comptian positivism, the CUP saw order and

Figure 2.1   The First Issue of *Kurdistan*.

progress as the means to reshape Ottoman society "scientifically" in order to ensure the empire's stability and integrity. The term "union" (*ittihad*) in the CUP's name was meant to underline the unity of all ethnic and religious elements within the empire, analogous to the Young Ottoman notion of *Ittihad-ı Anasır*, or Unity of the Elements.[5] Soon after its establishment, the organization grew, and people from various ethnic and religious backgrounds, including Turks, Arabs, Kurds, Albanians, and Armenians, joined its ranks in a bid to bring an end to the Sultan's absolute monarchy and reinstate the constitution. To appeal to both non-Turkish and non-Muslim constituencies, the CUP proposed a secularized form of Ottomanism that allegedly embraced all ethno-religious identities under the banner of Ottomanism. These seemingly liberal ideals of Ottomanism, coupled with the sociopolitical realities of the period—in which ethnic secessionism seemed a difficult if not impossible option—provided the impetus for both non-Turkish and non-Muslim groups to subscribe to the CUP's version of Ottomanist ideas. They saw the CUP movement as an opportunity to defend their own national individuality and to advance their own respective nationalist agendas within an ostensibly liberal Ottoman political framework.[6]

Sultan Abdulhamid II adopted severe measures when faced with the increasingly open defiance of his administration. Members of the CUP were arrested, while others were forced into exile in Paris, Cairo, Geneva, Folkestone, and Athens. CUP members continued to confront the Sultan from exile via pamphlets and periodicals. Kurdish nationalists acted jointly with the CUP. After years of preparation, the first meeting of the CUP, or the "Young Turks Congress," was held in Paris in 1902. The Kurdish delegation included Hikmet Baban and Abdurrahman Bedir Khan.[7] It is important to note that while the Young Turks and the CUP espoused a rational Ottomanism, they also were firmly attached to a romantic Pan-Turkish nationalism, which they would express overtly following the 1908 Revolution.[8]

Bedir Khan Brothers: Patterns of Ownership and the Control of the Media

Media ownership is a crucial aspect at the sociocultural level because the views, concerns, and circumstances of the owner play a pivotal role in a particular media's discursive practices, which ensures that particular political views become dominant in line with the interests of the owners and at the expense of other views.[9] Thus, analysis of the journalistic discourse in *Kurdistan* should also include an examination of the circumstances of the individuals and groups involved in its production. Economic and political conditions are two essential dimensions of the sociopolitical context in which media operates. Given their profound effect, these two dimensions must be considered in the analysis of media discourse to determine: who has access to mass communication; in what type of political regime the media operates; what type of affiliations media owners have with the state and the general audience; what kind of relations the media tries to create between itself, the state and its audience; what motivates the media to participate in this process; and, most importantly, whose interests are being served? Does a medium's discourse reproduce the existing power structure, or does it challenge it? Does it constitute a substantive egalitarianism, or does it primarily have a legitimizing role in respect to existing power relations?

It is important, therefore, to understand the nature of relations between the Bedir Khan Brothers and the Sublime Porte. In the new Ottoman political situation, loyalty to his person became Sultan Abdulhamid II's overriding concern, which led to a network of royal patronage: the Sultan tried to win over Kurdish tribal leaders and the princely families of Kurdistan, including the Bedir Khans, through lavish gifts, medals of honor, and prestigious administrative and military posts, thus integrating them into the Ottoman bureaucracy.[10] Many Bedir Khans bore the title of *paşa* and served as public prosecutors, local administrators (outside Kurdistan), military officers, and judges. As such, they were on the payroll of the Ottoman Empire.

Miqdad Midhat Bedir Khan (1857–1915)

M. M. Bedir Khan (Figure 2.2), the founder and first editor of the journal *Kurdistan*, was born in Crete in 1857. He was one of the sons of Bedir Khan Bey, the last prince of the Botan Emirate. On graduation from *Mektebi Sultani* (Galatasaray Imperial Hight School), he spoke Kurdish, Turkish, Arabic, French, and Persian.

He assumed various positions within the Ottoman bureaucracy, including the positions of executive assistant to the attorney general in Ankara, Izmir, and İsparta, and attorney general in Kırşehir.[11] M. M. Bedir Khan and his older brother Emin Ali Bedir Khan were involved in an unsuccessful revolt in 1889.[12] Due to his anti-government activities in the following years, he fled to Cairo in 1898, a city that had become one of the safe havens for many Ottoman dissidents. Because of the British occupation that began in 1882, the Sultan's power was less effective and even nonexistent. In Cairo, M. M. Bedir Khan published the first issue of the journal *Kurdistan* on April 22, 1889. After the 5th issue of the journal, he returned to Istanbul due to the pressure and extortions by Sultan Abdulhamid II's administration.[13] Upon arrival in Istanbul, to keep a close eye on him, the Hamidian regime appointed him as the Sultan's second town clerk. In 1906, following the assassination of the mayor of Istanbul, Rıdvan Paşa, M. M. Bedir Khan, along with Abdurrahman and a number of his family members, was sent into exile in Mecca.[14] Like other dissident figures, he returned to Istanbul after the July Revolution of 1908. He was a founding member of *Kurd Neşr-î Maarif Cemiyeti* (Kurdish Society for the Diffusion of Education) in Istanbul, and together with his brother, Emin Ali, he participated in the Ottoman political system and supported the *Hürriyet ve Itilâf Fırkası* (Freedom and Accord Party).[15] During the short-lived government of *Hürriyet ve Itilâf Fırkası*, he was appointed governor of Dersim, but it is not clear if he ever actually took up the position.[16] M. M. Bedir Khan was also a member of the *Kürdistan Teali Cemiyeti* (Society for the Rise of Kurdistan) (1918), which sought an independent Kurdish-state.[17]

Figure 2.2   Miqdad Midhat Bedir Khan.

Abdurrahman Bedir Khan (1868–1936)

Abdurrahman Bedir Khan, the second editor of *Kurdistan* and the brother of M. M. Bedir Khan, was born in 1868. Like his brother, he was admitted to Galatasaray Imperial High School in 1877. After studying political science, he assumed the prestigious position of chief secretary to High Schools Administration, which he held until 1898. The same year, he left for Geneva to participate in the CUP's anti-Hamidian activities and to take over the journal *Kurdistan*. As the new editor of *Kurdistan*, he moved the journal from Cairo first to Geneva, then to various places in Europe.[18]

Abdurrahman Bedir Khan was in close contact with Dr. Abdullah Cevdet and Ishak Sukuti, two Kurdish founding members of the CUP. In an article published in the Armenian journal, *Nor Dar* (1900), Abdurrahman Bedir Khan is introduced as "an active Young Turk leader."[19] In his writings, he frequently referred to the CUP as "our society."[20] As mentioned above, together with Hikmet Baban, he attended the first CUP Congress in 1902 as the Kurdish delegate. He also penned two articles—one in Turkish and one in Kurdish—about this congress for his journal *Kurdistan*.[21] Abdurrahman Bedir Khan was closer to Prince Sabahattin's faction of the CUP, which advocated *ademi merkeziyetçilik*, or political decentralization, instead of the more centralist and Turkish nationalist faction led by Ahmed Rıza. It is also important to note that *Kurdistan* did not represent or promote the views of any nationalist Kurdish political organization as it came into being due to the endeavors of the Bedir Khan Brothers.

The Bedir Khan Brothers saw nationalism as an interest-serving response to the conditions of modernity. That is, the Kurdish elite, in the person of the Bedir Khans, was quick to react to the opportunities presented by this new ideology, because in the age of nationalism, the quest for political power was concomitant with the rise of nationalism, and nationalism was instrumental in justifying political ends.[22] In a similar manner, as this book argues in the subsequent pages, the Bedir Khan Brothers saw nationalism as an ideal concept, a project, and a distinctive form of politics to recover and possibly expand the traditional power that their princely family had enjoyed before the destruction of their Kurdish emirate by the Ottoman Empire. The same political attitude was true of many Ottoman-Arab notables who previously had a privileged position. Several studies on the political power of the Arab notables have found that their loss of privileged positions within the Ottoman state was the primary motivation for the emergence of Arab nationalism in places such as Syria.[23] After all, politics as the exercise of power is what nationalism is really about, even though nationalist narratives attempt to justify and legitimize the nationalist cause by presenting it as the political expression of the nation. In this regard, nationalism, as an ideology that had near-universal support, served as a tool through which local elites attempted to mobilize people and channel their energies to legitimate, regain, or seize political power.[24] However, the Bedir Khan Brothers' use of nationalism as a practical tool to restore their former power does not necessarily imply that they were not genuine nationalists or that they did not sincerely believe in the national rights of the Kurds. On the contrary, they had a strong sense of Kurdish nationalism as they started at an early age to develop nationalist sentiments under the tutelage of Haji Qadir Koyi.[25]

Production and Distribution of the Journal *Kurdistan*

The Bedir Khan Brothers were in close contact with the key members of the CUP, who supported their journal from the very beginning and particularly after it was forced to move to Europe under Abdurrahman Bedir Khan's editorship. *Kurdistan* was mostly printed at CUP-affiliated printing houses in European cities where CUP centers were based. For instance, *Kurdistan* and such Ottoman journals as *Osmanlı*, *Selamet*, and *Dolab* were printed in Folkestone around the same time (*See* table 2.1).

Although Abdurrahman Bedir Khan moved the journal *Kurdistan* back to Cairo because he could not bear Geneva's harsh winter, according to an article published in the 49th issue of *Osmanlı*, it seems that Abdurrahman Bedir Khan's financial problems, as well as Sultan's pressure on European countries to suppress the CUP and the other opposition activities, played the central role in *Kurdistan*'s constant relocation.[26] For instance, while the spies of Sultan Abdulhamid II intimidated members of the CUP movement in Europe, Ottoman ambassadors to Europe filed complaints in European courts against CUP members to deter their activities or even to have them arrested and handed over to the Hamidian regime. Moreover, as reported in the 55th issue of the journal *Osmanlı*, Sultan Abdulhamid II's spies and Ottoman state ambassadors put pressure on the owners of European printing houses to deny or terminate contracts with dissident Ottoman journals.[27] Consequently, because *Kurdistan* mostly depended on CUP printing houses, when the CUP centers or printing houses had to move, so too did *Kurdistan*.[28] Owing to relocation and limited resources, *Kurdistan* was unable to appear with regularity after the 5th issue. Meant to be published fortnightly, as indicated on the cover pages of the 1st–23rd issues, subsequent issues changed this notice to "Monthly Kurdish Newspaper" [Ayda bir neşrolunur Kürdçe gazetedir].[29] Nonetheless, there were times when the journal went four or five months between issues.

While there is no statistical data on *Kurdistan*'s overall circulation, we know that the editors sent at least 2,000 copies to Kurdistan, as indicated in the folio section of the journal. What is more, those who had access to the journal received it enthusiastically, as evident in a reader's letter sent from Adana: "I was astonished when I read this newspaper. I could not put it down.

Table 2.1   Journal *Kurdistan*'s Publication Dates and Places

Issue Number	Year	Printing House	Place
1–3	1898	Al-Hilal	Cairo
4–5	1898	Kurdistan Gazetesi	Cairo
16–19	1898–1899	The Society for the Union and Well-being of Muslims[30]	Geneva
20–21	1899–1900	Not Specified	Cairo
22–23	1900	Hindiye	Cairo
24	1900	Not Specified[31]	London
25–27	1900–1901	Not Specified	Folkestone
28–31	1901–1902	Vengeance[32]	Geneva

I called Kurds [Kurd û Kurmanca] and read it to them. They were speechless with delight. In a few days, they collected and handed me enough money to buy twenty issues of the paper."[33] Although the Ottoman state issued the "Press Regulations" law as early as 1864, state-imposed censorship was strictly enforced only under the Hamidian regime.[34] Therefore, *Kurdistan*, like the publications of other dissidents, entered the empire's territory through Syria and was circulated clandestinely.[35] Since *Kurdistan* and most of the CUP journals were small enough to fit into envelopes, they were also distributed via the Ottoman postal system.[36] Still, Sultan Abdulhamid II paid particular attention to the journal *Kurdistan* and its circulation. For instance, on March 30, 1898, the Ministry of Interior enacted a government order banning the circulation of *Kurdistan* in Ottoman territory even before the second issue of the paper came out. Moreover, according to correspondence between Ottoman officials, Kurds returning from the pilgrimage to Mecca were subject to a thorough search as they were suspected of smuggling in copies of *Kurdistan*.[37] Not only did the Ottoman state persecute the publishers, but it also targeted readers. A reader's letter from Diyarbekir reported the following: "The newspaper *Kurdistan* has been circulating in our country for the last two to three months. However, government officials do not let us read it freely; they take it away from us, and when they find it in someone's possession, they torture and imprison the person."[38]

In addition to state restrictions, from its inception, Kurdish journalism suffered from the lack of financial resources and limited professionalism. As such, early examples of Kurdish journalistic activities reflect the concept of *citizen journalism* practiced by part-time, nonprofessional journalists or political activists. Under such conditions, the Bedir Khan Brothers had to shoulder the duties involved in journal publication, including editorial responsibilities, correspondence, reporting, writing, typesetting, printing, distribution, and so forth, all without professional assistance. Most articles published in the Kurdish journals were editorials or opinion pieces—as opposed to hard news—that critically examined social and political developments in the Kurdish community and the Ottoman Empire. As a matter of fact, even the few hard-news items that appeared did so in an editorial format because the events were not merely "reported" but rather were presented from a particular personal perspective. The subsequent Kurdish newspapers also lacked many of the typical characteristics of professional newspaper publishing.[39] The same was true for the first Turko-Ottoman journals published in exile. The editor Ali Suavi, for instance, had to tend to every task involved in newspaper publication, including writing all the articles for the first Turko-Ottoman journal, *Muhbir*, published in London in 1867.[40]

Still, the greatest obstacle to the dissemination of the journal *Kurdistan* was the high illiteracy rate among Kurds, as the literacy rate in Kurdistan did not exceed 10 percent.[41] However, reading circles in coffee houses,[42] medreses (mosque schools), and guest houses/lounges (*diwanxane*) alleviated this narrow reader base as the literate would read newspapers aloud to those present.[43] Pictures published in the journals, as well as word-of-mouth transmission, were also effective in disseminating the journals' message among the illiterate. Nevertheless, these challenges, among others, prevented the journal from reaching a broader readership necessary to bring about fruitful results similar to those described in Anderson's notion of print-capitalism or Habermas's concept of the public sphere. In other words, it never reached that critical mass that would facilitate the spread of nationalist ideas among broad segments of the Kurdish community.[44]

THE DISCURSIVE PRACTICES AND TEXTUAL ANALYSIS OF THE JOURNAL *KURDISTAN*

This section concerns the close analysis of discourse samples taken from *Kurdistan* in terms of their content, themes, discursive structures, and formal properties, such as lexico-grammatical choices in the framework of the following overlapping semantic macro-areas: the discursive construction of a common political present and future; the discursive construction of a common language; the discursive construction of shared history and political past; the discursive construction of collective culture; the discursive construction of a national body; and the discursive construction of identities and relations between the Kurdish elite and commoners.[45]

Journal *Kurdistan* under Sultan Abdulhamid II and His Turkish Brand of Pan-Islamism

This semantic macro-area will explore the common political present and future of the Kurds around such themes as contemporary sociopolitical problems and their implications for future political achievements, crises and dangers, future political objectives, and so forth. Seeing themselves as the custodians of the Kurds, the editors of *Kurdistan* took the responsibility upon themselves to determine what constituted social, cultural, political, and national problems by making reference to the common worries and possible solutions and their implications for the future of the Kurdish community as a distinctive ethno-national community. Some of the essential issues and problems identified by *Kurdistan* that are relevant to this analysis includes matters related to the ethnic domination of the Turks over the Kurds; Ottoman state officials' unjust treatment and ethnic discrimination directed against Kurds; the notion of Pan-Islamism/Ummahism, and Ottomanism among the Kurds; the political future of the Kurds and Kurdistan; the lack of modernization/Westernization among Kurds and the industrialization of Kurdistan; education and literacy; the lack of unity and inter-tribal rivalries; Kurds' deteriorating relations with and hostilities toward Armenians; among others. Although *Kurdistan* problematized various other issues that were not exclusively Kurdish concerns but common to all Muslims and the Ottoman state, the journal still distinguished itself by addressing these issues from a nationally oriented Kurdish perspective.[46] Hence, analysis at this level is most revealing for the politics of *Kurdistan* in terms of the journal's assessment of the political situation and the course of action it envisaged for the collective present and future of the Kurds.

It should be emphasized at the outset that under the impetus of the era's fast-changing social and political realities, the discursive practices of *Kurdistan* pertinent to the collective political present and future of the Kurds remained ambiguous for the most part, as the politics of journal oscillated between Pan-Islamism/Ummahism as a mode of identification, on the one hand, and a secessionist, statist Kurdish nationalism on the other. That is, in an essentially pragmatic manner, *Kurdistan* adopted different ideological characters and courses of action that corresponded to different sociocultural and political instances and historical contexts. What is more, they did not shy away from playing both sides by also cooperating with the CUP. That is, the editors of *Kurdistan*, but notably Abdurrahman Bedir Khan, hedged their bets and maintained contacts with both the Sultan and the CUP, in part because it did not matter to them who controlled the empire as long as they could cut a deal with the state on behalf of the Kurds. Usually, both editors of *Kurdistan* refrained from criticizing or opposing the Sultan and the state directly and instead tried to ally themselves with both. Despite their close relations with the CUP, in most of their open letters to the Sultan, the editors of *Kurdistan* often praised and even defended Abdulhamid II against criticism and pinned the blame for administrative misconduct against Kurds on Ottoman statesmen and officials. M. M. Bedir Khan went so far as to suggest that he could change the content of his journal following the Sultan's wish if the state removed the restrictions on the distribution of his journal. This was expressed in the following two excerpts from the 4th and 5th issues: "in fact, as there is nothing harmful in its content, it is possible to make its content more compatible with the noble government's views and desires"[47] and "as was stated in my first humble petition submitted previously, since it is possible to publish my newspaper in a manner that your noble government would see fit."[48]

Religious Intertextuality in Kurdistan's *Nationalist Discourse*

In an attempt to counter the impact of interventionist European colonialism as well as the strong liberal and ethno-nationalist currents within the empire, Sultan Abdulhamid II nationalized Islam by fashioning a strong link between Islam and Ottoman Turkish imperial identity, which can be regarded as an Ottoman Turkish Pan-Islamism. This particular brand of Ottoman Turkish religious nationalism was an integrative ideology that replaced the seemingly secularized Ottomanism of the *Tanzimat* period. Sultan Abdulhamid II's use of Islam or Pan-Islamism as an ideological tool against nationalist sentiment constituted a major reason that *Kurdistan* made extensive use of religious nationalism by way of religious intertextuality, that is, the use of Islam and Islamic references in its Kurdish nationalist discourse. This endeavor on the part of the Bedir Khan Brothers was meant to counter the Sultan's Pan-Islamist strategy, which appealed to the religious Kurdish constituency. By adopting religious intertextuality in their discourse on Kurdish nationalism, the Bedir Khan Brothers did not only confirm with state-sponsored notions of Ottoman Pan-Islamism, but they also used the same approach to address the predominantly socially and religiously conservative Sunni Muslim Kurdish society. Thus, it is fair to argue that during this historical period, *Kurdistan* used religious intertextuality by means of religious allusion for novel needs.

Consequently, the editors of *Kurdistan* promoted Kurdish nationalist ideas as well as the modernization/Westernization and progress of the Kurdish society in a religiously tinged language. For these reasons, almost everything *Kurdistan* stood for was justified through Islamic religious intertextuality, either by citing a relevant hadith or Qur'anic verse.[49] Education, for instance, was presented as a religious virtue because hadiths and Qur'anic verses said so; literacy was necessary to be able to say one's prayers. Inter-tribal disputes were "evil" because all Muslims were brothers. Progress in science and technology was desirable because, in this manner, Kurds could serve not only their own community but also the wider Islamic ummah in a better capacity. Kurds had to improve their combat skills and abilities to face the "infidel" Russians, and so forth.

In one article suggestively entitled "Al Mu'minun Ikhwatun" (All Believers Are Brothers), Abdurrahman Bedir Khan wrote: "O ulema of Kurds! . . . I feel sorry [that] I have come across Kurds [Kurmanca] [who] cannot even recite the verses of Qur'an to say their prayers; this is a sin [guneh] for all of us."[50] Although in this dense and manifest religious intertextuality, the editor's primary concern was underlining the lack of literacy, he painstakingly drew the audience's attention to the fact that they could not practice their religion without literacy, the lack of which was presented as a sin (*guneh*). In reality, however, one does not need schooling or even literacy to learn Qur'anic verses to say the prayers, as many illiterate Muslims simply memorize them. The title of the article, which is a verse from the Qur'an, reinforces the author's religious argument.

In the same vein, M. M. Bedir Khan wrote:

O ulema and mîrs and aghas of Kurds! [. . .] for God's sake [ji xêra Xwedê], take action, educate Kurds, teach your children the sciences, literature, and the arts. Muslim people should be educated; they should learn their religion [. . .] From now on, I expect from the ulema of the Kurds to read this newspaper of mine to the mîrs and aghas and Kurds [Kurmanca], and explain to them what Almighty God and His Excellency the Prophet, may peace be upon him, have commanded.[51]

Clearly, education and literacy are presented as essential parts of religion and religious duties, as the editor urges Muslim Kurds to educate themselves *merely* "for the sake of God" and his Prophet to become good Muslims. Here, the editor transformed the voice of *Kurdistan* into the voice of Islam, in that, the voice of the journal and that of the faith were intermingled. Conveying his message via the voice of God and the Prophet is meant to aggrandize and glorify his own voice: the voice of *redemption*. Abdurrahman Bedir Khan reinforced this point in the 9th issue when he wrote: "All the things that I am writing in this newspaper are the things that have been commanded by God and the Prophet. The thing that is commanded by God and practiced by the Prophet, without a doubt, is for your benefit."[52] Again, the editor attempted to transform the sacred and authoritative voice of religion into the voice of the journal as if God and the Prophet were speaking through the journal *Kurdistan* or as if the journal itself is the voice of God and the Prophet. This impression, in turn, is meant to transform the message of *Kurdistan* into an authoritative divine text, which is intended to convince the Kurdish masses to become literate as a first step toward the type of modernization and Westernization that the authors envisaged.

Hostilities between Kurds and Armenians were another realm where the journal made recourse to religious forms of nationalism via religious intertextuality to persuade Kurds not to attack the Armenians. In one article, Abdurrahman Bedir Khan asserted:

Instead of coming to the help of the oppressed [mezlûm] Armenians, you kill them. This is a very *sinful* situation [Ew hal gelek *guneh* e], and it is a great disgrace. God and the Prophet do not approve of this situation. Almighty God has commanded in His book: "We izzi we jalali ilkh [ilaakhirihi]," which means, I swear on my greatness and glory that I will revenge those who see an oppressed person but do not help.[53]

In this manifest intertextuality,[54] the religious texts—a hadith and a Qur'anic verse—are overtly present in the form of the words of the Prophet and God. Besides, the editor labeled Kurdish antagonism toward Armenians as *sinful* acts to render a more convincing argument from a religious perspective.

Although it does not necessarily mean that they were not religious, it should be noted that neither of the editors was particularly devout and that *Kurdistan* was in no obvious sense religious, insofar as it did not propagate religion for the sake of religion. The editors might have simply wished to preserve the essence of their Islamic heritage and religious traditions. But what is evident is that their religiously tinged language and their constant use of religious intertextuality—or the instrumental use of Islam—was part of their *strategy of persuasion and manipulation*. This supplemented and backed up their profane and modernist views and nationalist arguments that were quite foreign to Islam and Muslim Kurds. They simply utilized religion as a way of framing political claims, as an instrument to promote Kurdish nationalism and the modern needs of the Kurds through the Holy Scripture and the hadith. In any case, in an Islamic society, political leaders and intellectuals have generally found it wise to profess and sponsor religion regardless of the depth of their own belief and commitment. This practice justifies and legitimizes their authority because authority is seen as legitimate when it is supplemented by religious rhetoric.[55] Analogously, the Bedir Khan Brothers resorted to religion as the rhetorical form for their politico-nationalist claims. If the journal *Kurdistan* were isolated from its nationalist nature, its corpus would resemble a collection of leaflets or a propaganda tool that encouraged literacy and education for purely religious purposes. However, in *Kurdistan*, the editors did not make any claims about ordering and regulating public life in a manner that conformed with religious principles. In intertextuality, "it is not just a matter of which other texts you refer to, but how you use them, what you use them for, and ultimately how you position yourself as a writer to them to make your own statement."[56] Comparably, when *Kurdistan* made use of other texts, for example, religious texts, the editors adopted a particular attitude as they commented and evaluated the original text in a new—modernist and nationalist—context. Thereby they used other texts in the service of novel social, cultural, and political ends, that is, the progress of the Kurdish community as a nation in the age of nations. What is more, Abdurrahman Bedir Khan, a Western-oriented intellectual, who received a secular education in Istanbul, worked to undermine the authority of the Sultan Abdulhamid

II, the caliph of Islam. More importantly, Abdurrahman Bedir Khan married Elisabeth-Eugénie van Muyden, a member of the Genevan aristocracy, who did not convert to Islam even after their marriage. She converted to Islam only in 1940 and changed her name to "Emel" simply to be buried next to her husband as only Muslims were allowed to be buried in a Muslim cemetery.[57]

As far as the concept of *Ottomanism* is concerned, although as I argue later, Kurdish intellectuals' ostensible Ottomanist stance found its true manifestation in the discourse of *Kürd Teavün ve Terakki Gazetesi* (*KTTG*), the journal *Kurdistan* also blended Ottomanism—albeit a more Islamic version of it— into its discourse. For instance, one of the political issues of the day that was problematized frequently by *Kurdistan* was the Russian threat on the eastern borders of the empire, that is, Kurdistan. In the very first open letter to the Sultan,[58] M. M. Bedir Khan underscored the strategic location of Kurdistan as a vulnerable Ottoman territory in the east. He urged the Sultan to improve the situation of the Kurds so that they could defend the empire's eastern borders, allegedly one of the goals of the Ottoman reform and modernization project since the Tanzimat.[59] He wrote:

> My Padishah,
>
> As your Excellency knows, the Kurds are the most distinguished of all the people [akvam] that compose your Ottoman empire, which will live forever; and as Kurdistan is located on the borders of two neighbouring states, [Kurds] can prevent any attack on Anatolia and even have the ability to threaten the enemy from that direction; although Kurds have long occupied an important place in the [Ottoman] political realm and have been proud Ottomans, somehow the means and methods that would enable Kurds to receive education and instructions were neglected until you, the Padishah, ascended the throne.[60]

Regardless of whether Russian ambitions posed a formidable threat to the Ottoman state's integrity, the primary objective of the letter is the consolidation and empowerment of the Kurds by exploiting this real or putative threat and the presentation of the Kurds as the only viable option to oppose Russian aggression.[61] Especially when read in the context of the journal's entire corpus, the exploitation of the danger posed by Russia becomes more evident, given the fact that presenting Russia as the *other* was a discursive act to convince the Sultan to improve Kurdistan. At the same time, the editor probably aimed at persuading Muslim Kurds to improve themselves against such a *Christian threat*. Hence, the message was meant not only for the Sultan's ears but also for the Kurds. In any case, memories of the destructive Russo-Turkish War of 1877–1878 were still vivid in Kurdish minds.[62] In this context, it is also interesting to see that subsequent Kurdish journals never expressed any particular concern about Russia, even though Russia did remain one of the states hostile to the Ottoman Empire, particularly Ottoman Kurdistan. More importantly, it should not go unnoticed how in his letter, M. M. Bedir Khan reassuringly presented the Kurds as loyal Ottomans and Kurdistan as an extension of Ottoman lands as a means to put the Sultan's mind at ease by leaving no room for any suspicions about Kurdish nationalist aspirations or *Kurdistan*'s nationalist intentions. In this particular representation of the Kurds and Kurdistan, the political present and future of the Kurds were linked to the present and future of the Ottoman state.

In several other articles, M. M. Bedir Khan and Abdurrahman Bedir Khan tried to further consolidate their argument about the Ottoman identity of the Kurds and their loyalty to the state to secure the Sultan's support for the modernization of the Kurdish community. Appealing to the Sultan for the free circulation of the journal *Kurdistan*, M. M. Bedir Khan wrote: "if such a journal existed ten years ago, the *foreigners* [ecanibi] would not have been able to cause chaos in Kurdistan. It would have prevented the interventions and disturbances by the *foreigners*; it would have contributed to the achievement of total progress and development (my emphasis)."[63] Similarly, after warning the Kurds against possible attacks from Russia, Abdurrahman Bedir Khan explained the potential consequences of such attacks: "Kurds will see that the land lovingly raised their children falling into the hands of *foreigners* [biyanî]" (my emphasis).[64] As far as the first extract from M. M. Bedir Khan's article is concerned, although the progress of the Kurds is the central issue of this article, an important discursive act is embedded in the noun *foreigners*, which is meant to create or reinforce the assumption that Ottomans are *not foreigners* but an integral part of the Kurdish self. In the second extract, editor Abdurrahman Bedir portrays Russians as *foreigners*, while instinctively establishing Ottoman domination in Kurdistan as a non-foreign rule. This presumption suggests that the Ottoman identity is a part of the Kurdish self.

A parallel Ottomanist and pro-Sultan tendency is evident in the journal's treatment of the hostilities between Armenians and Kurds. After presenting this conflict as an internal matter between the two Ottoman communities, M. M. Bedir Khan argued: "For the last two or three years, Armenians and Kurds have been entangled in quarrels. This is not a good situation. The state doesn't approve [ne razî] of that."[65] In this excerpt, the author's conformism goes so far as to claim that the Ottoman state does not approve of the killing of the Armenians. It does not seem possible that M. M. Bedir Khan, a well-educated and well-informed intellectual, would sincerely believe what he says, given the fact that the state was the actual perpetrator or encourager of violence against the Armenian community. Not only that, one of the primary reasons behind the establishment of the *Hamidian Cavalries* only nine years earlier was the oppression of the Armenians.[66] It is important to note that the editor was not unaware of the true nature of Sultan Abdulhamid II's manipulative

policies. As a matter of fact, M. M. Bedir Khan, along with Emin Ali Bedir
Khan, his older brother, organized an unsuccessful revolt against the same
Sultan Abdulhamid II in 1889, ten years before the publication of *Kurdistan*.
It is also noteworthy that later under the editorship of Abdurrahman Bedir
Khan, *Kurdistan* would directly blame Sultan Abdulhamid II in the harsh-
est terms for the atrocities inflicted on the Armenians. For instance, in the
28th issue of the journal, Abdurrahman Bedir Khan condemned the Ottoman
government for encouraging the misconduct and unlawful acts of Hamidian
Cavalries.[67] Returning to the excerpt above, the author either assumed that the
state's disapproval would be more convincing for the Kurds not to target the
Armenians, or he simply intended to curry favor with the Hamidian regime,
or both.

Nevertheless, despite the emphasis on Pan-Islamism/Ummahism—as
a mode of identification and social organization—and the legitimacy of
Ottoman rule in Kurdistan, the journal never hesitated to present Kurds and
other Ottoman communities as distinct ethnic groups or nations, albeit in a
subtle way and within the Ottoman political framework. M. M. Bedir Khan
wrote: "There are many nations [milet] that are not half as much as us; they
all possess newspapers, books [and] schools. Kurds are stronger and more
hardworking than other nations [qawm]; therefore, the lack of book[s] and
literacy brings shame on us."[68] Here the editor situates the Kurds in the world
of nations by comparing the Kurds to other nations, which inevitably creates the assumption that Kurds, *too*, constitute a nation. The dichotomy of
us versus them in the phrase "all nations" [hemî qewm] and "us" [me], does
not only reinforces this assumption, but it also constructed all other nations
outside the realm of the Kurdish self as non-Kurdish *others*. It is remarkable
that M. M. Bedir Khan remained ambiguous in his articulation of the *others*
when he referred to other national. Nevertheless, in his continuation of the
same article, he clarified this ambiguity by appealing to the following radical
words from Ahmad Khani's (1650–1706) *Mem û Zîn* (1695):

Only if we had a unity
If we obeyed each other
The entirety of the Turks [Rom], Arabs and Iranians ['Ecem]
They all would have become our servants/subjects
We would have achieved perfection in religion and worldly affairs
We would have learned knowledge and wisdom[69]

Mem û Zîn (Mem and Zîn) is a narrative poetic romance by Ahmad Khani,
who adopted it from *Memê Alan* (Mem of Alan), an orally composed and
transmitted Kurdish folk romance. The plot of the romance revolves around
the story of Mem and Zîn, who are in love with each other but whose union

is prevented by the villain Bekir. Although the epic is a classic love story, it is believed that the story is an allegory for the tragic fate of the Kurds. In this view, Mem and Zîn represent the two parts of Kurdistan divided between the Safavid and Ottoman Empires, while Bekir represents the discord and disunity among Kurdish rulers. Khani's *Mem û Zîn*, as recognized by many scholars, was a clear expression of premodern Kurdish ethnic awareness and even the first appearance of an embryonic national awareness if not an unequivocal national consciousness.[70]

Abdurrahman Bedir Khan also resorted to the same voice. However, first, he brought up the unjust treatment of the Kurds by state officials and encouraged Kurds to appeal to the Sultan's authority through petitions: "If the state officials did not listen to you . . . you should write your complaints to the Sultan . . . The Sultan will remove them. If he did not, write to him again . . . Hence, stop waiting. Raise your voice; cry out, demand justice from the Sultan."[71] Abdurrahman Bedir Khan, from a seemingly Ottomanist perspective, urged the Kurds to appeal to the Sultan in the face of government officials' unjust treatment. This argument contributes to the validation and legitimization of the Ottoman regime and the Sultan's authority in Kurdistan. Nevertheless, later in his article, the editor resorted to the following verses from Khani, much as his brother M. M. Bedir Khan had:

If our fortune favoured us
If we could wake up from this sleep
If a protector could rise among us
That we could find a king
[. . .]
These Turks wouldn't dominate us
We would not fail at the hands of the owl
We would not be miserably oppressed
We would not be defeated and obedient to the Turks and Iranians[72]

Notice how both editors were careful in their wording so as not to sound too nationalist, radical or rebellious against the sacred authority of the state and the Sultan Caliph, the leader of the Muslim ummah, and "the shadow of Almighty on earth." However, via an act of ventriloquism, they allowed the more radical words of a higher religious figure of authority, that is, Khani, to speak to the audience on their behalf. This radical voice, in stark contrast with the seemingly Ottomanist attitude of the journal *Kurdistan*, communicated "the actual" or "the desired" political solution: that Kurds under the "yoke" of the Ottoman Turks, Arabs, and Iranians should overcome their internal enmities, unite and revolt under the leadership of a Kurdish king to establish a Kurdish state, whereby Kurds would subjugate the Iranians, Arabs, and

Turks. The voice of such a well-respected clergyman, whose "discourse on the Kurds was one of the state of politics and governance,"[73] was much needed for two reasons: first, the voice of a third party was instrumental for an indirect expression of such radical measures, that is, setting up a Kurdish state, as the Bedir Khan Brothers refrained from taking an open or radical position, at least in the early issues of *Kurdistan*; and second, the Bedir Khan Brothers felt that they should supplement their tribal authority by relying on the voice of a highly venerated religious scholar to justify and legitimize their nationalist argument among the predominantly Muslim Kurdish community.[74]

Kurdistan was not and could not be as radical as Khani's *Mem û Zîn* for many reasons. First, Khani produced his work in Kurdish medreses in an agrarian Kurdish society during the premodern and pre-nationalism era, while the Bedir Khan Brothers were the products of the modern Ottoman school system in the age of nationalism. Second, *Mem û Zîn* and *Kurdistan* differed in form—the former was poetry, the latter was prose—and thus targeted different audiences employing two different genres within two distinct historical contexts.[75] Khani was a patriot, and his work was an expression of his personal grief in the form of poetry, meant, with its few copies, for the small Kurdish elite of the seventeenth-century medrese who were bestowed with the prestige of literacy, while *Kurdistan*, which appeared in the era of nationalism, was a prosaic newspaper produced on a large scale by printing press for the largest audience attainable, targeting the political and cultural elite and non-elite, including the Young Turks as well as the Sultan and Ottoman state officials. What is more, *Kurdistan* was published under the reign of Sultan Abdulhamid II, who did not tolerate any form of non-Turkish ethnic nationalist inclinations. In sum, the social and political realities of the late Ottoman period coupled with the personal and familial interests and concerns of the editors, played a significant role in setting the tone of their journal. Thus, the Bedir Khan Brothers made full use of Khani's radical political tone.

Discursive Shifts from Pan-Islamism to Full-fledged Kurdish Nationalism

In the later issues of *Kurdistan*, Abdurrahman Bedir Khan embraced a more radical political line by directly criticizing the Sultan himself and holding him responsible for the misconducts of the state officials in Kurdistan. Furthermore, he drew a clearer line between Kurds and Turks, defying Ottoman Turkish political domination over the Kurds and Kurdistan. Similarly, the importance and objectives of education and modernization shifted from turning the Kurds into capable Ottoman Muslims to the consolidation of Kurdish national identity and the protection of the Kurdish homeland at the expense of the Ottoman state. Moreover, the editor continued to problematize the Russian threat, this time not

as a part of his strategy to convince the state to empower the Kurdish component of Ottomanism against Russia, but rather as a *strategy of delegitimization
and discrediting* of the Sultan and Ottoman rule in Kurdistan.[76] Evoking the
fate of Muslims in Crete[77] at the hands of Christian Greeks, the editor asserted
that the same situation would befall Kurds when Russia invaded Kurdistan:[78]

> Then, O Kurds [Kurdino], you should come to your senses. Alas, if you are not
> cautious, if you do not wake up, this situation, before long, will befall you too
> . . . If Moscow sends its soldiers against you, the [Ottoman] state will not come
> to your aid. The soldiers of Moscow outnumber you; you do not possess the
> cannons and rifles they do . . . They will kill twenty of you by the time you kill
> one of them. I know Kurds are manlier [mêrtir][79] than Moscow. However, in the
> face of those cannons and rifles, your manliness will not suffice.[80]

The editor achieved two aims at once; first, he delegitimized the Sultan's
authority by condemning his regime for being oblivious to the plight of his
subjects; needless to say, the object of his concern is the Kurds. Second,
employing the *strategy of negative-self presentation,*[81] he criticized the
backward situation of the Kurds and encouraged them to take matters into
their own hands by modernizing themselves so that they could confront this
imminent "Christian" danger on their own, without help from the Ottoman
state. In this context, the most important political implication of the passage
is that the fate of Kurds no longer lies with the Ottomans or the Ottoman
state, which invalidated one of the strongest ties between the Kurds and the
Ottoman Turks.

A parallel discursive shift took place in the journal's treatment of the
Armenian issue. The Sultan, who was previously claimed to be against the
killings of Armenians, was now the very entity responsible for such acts:
Abdurrahman Bedir Khan wrote: "you . . . are murdering innocent women
and children of Armenians. The Prophet has said: 'Give glad tidings to the
killer [that he too will be killed] [. . .]' You follow Abdulhamid's orders
[emrê Ebdulhemîd] [and] kill Armenians. Do you think Abdulhamid's order
is greater than the Prophet's hadith [or] superior to God's commands?"[82]
In this dense religious allusion, obeying the Sultan's commands to kill
Armenians is the same as going against God's will. Moreover, Abdurrahman
Bedir Khan not only condemned Kurdish hostilities toward their Armenian
neighbors in religious terms, but he also defied Sultan Abdulhamid II who he
openly blamed for ordering the killings.

Furthermore, in another article, Abdurrahman Bedir Khan explicitly and
with great resentment equated the Ottoman state and the Sultan Caliph,
two so-called supra-ethnic or supra-national entities, with Turkish national

identity and Turkish nationalism, creating an explicit ethnic *other* in discernible nationalist terms:

> Rom [Turks] establish great schools in places inhabited by Turks [Tirk]. The government takes money from Kurds and spends it on Turks. Poor Kurds are captives [esîr] of that government . . . I want to come to my homeland [welatê xwe] and sacrifice myself for my nation [milet]. But the Turkish government would not allow me; it does not want Kurds to become learned and strong.[83]

This was undoubtedly a breaking point in the discourse of *Kurdistan* from an ostensibly Ottomanist position to a more anti-Turkish, Kurdish nationalist line. The excerpt is an unequivocal expression of Kurdish ethno-national consciousness directed against the domination of the Turks, whereby the Ottoman Empire is presented as an unjust despotic Turkish state who "takes it from the Kurds and spends it on Turks." The author's word choice is also important in that he referred to the Turks as *Rom*. Although the term *Rom* or *Roma Reş* (the Black Rom) was previously applied to the Byzantine Empire, Kurds used the same term to refer to the Turks with its derogatory connotations—a hostile non-Muslim entity.[84] Earlier, in the 6th issue of the journal, Abdurrahman refers to Turkish as *Romî* (the language of the *Rom*).[85] It is important to note that even today, Kurds sometimes refer to the Turks as the *Rom* or *Roma Reş*. Perhaps Kurds have perceived the Ottomans as "the Romans of the Muslim world."[86]

Nonetheless, the most fundamental and overt manifestation of Kurdish nationalism only appeared in the 27th issue of *Kurdistan*, when Abdurrahman Bedir Khan wrote:

> O Kurds! [Gelî Kurdno] As you know, all nations are working toward their own welfare. It is very bad that Kurds have always served the *foreigners* [biyanî]. You have been serving the Turks for so many years, what benefit have you gained from it? When you receive a badge or a military rank in return for all the cruelty of the government, you forget all about the unjust treatment. Many Kurds have been killed in wars for the sake of this government; however, not a [single] Kurd, until today, has made an effort for his/her own homeland [weten]; as if we have been created to serve the *foreigners*. Five hundred years ago, there was not a single Turk in our country [welat]. All these Turks came to our country from Turan, and they dominate over us in our own country. Their padişahs, who are bloodthirsty tyrants [xwînrêjên mustebid], call themselves Caliph and as such they carry out all types of cruelties that exist. However, the truth is that they are not caliphs; they are cruel padişahs who should be dethroned. You are not aware of this situation because you are ignorant; the government keeps you that way lest you become aware of the situation.

Turks and the Sultan might use whatever name or title they desire; however, God has not created Kurds for their service [. . .]

The time has come; we should work for our own and our children's salvation. It is a shame if Kurds, who are known for their bravery and generosity, keep being servants to a cruel government. A while back, we also possessed a state; we were free. However, it is a shame that that happiness slipped through our fingers; now, we are in the hands of clowns. Our disunity is the major reason for this situation. Because we Kurds are enemies of one another, Turks are taking advantage of this situation [. . .] Among us, there are good, kind-hearted and just rulers; let our leader be a Kurd. Why should we stay under the [rule of the] Turks?

I have written to some Kurdish aghas and begged them to unite so that they can find a cure for this disease. I am telling you via my newspaper too[that] you should unite. Given their situation, the Armenians [are ready to] ally with you. Together you will formulate a good future [and] you will together liberate yourselves from the cruelty of the Turks [. . .] God willing, one day, I myself will seize an opportunity [and] enter Kurdistan from the Iranian side. Then, God willing, I will liberate the Kurds from the Rom [Turkish] servitude, and I will show the world that Kurds are not the killers of oppressed people, the way Abdulhamid claims.

May God give us success.[87]

First, through a number of presuppositions, the editor designated the Kurds to be a national community. In the first line, he conveyed an "invisible meaning": he lamented the fact that all nations work for their own welfare except the Kurds, presupposing that Kurds constitute a single, coherent, and unified entity in the form of a nation just like other nations who *do* work for their common national present and future. Second, we observe a radical shift not only in the referent but also the meaning of the term *foreign*; while the term "foreign" used to denote the Russians as a non-Muslim *other* in a religious intertextuality, here, the term unambiguously refers to the Ottoman Turks, expressively designating them as *foreigners* with the political connotation of an entity that is *nationally alien* to *us* Kurds. In the age of nationalism, there remained only one, univocal, modern, and acceptable definition of foreignness: *those* that do not have the same ethno-national identity as *us*.[88] Third, the editor portrayed "these Turks" as a colonizing foreign entity who came from their native land of "Turan" and colonized Kurdistan to dominate over "us" in "our own country." Here, the editor not only imagined and articulated Kurdistan as the Kurdish national homeland, but he also portrayed the Ottoman Turks as a colonialist entity which reinforced the construction of the Turks as a foreign entity.

Another central argument pertains to the rejection of the office of the Islamic caliph held by the Turks. Using the *strategy of delegitimization and discrediting*, the editor labeled all Ottoman sultans as "bloodthirsty Turkish tyrants" who do not deserve the title of caliph. Therefore, he suggested that Kurds cut all bonds with the Turks and free themselves from this relation of slavery [xulamî]. In this particular reconstruction, the Ottoman Turks were deemed an outgroup in derogatory terms such as "barbarian" and "inferior." Interestingly, around the same time as the journal *Kurdistan*, dissident voices were rising from the Arab world that questioned the legitimacy of the Ottoman Turkish monopoly over the office of the Caliphate. For instance, Abd al-Rahman al-Kawakibi (1849–1903), an Arab nationalist of Kurdish descent, called into question the legitimacy of the caliph and problematized Turkish despotism embodied in Sultan Abdulhamid II. Kawakibi went so far as to suggest the replacement of Sultan Abdulhamid II with an Arab caliph, for which he paid with his life.[89] A notable discursive practice in this excerpt is that the editor assigned an ethnicity not only to the Ottoman state but also to the caliph, a position that had always been perceived as universal and supra-ethnic by all Muslim subjects of the empire. Hence, evading the notion of Pan-Islamism, the caliphate, and shattering the myth of Ottomanism, which constituted the cement that held together the divergent ethnic communities, the editor presented the entire Kurdo-Ottoman history as a history of master-servant, whereby Kurds served their *foreign Turkish masters*. In this particular reconstruction of the past and the present from a particular Kurdish nationalist standpoint, the editor invalidated the centuries-old bond of so-called brother-hood, common faith, and common fate among the Muslim constituents of the empire, for example, Turks, Kurds, Albanians, Arabs. What is more, from a romantic nationalist perspective, the editor "reminded" the Kurds of their glorious past in their own country prior to the Turko-Ottoman rule.

The metaphorical representation of disunity among Kurds as a disease is also noteworthy. Fairclough argues, "the ideological significance of disease metaphors is that they tend to take dominant interests to be the interests of society as a whole."[90] As a way of ridding the organism of this disease, the editor rejected the rule of the Ottoman Turks by offering an action-oriented suggestion: Kurds as a single organism should work toward "their own future" by uniting under the leadership of a Kurd, perhaps himself, along with people from his princely family. As a matter of fact, later on, he explicitly designated himself the leader of the Kurds who, given his princely familial past, was qualified to deliver the Kurds from their Ottoman *servitude* or *slavery*. Strikingly, this is the very first discursive manifestation of what might be called Kurdish *political nationalism* in the Kurdish journalistic discourse of the late Ottoman period. Another fundamental, action-oriented proposal by the editor was to seek the future of Kurds in alliance with the Armenians, even though suggesting a common front with the Armenians—a non-Muslim Christian community—against the Sultan Caliph, the leader of the Muslim ummah, was for the most part unthinkable in the Pan-Islamist narrative. This was clearly another blow to Pan-Islamist and Ottomanist bonds which were already on the wane.

There is a case for saying that nationalism is, above all, an ideology of the first-person plural, that is of the "we," which is the antithesis of similar binary opposition of the "us and them" in the rhetoric of nationalism.[91] Correspondingly, the use of deictic words constitutes another central aspect in the article above. As textual properties, these deictic words or deixis are crucial in nationalist discourses, too, in terms of the meaning-making process. That is, not only memorable grand words and phrases, but also small deixis such as "we," "you," "this," "here," "there," "them," "us" and so on can be powerful, albeit barely conscious, reminders of nation and nationalism. In this sense, nationalism is the ideology of both the first-person plural as well as the third person plural because "there can be no 'us' without 'them.' "[92] Hence the use of deictic words should also be analyzed for a complete close textual analysis.[93] Abdurrahman Bedir Khan used the Kurdish pronoun *em* (we/us) and *me* (we/us/our) in sixteen instances in the excerpt above, registering solidarity and communality of experience among his readers, who are presented as a national audience. For example, he said: "as if *we* have been created to serve the foreigners"; "*we* should work for *our own* and *our* children's salvation"; "why should *we* stay under the [rule of the] Turks"; "*they* dominate *us* in *our own* country." Then, in stark contrast to the deictic *we*, *our*, *us*, *own*, the author used such deictic words as *them*, *their*, *they*, and so forth in reference to the Turks that are deemed as the *other*, often accompanied by derogatory terms such as "cruel," "barbarian," and "bloodthirsty." One should observe that the deictic "we" and its Kurdish variants in the extract above are *addressee inclusive*. As such, they are expected to be read as a particular "we," that is, "*we* the Kurdish nation." As Volmert astutely put it, "a speaker can unite himself and his audience into a single community sharing a common destiny' by letting fall into oblivion all differences in origins, confession, class, and lifestyle with a simple 'we' "[94] In this regard, the inclusive "we" helped the editor, a member of the Kurdish aristocracy, to claim co-membership with a lay audience and the right to talk on behalf of "us" as one of "us."[95]

The use of the exclusive deixis *you* (hûn/we) that occurs on fourteen instances in the extract is also fundamentally important as it distinguishes the speakers from the addressee.[96] The author Abdurrahman Bedir Khan made extensive use of the exclusive deixis *you* in the first paragraphs (nine occurrences) in order to exclude himself from the mistakes of the past. Consider the following sentences from the extract: "*you* have been serving the Turks for so many years, what benefit have *you* gained from it"; "when *you* receive a badge or a military rank in return for all the cruelty of the government, *you* forget all about the unjust treatment"; "*you* are not aware of this situation because *you* are ignorant." Notice how in all of these sentences the exclusive "you" creates a distance between Abdurrahman Bedir Khan and the audience. These sentences exonerated him from criticism, even though before his departure to Cairo, Abdurrahman Bedir Khan himself had worked for the Ottoman Ministry of Education for several years as the chief secretary, in addition to his previous service to the Ottoman state.[97] Exempting himself from the mistakes of the past consolidates his role as the savior with a "clean personal record" who could liberate the Kurds from Turkish domination. This approach ruled out alternative reasons for Kurds' servitude, including the accountability of the Kurdish elite represented by the Bedir Khans.

Another noticeable discursive practice in this and the two previous extracts is that Abdurrahman Bedir Khan abandoned the use of honorific titles before and after the Sultan's name. Although the editor used to refer to the Sultan by such honorific titles as "your excellency; you, the Sultan; your excellency the Sultan; Sultan Caliph; His Excellency Sultan Abdulhamid Khan" and so forth, starting from the 9th issue, he began to refer to the Sultan by his given name only, that is, Abdulhamid. Later, he referred to the Sultan with such insulting words as "cruel" (zalim), "bandit" (şakî), "that man" (o adam), "hypocrite" (minafiq), and "thief" (diz).[98]

The final sentence of this extract reads: "I will show the world that Kurds are not the killers of oppressed people, the way Abdulhamid claims." What caused the author to make such an assertion might be best explained through Deringil's notion of "borrowed colonialism" and Makdisi's "Ottoman Orientalism." Deringil argues that toward the end of the nineteenth century, as a survival tactic, the Ottoman Empire adopted a colonialist stance toward the people of the empire's periphery in a bid to present itself as an equal player on the world stage vis-à-vis the European colonial powers. In other words, the Ottomans used colonialism as a survival tactic because they were fully aware that if they were not to become a colony themselves, they had to at least qualify for the status of a colonialist state.[99] As a part of this colonialist or "borrowed colonialist" attitude, the empire also adopted the Western notion of "Orientalism," which Makdisi calls "Ottoman Orientalism."[100] Accordingly, the Ottoman imperial or "colonial" center in Istanbul generated its discursive opposite in the form of a backward premodern periphery within the empire that resembled the relationship between the "civilized" European colonial states and their "lawless," "savage," premodern colonial subjects. This attitude manifested itself in the Ottoman reaction to sectarian clashes in the periphery, including those that erupted between Kurds and Armenians, the Druze and Maronites in Mount Lebanon and Muslim riots in Damascus that resulted in the massacre of the province's Christian population. It is beyond the scope of this book to discuss these clashes in detail. Still, it suffices to say that the Ottoman Empire explained these incidents as the savagery of the Oriental inhabitants of its periphery and as a "civilized" colonist distanced itself from these "primitive," "religiously confused" subjects. Thus, the last sentence of the extract above reflects how the Ottoman imperial center presented ethnic and sectarian clashes in Kurdistan to the outside world, that is, the European colonial powers. In these representations, the Ottoman Empire assumed the role of a modern state and a colonialist "civilizer," much like the West, while the "savage" Kurds—or any other society on the periphery for that matter—were presented as the "Ottoman man's burden" that needed to be disciplined and civilized.[101]

Nonetheless, Abdurrahman Bedir Khan's harsh criticism of the Ottoman Turks, the Ottoman state, and the Sultan Caliph should not be interpreted as the expression of a widespread and organized attempt on the part of the editor to break from the Ottoman Empire to establish an independent Kurdish state. It seems that his rage was directed at the increasing hegemonic power of the Turks and Turkish nationalism over the Ottoman state apparatus at the expense of the Kurds. Even though in the extract above and elsewhere in *Kurdistan* the editor called upon Kurds to take up arms against the Turks, the state, and the caliph, he did not openly propose a well-defined course of action such as an armed struggle that could lead to Kurdish national independence. It is important to note that all non-Turkish Muslim leaders and intellectuals in the empire found themselves in a similar political and emotional "ambivalence"[102]—to use Homi Bhabha's term—toward Ottomans, particularly when Ottoman policies went against the vital interests of their people and region, as in the case of Palestinian Arab leaders and intellectuals.[103] Perhaps this "ambivalent" state can be attributed to the peculiarities of the "Ottoman colonial project," which differentiated itself from Western colonialism given the fact that Kurds—and the majority of other non-Turkish Ottoman subjects—shared the same religion as the ruling Ottoman Turks and some similar goals. These idiosyncrasies made things complicated when it came to opposing the Sublime Porte.[104]

Kurdistan was a bilingual journal published in Kurdish and Ottoman Turkish. Therefore, it is imperative to point out that when the corpus of *Kurdistan* is considered as a whole, the articles written in Kurdish seem to be more radical when compared to the more moderate articles written in Turkish. The articles in the 27th issue of the journal constitute a good case in point. Compared to the Kurdish article analyzed above, two Turkish articles that appeared in the same issue of *Kurdistan* were much more moderate in their content and tone. The author, in line with Young Turks/CUP discourse, adopted a more Ottomanist tone by limiting his criticism to the personality of Sultan Abdulhamid II and his destructive policies in Kurdistan, and not criticizing the increasingly

Turkish nationalist character of the empire or the Sultan. Furthermore, in Turkish-language articles, his criticism revolved around the manipulation of the Kurds against Armenians, another ethnic group vigorously involved in CUP activities. Given the fact that CUP members and the Turkish members, in particular, were the "unaddressed recipients" of *Kurdistan*'s messages, the journal naturally tried to stay on the good side of the CUP by toning down its criticism of the Turks in Turkish-language articles. This policy can be observed in other Kurdish journals, as we will see in the subsequent chapters.

As stated earlier, far from representing the general voice of *Kurdistan*, the radical political attitude in the above extract only occurred in a few instances that stand out in the entire corpus of the journal. Later, in complete contrast to his previous radical tone, the editor Abdurrahman Bedir Khan went back to his earlier moderate political stance in which he fostered Kurdish identity as a part of the larger Islamic and Ottoman identity. Below are excerpts from different issues of the journal to illustrate this more dominant Ottomanist attitude:

> Last year *our* state and the Greeks fought. Thank God, *our* state defeated the Greeks; the *soldiers of Islam* took six large cities and more than one hundred villages from the Greeks in a month. Thereafter, Moscow intervened and did not let *us* proceed; *we* made peace (my emphasis).[105]
>
> *We* all know that in every sector of *our* government misery and disorder prevail (my emphasis).[106]
>
> Kurdistan constitutes a very vast and important region for *our* state on the borders with Russia and Iran (my emphasis).[107]
>
> All Muslims should wish for the eternity of the Ottoman State.[108]

Notice how the Islamic Ottomanist or Ummahist content of these extracts is consolidated by using such deictic words as "we," "us," and "our," all of which refer to "us Ottomans" or "us Muslims," "our state" and so on.

I conclude my analysis of this section by examining a few fascinating remarks made by Abdurrahman Bedir Khan on the Armenian issue. His treatment of the Armenian issue represents a relevant instance that typifies his inconsistent manner of jumping from one extreme to another throughout the corpus of *Kurdistan*. As we saw, on several occasions, the editor praised the Armenian struggle against the Ottomans and shamed the Kurds for not following suit or for not forming an alliance with the Armenians in a war against the Sultan Caliph and the Ottoman state. The excerpts below illustrate his inconsistency and sharp turn from being a zealous supporter of the Armenian struggle to a staunch opponent:

> There is no one province [in the empire] in which the Armenians would outnumber the other nations [milet], such as Kurds or Turks. Therefore, the ambition

for Armenian independence is an impossible dream [xiyalek mustehîl] . . .
Armenians should eventually seek their happiness with our [Ottoman] state. . .
If our state survives, so will the Armenians. If not, the Armenians will be
destroyed entirely. Our state can still survive on its own should the Armenians
break away; we would only be left with sadness [for Armenians].[109]

It is remarkable to see how the editor, who had previously condemned
Turkish racial dominance and called upon the Kurds to take up arms against
"cruel," "barbaric," "bloodthirsty," and "foreigner" Ottomans under his very
own leadership, urged the Armenians to work toward the unity and welfare
of the Ottoman state, pursue their happiness within the Ottoman framework
and give up all hopes for independence, which he described as "an impossible dream."[110] As stated at the outset of this section, on account of rapid
changes in local and global sociopolitical circumstances and shifts in the balance of power, the Bedir Khan Brothers, but especially Abdurrahman Bedir
Khan, could not maintain or at least express a coherent and consistent political attitude. Instead, in a pragmatic manner, his Kurdish nationalist project
and discourse tended to ebb and flow over time following local, regional,
and global conjunctures, his personal concerns and his frame of mind. As a
consequence, the political present and future of the Kurds in the discourse of
Kurdistan fluctuated between two extremes: An Ottoman Pan-Islamist policy,
one on the one hand, and an anti-Turkish, anti-Ottoman separatist Kurdish
nationalism, on the other.

They Don't Speak Our Language

Language has been perceived as the *national soul* or *Volk* and hence the primary marker of national identity since the mid-eighteenth century when the
German romantics first elaborated the idea of nationalism. The fundamental
role of language is even more vital in the Kurdish case, since Kurds share
many cultural traits with neighboring ethnic groups such as Turks, Persians,
and Arabs, leaving language as the major exclusive marker of Kurdish
national identity.[111] Therefore, the Kurdish language has been conceived as
an essential part of the spiritual "inner" domain of Kurdish cultural sovereignty.[112] Consequently, the editors of the journal *Kurdistan*, aware of the role
of Kurdish as a *natural* divide between Kurds and non-Kurds, transformed
the Kurdish language into a collective cultural element in a politico-linguistic
framework as a crucial component of Kurdish national identity. Due to their
vernacularization through the printing press, Kurdish language texts acquired
the essential function as tools of inclusion and exclusion regardless of their
content. Hence, thanks to the "identity integrating power" of the Kurdish
language, Kurds were imagined as a distinct entity both *in* and *around* the

Kurdish language, instead of Ottoman Turkish, the *lingua franca* of the empire.[113]

The Politico-Symbolic Function of Kurdish as a Tool of Inclusion and Exclusion

The use of Kurdish as the sole basis for identity was a primary discursive practice in *Kurdistan*. The use of Kurdish as such presented *Kurdistan* with the opportunity to make an unmistakable distinction between Kurds and their linguistic "others."[114] That is, the use of Kurdish language for *Kurdistan* was a *tactic of dissimilation* or *dis-identification*[115] in the journal's strategies of *inclusion* and *exclusion* in the power struggle for themselves and the Kurdish people. Thus, it can be argued that through this multifaceted strategy, *Kurdistan* illustrated how the use of *the language of the self* could be a powerful boundary-maker and an instrument of *othering* in a linguistic nationalism framework. In this context, I argue that the chief reason for the Bedir Khan Brothers' preference for Kurdish as the dominant medium of communication in *Kurdistan* was not the purely pragmatic communicative function of this language, neither was it the result of a theoretical or academic interest in this vernacular, but was a powerful politico-symbolic function of Kurdish as the most salient marker of Kurdish national identity. *Kurdistan*'s use of Kurdish language as an exclusive Kurdish cultural property engendered a new social interaction and an imaginary connection exclusively among Kurds as the readers of the same journal *in* and *around* their own language. In other words, *Kurdistan* offered something that only Kurds had in common or something to which only Kurds had privileged access, which in turn caused Kurds to feel that they possessed something exclusive that they did not share with *other* Ottomans for the simplest reason: "They do not speak Kurdish." Although the readers of *Kurdistan* had never seen each other or heard of each other, in an Andersonian sense, they all believed with great conviction that the ceremony of reading the same newspaper in Kurdish was being replicated simultaneously by their fellow Kurds elsewhere.[116]

At this juncture, it is noteworthy that the content of the text in mass communication is as important as the form of vernacularized language in the construction of national identities. In the Kurdish case, the discursive practice of inclusion and exclusion was not limited to the mere use of the Kurdish language, but was also produced in the content of the text. Consider the following Kurdish phrase, which appeared in the folio section of the journal: "Bi-weekly published Kurdish [Kurdî] Newspaper."[117] Another note, this time in Ottoman Turkish placed right beneath the phrase mentioned above, read: "For now, bi-weekly Kurdish newspaper for awakening and encouraging Kurds to education in arts and skills."[118] In both phrases, the editor significantly and overtly *flagged* the fact that the paper was a Kurdish journal for Kurds.[119]

Nevertheless, *Kurdistan* also employed Ottoman Turkish, which suggests that more complex dynamics were at play than the notion of *linguistic nationalism*. Chief among them was that the editors tried to convey their politics to non-Kurdish Ottomans, for example, Turks, Armenians, Arabs who spoke Turkish, and to those Kurds who were illiterate in Kurdish or Kurmanji-Kurdish.[120] Turkish was instrumental particularly when the issue at hand was of concern to all Ottomans, although dealt with from a Kurdish perspective. The number of Ottoman Turkish articles in *Kurdistan* increased only after the 18th issue, following the request of its readers. In a note appearing in the 18th issue of the journal, the editor stated: "Many people wrote to me [saying] that they cannot read Kurdish and therefore they asked for a Turkish section in my newspaper. On their request [and] God willing, I will, from now on, publish half of my newspaper in Turkish."[121]

In the 4th issue of *Kurdistan*, M. M. Bedir Khan wrote: "The text above, which I have written in *Turkish* [Tirkî], is a letter for His Excellency Sultan Abdulhamid Khan. In this letter, I [express my] hope that he grants permission for the free circulation of my newspaper in Kurdistan . . . Because *[they] don't speak Kurdish* [Kurmancî], [they] think I have written something [bad] about them (my emphasis)."[122] There are key discursive practices at work in this extract. First, the author highlighted the fact that the letter in question was addressed to the Sultan Abdulhamid II in Turkish, which might, at first, seem a trivial if not a redundant explanation. However, in this discursive act, the author implicitly associated the Sultan with the Turkish language and hence with his Turkish identity. Then, he added the other state officials to the same category, referring to them using the plural third-person pronoun *they*, an essential term in the strategy of othering or creating *out-groups* in nationalist terms. The Sultan Caliph and his state officials are portrayed not only as non-Kurds but also significantly as *Turks* who do not speak Kurdish language, a "justification" as to why the author had written the letter in "their" language. The author explicitly designated the Sultan—and his statesmen—as members of a particular ethnic and linguistic community, that is, Turkish, disregarding the Sultan's and the Ottoman state's allegedly supranational position in the *Ummah*. This creates a subtle distance between the Sultan Caliph and Ottoman Turks on the one hand and Kurds on the other. Similar discursive acts can be observed in other issues of *Kurdistan*. In the 6th issue, the editor Abdurrahman Bedir Khan wrote: "In this [issue of] the newspaper I have written a *Turkish* [Romî] letter for Sultan Abdul Hamid Khan"[123] (my emphasis). Similarly, the readers were aware of and underlined this fundamental linguistic difference. A reader's letter stated: "We Kurds hope that you write to the Sultan *in Turkish* and [publish it] in your paper so that he would consider the situation of the Kurds [Kurmanc]."[124] Here not only the editor but also the reader has assigned an ethnicity to the Sultan Abdulhamid II and the Ottoman state around Turkish language. Language, both for the Kurds and the Ottoman Turks, who held state power, was not only a tool of communication but a significant element of national identity. Therefore, soon after he came to power, Sultan Abdulhamid II imposed Turkish as the sole language of instruction on Ottoman subjects throughout the empire.[125]

One aspect of the segregated nature of the Kurdish community stemmed from the sociocultural alienation of the Kurdish aristocratic stratum from the Kurdish masses. The Bedir Khan Brothers used Kurdish language as a strategy of interclass Kurdish solidarity by establishing a new bond between the elite and the commoners by "ethnicization" and "authentication" of both the Kurdish elite and the Kurdish masses around the Kurdish language, which became a strong identity-constitutive element.[126] The use of the Kurdish language illustrates the way the Kurdish elite, who led the nationalist project, was influenced by the commoners who spoke and took pride in Kurdish. Hence, the promotion of Kurdish as a common cultural property "is what made the Kurdish people (the masses) valuable in the eyes of the nationalists" and vice versa.[127] In other words, the functional dependence of the Kurdish elite on the Kurdish language reflected their need to communicate and activate the predominantly illiterate masses through the use of the Kurdish language.[128]

The Translation of Qur'anic Verses into Kurdish

A significant consequence of the Protestant Reformation in Europe was the translation of the Bible first into German and then into other vernaculars, which brought about the gradual demotion of Latin as the sacred script language. That is, vernacularization diminished the idea that only a sacred language could represent divine truth. Vernaculars, which previously had no religious attachments, eventually put an end to the politico-religious monopoly of Latin over the Bible. Thereby, vernacularization elevated German and other vernaculars to prestigious languages with the same status as Latin.[129] In a similar manner, after the arrival of Islam, Arabic became the medium of divine revelation and the sacred language of God, Persian remained the language of literature, while Ottoman Turkish, on the other hand, became the language of the palace and the state. This situation rendered Kurdish, along with a few other peripheral languages, inferior in rank and status.[130] Since the introduction of Islam, Kurds, like other non-Arab Muslims, perceived Arabic to be the language chosen by God to disseminate the divine message through the Holy Qur'an. There was a mutually reinforcing link between the linguistic and the spiritual importance of the Quran, particularly to native Arabic speakers. Thus, to safeguard the divine character of the book, it was believed that the Qur'an could not be translated, imitated, or reproduced in any form or manner because it was an inimitable miracle (i'jaz al-Qur'an).[131] The inimitability of the verses is justified through the claim that the meaning (signified) is inseparable from the form (signifier). It is for this reason that Muslims often prefer the term "tafsir" (interpretation) instead of "translation" for versions of the Qur'an in languages other than Arabic.

Although Islam was opposed to linguistic diversity,[132] *Kurdistan* became the first Kurdish journal to print Kurdish translations of Qur'anic verses.[133] Nonetheless, this was not for the religious purpose of propagating religion, but it was instead a part of the journal's strategy of religious intertextuality in an Islamic modernist synthesis to serve the novel needs of Kurdish nationalism and modernization efforts. In other words, from the perspective of "medium theory,"[134] the translation of the Qur'an was not meant to and did not necessarily consolidate the power of religion among the Kurdish community. Rather, it was a major discursive act—deliberate or not—that by reproducing the divine words of God affirmed the validity, prestige, and credibility of the Kurdish language. It also proved the literary credentials of Kurdish by elevating it to an equal ontological level with Arabic, "the holy language of Allah."[135] The translation and printing of sacred verses gave Kurdish all the sanctity that religious texts had. Hence it would be fair to argue that the translation of the Qur'an into Kurdish—and other vernaculars—was, in a sense, the manifestation of an "egalitarianism among languages" even though Arabo-Islamic culture "was not one of translation but of assimilation."[136] To put it differently, "if all languages now shared a common (intra)-mundane status, then all were in principle equally worthy of study and admiration. But by whom? Logically, since now none belonged to God, by their new owners: each language's native speakers- and readers."[137] Moreover, with the translation of the Qur'an, *Kurdistan* took the first step toward the nationalization of religion in the Kurdish case.

Promotion of Linguistic Works in Journal Kurdistan

In Europe, the nineteenth century was a golden age for the growth and reform of languages, with the promotion of national literatures, monolingual/bilingual dictionaries, grammar books, and so forth, which were intended to kindle the fire of national consciousness among the masses. Similarly, linguistic works became indispensable elements of nascent Kurdish nationalism during the last decades of the Ottoman rule as nationalist Kurdish intellectuals began to promote Kurdish literature, dictionaries, and grammar books. *Kurdistan* proudly announced the publication of Sheikh Yusuf Zîyaeddîn Pasha's Kurdish-Arabic dictionary, entitled *El-Hediyye't'ul-Hamidiyye fi'l-Lugat'il-Kurdiyye* (A Gift to Hamid in the

Kurdish Language), with an introductory section on Kurdish grammar.[138] The publication of this dictionary was particularly important, given that Arabic was the most prestigious and sacred language in the Muslim world and Zîyaeddîn Pasha's dictionary, much like the translation of the Qur'an, elevated Kurdish to the same ontological level as Arabic. Ironically, by order of Sultan Abdulhamid II, to whom the dictionary had been dedicated, the Ottoman Ministry of Education banned the dictionary and confiscated it from booksellers in June 1906.[139] Sultan Abdulhamid II had already banned Albanian-language books and correspondence, which indicated that the Sultan and his administration were concerned that the publication of such dictionaries and textbooks would bolster nationalist feelings among non-Turkish components of the empire. In any case, an aggressive form of Turkish nationalism hostile to non-Turkish communities' nationalist inclinations had been on the rise as early as the *Tanzimat* period. Basing his argument on Ottoman archival documents, Soleimani illustrates the uncompromising linguistic nationalism of the Ottoman Turks, who considered Ottoman constituencies that did not speak Turkish to be disloyal, untrustworthy, and a threat to the Ottoman state.[140]

As far as vernacular education was concerned, although *Kurdistan* devoted generous space to the importance of education in lengthy articles in almost every issue, it did not focus on vernacular education in Kurdish. However strange this preference might seem for a journal promoting linguistic nationalism; it was in line with *Kurdistan*'s overall stance on education. The editors of *Kurdistan* believed that without a certain degree of economic and industrial progress and modernization/Westernization, which could be accomplished only through literacy and education—in any language— Kurds would not be able to compete with more advanced neighboring ethnic groups, the Turks in particular. Perhaps schooling per se seemed more important than promoting Kurdish as the language of instruction as long as education was instrumental in the progress and modernization of Kurdish society. Thus, discourses of reform and modernity were always dominated by a discernible "sense of urgency," which also can be observed in Ottoman reform literature.[141] This aspect of Kurdish modernization, as envisioned in *Kurdistan*, was similar to the "material domain" in Chatterjee's analysis of anti-colonial nationalism.[142] Accordingly, in their political battle with the imperial power, nationalists divide their struggle into two domains: the spiritual and the material, the latter being the domain of social progress in economy, science, technology, and modern methods of statecraft. To defeat colonial domination, "the colonized people had to learn those superior techniques of organizing material life and incorporate them within their own culture."[143] Perhaps, the Bedir Khan Brothers felt the same way as far as the salvation of the Kurds was concerned.

Rapprochement between Kurmanji and Sorani
as the First Standardization Effort

Kurdish language does not constitute a unified standard language. Instead, as a *polycentric language*, to use Stewart's term,[144] it has a few speech varieties with *Kurmanji* and *Sorani* being the two major, and more or less standardized, dialects. Kurdish intellectuals of the period, influenced by the nation-state premise of *one nation, one language*, were aware of the linguistic division in their society and the need for a linguistically homogeneous unity. In the corpus of *Kurdistan*, we see a discursive strategy that could be seen as the first practice of deliberate innovative language cultivation and planning, or what Heinz Kloss has called *ausbaun*, in an effort to bring about a rapprochement between Sorani and Kurmanji varieties.[145] There are many techniques of language-shaping in *ausbau*. One such technique utilized in *Kurdistan* was the deliberate inclusion of some *Sorani* words in *Kurmanji* texts as illustrated in the sample sentences below.[146]

- God *has not created* [nekirdiwe] anything better [çaktir] than reason.[147]
- O Kurds! God and the Prophet and the imams and [other] notables *have shown* us [nîşa me kirdine] such useful advice and the right path.[148]
- In this [issue of] the newspaper, I have *addressed/sent* (rêkirdiwe) a Turkish letter to Sultan Abdul Hamid Khan.[149]
- Read Imam Ghazali's book; see what verses [and] what hadith he *has cited* [zikir kirdiwe] about ill-intentioned ulama.[150]

The editor's word choice in these sentences and elsewhere was an obvious discursive *strategy of rapprochement* that perhaps aimed to bring the two varieties closer to each other in an effort to create a roofing language or what Kloss calls *dachsprache*,[151] which might serve as a standard language for different dialects, like *fus'ha* (modern standard Arabic).[152] It is interesting to see that the editor Abdurrahman Bedir Khan limited himself to a few Sorani Kurdish words, perhaps because he himself did not have a good grasp of Sorani or even if he did, he might have felt that Kurmanji speakers might not comprehend his message if he used Sorani vocabulary extensively. What is more, the editors of *Kurdistan* often hinted at common origin for the two dialects, which probably was meant to create or reinforce the impression that the two dialects are merely two mutually intelligible varieties of the same language.

The publication of Sorani poetry side by side with Kurmanji seems to have been another technique of *ausbau* utilized by the editors of *Kurdistan* to create a similar assumption among its readers. Furthermore, when introducing a poem by Haji Qadir Koyi,[153] M. M. Bedir Khan stated: "His language is Sorani [ezmanê Sora]. That is why, not all Kurds know this language. . . [However] it is easily understood if read carefully."[154] Notice how the editor presented Sorani as a mere variety of Kurdish which can be understood easily *"if read carefully."* The author referred to Sorani as a *language* rather than a *dialect* perhaps due to the lack of a better term, such as *zarava*, a neologism in Kurdish that signified *dialect* or *variety*, which probably had not yet been coined. In any case, *dialect, speech variety*, and *national language* as terms and concepts belong to modernity.

Consequently, *Kurdistan* became the first Kurdish journal to take up issues concerning the dialectal nature of Kurdish by downplaying the differences between the two varieties and attempting to bring them closer to each other through language cultivation. In this way, the speakers of the two dialects could imagine themselves as the speakers of a common language belonging to a common nation, as was the case of Albanian with its dialects of Gheg and Tosk.[155] The utilization of a limited number of language-shaping techniques in *Kurdistan* was probably the result of the substantial lexical, but more importantly, grammatical differences between the two dialects, which without prior familiarity with the other dialect also undermines mutual intelligibility in different contexts. It is important to note that neither the *Dimilî (Zazakî)* nor *Goranî/Hawramî* varieties of Kurdish were included in the use of *ausbau*.

Kurdish Common History on Pages of *Kurdistan*

Nationalists utilize history to reconstruct collective national identities from real or invented essential cultural traits, including shared memories of great exploits or personages, myths of origin, genealogy, tradition, rituals, and so forth that tend to be socially, culturally, and politically binding. They characterize the persistent and recurrent aspects of collective continuity and difference. Pointing to this crucial role of history, Renan observed that "more valuable by far than common customs posts and frontiers conforming to strategic ideas is the fact of sharing, in the past, a glorious heritage and regrets. . . or the fact of having suffered, enjoyed, and hoped together. These are the kinds of things that can be understood despite differences of race and language."[156] Given the importance of history in nation-building, this section discusses *Kurdistan*'s historiographic nationalism and its role in forging a Kurdish national identity. Thanks to the flexible and open-ended character of narrative identity, revisiting the same events or occurrences in history and reinterpreting them in accordance with the requirements of the present day are standard practices among nationalist historians and politicians. Therefore, history as a glorious heritage and heroic past, among other preexisting

cultural attributes, becomes one of the most effective resources available for
the cultivation and articulation of national identity.

So far as the construction of Kurdish history is concerned, the first
time the journal *Kurdistan* made reference to Kurdish history[157] was in
its second issue when M. M. Bedir Khan made the following announcement: "God willing, from now on, I will talk about the history of the Kurds
[tarîxa Kurda], too; what is their origin and their descent; the intelligent
and famous people that have arisen among them; I will write [about] them
all."[158] Although this extract seems to be a simple announcement about a
future topic to be covered by the journal, it carries powerful implications
and ideologies. The phrase "history of Kurds" [tarîxa Kurda] along with
such lexemes as "esil" [origin] and "nesil" [descent] presuppose or take
for granted that Kurds are a distinctive community who possess a collective *national* history of their own without detailing the facts. In any case,
since history is, to a great extent, an ideological construct, in such historical narratives the factual details do not matter; what matters is the general
trajectory of the story. Hence the text imagines the Kurdish community as
a social and political entity that has persisted through time in an uninterrupted continuity since time immemorial. The following is another typical
example that illustrates a similar discursive practice: "O Kurds! For once,
look at your state of being and that of your neighbour Moscow. Kurds are
the same today as they were a thousand years ago. But your neighbours have
attained merits and skills; they possess states [of their own]. [Conversely]
Kurds have remained weak and miserable [jar û reben]."[159] On the surface,
the excerpt is a lament about the Kurds' lack of progress in comparison
with Russians (Moscow). However, there are three underlying, but subtly
conveyed, messages that rest on a set of assumptions: first, it is assumed
that there exists a unified collective community that possesses a collective
proper name: Kurds; second, Kurds as a coherent ethnic group are rooted in
a history whose past can be traced back to antiquity—or more specifically
to "a thousand years ago"—that has remained unchanged. This is a common strategy in the historicization of nations, for nationalists attempt to set
the birth of their nation as early as possible to underscore the fact that their
nation is not a newly emerging "invented" entity, but rather a historical and
thus inevitable "natural" reality. The third presupposition embedded in the
extract is that Kurds not only constitute a nation, but they also deserve a
state of their own. While it has not been attained *yet*, a point *implied* in the
statement that argues that the "neighboring nations," significantly Moscow,
have already achieved statehood, Kurds have lagged behind merely because
of their "weakness and misery."

The Presentation of the Bedir Khan Family's Political Past as Kurds' Collective History

As we saw earlier, patterns of media ownership are crucial in determining the formation of a media discourse in accordance with the interests of owner(s).[160] The Bedir Khan Brothers, equipped with privileged access to newspaper publication, had the power to imagine, construct, and disseminate a particular version of Kurdish history in line with their own personal and familial interests. With this goal in mind, they attempted to formulate a specific version of Kurdish history as the history of their dynasty, which had ruled the Botan Emirate until the mid-nineteenth century. Consequently, one of the most remarkable discursive acts of *Kurdistan* was its reconstruction of Kurdish history as the familial history of the Azîz or Azîzan, the editors' princely family. Comparable history writing practices have been observed in other places, which demonstrate the contestation between tribes and their attempts to create official histories out of their respective tribal accounts.[161] One such example is in Jordan where ethnographers have promoted their particular tribal history as the history of Jordan.

In *Kurdistan*, a particular version of Kurdish national history was forged in the process of selective memory by manipulating the "collective act of remembering as well as the collective act of forgetting."[162] The following extract is a good case in point: "I know that Kurds don't know anything about the history of Kurdistan. Therefore, in every [issue] of my newspaper, I will very briefly write about the history of Kurdistan and that of the ancestors of the Aziz [Azîzan]."[163] Here, through the use of collocation or the proximity of the phrases[164] "the history of Kurdistan" and "the [history of] Azîzan" in the same sentence, Abdurrahman Bedir Khan equated or associated Kurdish history with the political past of the Azîzan. What is more, he also started a Kurdish history series entitled *Hukkamên Cezîretu ibni Umer [The Rulers of the Jazirat ibn Omar]* in the 8th–14th issues of *Kurdistan*, where he introduced a total of twenty figures from his family's lineage who ruled their Botan principality.[165] In the first article in this series, he provided a brief account of the foundation of his dynasty:

The [full] name of Jazira is Jazira of ibn Omar [Jazira of Omar's Son]. This city was established two hundred years after the Prophet, may peace be upon him, under the auspices of Abdulaziz bin Omar Al-Barqamidi.[166] In 680,[167] Prince Suleiman established his dynasty around Jazira. Prince Suleiman was a Kurd. This Prince Suleiman, may he rest in peace, is the ancestor of Bedir Khan Beg and all the emirs of Kurdistan.[168]

First, to attribute an antique value or a primordial quality to his family, the editor provided the date on which Jazeera was established. Second, he suggestively highlighted that Prince Suleiman was a Kurd and not only the ancestor of the Bedir Khans, but the ancestor of all the other princely families of Kurdistan, which by default incorporated all Kurdish rulers as the offspring of the Bedir Khan family. This particular representation implied that the history of Kurdistan was the same as the history of his family.

Another meaningful aspect of this history is that the editor cited Sharaf al-Din [Sharaf Khan] Bidlisi's (1543–1598/99) *Sharafname* (1596 [2005]) as a source. Still, interestingly, he used only the parts of the book that pertained to his own family, although Sharaf Khan recounted all the Kurdish dynasties founded until his time (1596), including the Bitlis Principality, which was ruled by Sharaf Khan himself.[169] Moreover, it should be noted that Abdurrahman Bedir Khan introduced Sharaf Khan as a mere "alim" (scholar) and overlooked his aristocratic/princely background.[170] In contrast, when talking about Shah Ali Beg, one of his own ancestors, the editor stated that Shah Ali Beg, along with Amir Sharaf of Bidlis, accepted Sultan Selim's suzerainty. It seems like the editor was not aware that Amir Sharaf of Bidlis penned the Sharafname.

What is more, Abdurrahman Bedir Khan was very selective when using Sharaf Khan as a source. For instance, he disregarded Sharaf Khan's claims that the Azîzan family used to practice the Yezidi religion.[171] Here, the author not only omitted a crucial piece of information and an inconvenient fact about the previous religion of his ancestors, but he also highlighted their Islamic heritage to present a more favorable image of the Azîzan among the predominantly Muslim Kurds.

This brings us to another outstanding discursive practice of the journal *Kurdistan*: the Bedir Khan Brothers claimed a *silsila* or investiture in a long line of descent from the Prophet. They traced their family lineage back to Khalid ibn al-Walid, an Arab Umayyad military general and a companion of the Prophet, who conquered Kurdistan in a bloody campaign under the banner of Islam in the seventh century. M. M. Bedir Khan wrote, "O ulema and mîr and aghas of the Kurds! You all know my origin and descent. My ancestor is Khalid ibn al-Walid, may God be pleased with him, our tribe is Botan, we are known as the Azîzan."[172] In the same way, Abdurrahman Bedir Khan claimed: "There was a scholar of merit, his name was Sharaf bin Shemseddin. . . . In his history of Kurdistan, he wrote that Prince Suleiman is a descendant of Khalid ibn al-Walid [and] that he is from the Botan tribe."[173] This claim to prophetic ancestry at first seems to contradict and undermine Bedir Khan's claim to Kurdish national leadership. Nonetheless, as stated above, the factual details matter less than the general course of the narrative. When a historic situation takes on a mythical character, contradictions are forgotten or at least relativized.[174] The same practice was true of Iranian and Ottoman rulers who also used this religious allusion as a way to frame political claims or legitimize their rule.[175]

The more contemporary history of the Bedir Khan family was also at the center of *Kurdistan*'s production of Kurdish history. Bedir Khan Beg (1802–1870), the last prince in the genealogy of the Bedir Khan dynasty and the father of the editors of *Kurdistan*, received extensive attention in the journal. Abdurrahman Bedir Khan narrated his father's rule (1821–1847) in two lengthy articles, one in Kurdish and another in Turkish. In the Kurdish article, he said: "Bedir Khan Beg became the Ruler of Kurdistan [Hakimê Kurdistanê] in 1250 (1835) . . . At that time, the [Ottoman] state officials were plundering Kurdistan . . . However, when Bedir Khan Beg took control, he rescued all tribes and clans from the cruelty of the officials . . . and ruled over his tribes with justice . . . . All Kurdistan, including the Hakkari region, fell under his rule."[176] The author venerated Bedir Khan Beg and portrayed him as a heroic Kurdish leader and national savior who protected the Kurds from the corrupt Ottoman governors. Next, he asserted that his father ruled over all Kurdistan, a claim meant to attribute to Bedir Khan Beg the role of a national leader. However, in reality, he ruled over a considerable territory, not all of which was considered to be Kurdistan. Contrary to the journal's effort to present Bedir Khan Beg as a Kurdish national leader, he was not necessarily motivated by nationalist sentiments when he opposed Ottoman officials.[177] Rather, his and other Kurdish emir's major concern was to preserve their tribal authority and privileges and expand them when possible. Presenting Bedir Khan Beg as a Kurdish national leader should come as no surprise. When crafting their histories of the past, historians, nationalists, politicians, and so forth, always manipulate their national histories by eliminating or modifying inconvenient or burdensome facts and historical periods, and by promoting or even inventing favorable events and moments. Thus, "getting its history wrong" is indeed a part of being a nation. Nonetheless, it is remarkable that the journal *Kurdistan* treated Kurdistan as a nation-state and Bedir Khan Beg as a national ruler of that state. What is more, the Kurdish article mentioned the Armenian struggle against corrupt Ottoman state officials. It urged the Kurds to ally with the Armenians against the Ottoman state, a point utterly absent from the Turkish article.

Due to space limitations, I am unable to discuss the Turkish article at length, but suffice it to say that although the Turkish article was presented as a "translation" of the original Kurdish article, there are glaring discrepancies between the two. Most noticeably, the tone of the Turkish article was much softer, as it revolved around: (1) the unjust practices of the state officials—not the state itself—in Kurdistan; (2) the Ottoman state's misunderstanding of Bedir Khan's "alleged" defiant stand; and (3) the general bitterness—not antagonism—of Bedir Khan Beg, who was portrayed as a Kurdish leader loyal to the Muslim Ottoman state. This deliberate discursive act can be observed in other Turkish articles in which the Bedir Khan Brothers mitigated their Kurdish nationalist tone in favor of the Ottoman state to avoid antagonizing the Sultan or the Young Turks/CUP. Nonetheless, a fascinating sentence in the Turkish article stands out: "Before setting out for Jazeera along with around 30,000 troops from the regular army, 15,000 militias and 40 cannons, the Sublime's decree, which included the reasons for the *War of Kurdistan* [Kurdistan muharebesi], was announced" (my emphasis).[178] Despite his relatively softer tone in the Turkish article, the author suggestively used the phrase "War of Kurdistan" to present the conflict as a war between two states, which implicitly portrayed Bedir Khan Beg as a national leader of Kurdistan.

Construction of Kurds as a Primordial Nation

The construction of ancient history as a significant constituent of national identity can be found in all nationalist narratives. However, *Kurdistan*'s treatment of ancient Kurdish history had to wait until the 24th issue of the journal, that is, after the editor finished articulating Kurdish history as the tribal history of his princely family. In an article that traced the history of the Kurds back to antiquity, the author presented the main points of the rather complex topics of the history of the Kurds and Kurdistan in a condensed fashion, without going into factual details:

> Although the political borders [hudud-i sîyasîye] of Kurdistan are not clearly defined, today, Kurds dwell in Media [Medya] and parts of ancient Assyria [Asuristan]. The region that includes Erzurum, Diyarbekir, Mosul . . . Ardalan region and Kermanshah territory, Lower Zab, Bitlis and Batman cities as well as the Lake Van vicinity are the ancient territory [cevelângâh] of this courageous nation [millet] [. . .] Regrettably, we cannot come across any important Kurdish source to investigate the beginning of the Kurdish presence in these areas. [Thus] it is imperative that we turn to . . . the Assyrian and the Chaldean historical remnants. [. . .] In their history, we come across one of the enemies of the Assyrians known as "Kardu"; the ancient Iranian sources prove that these Kardus were the present-day Kurds. In ancient Iranian sources, too, Kurds were known as Kardu or Kardyen. In Sanskrit, which is the mother of the Zend language, Kardu and Kardyen constitute the origin of the modern term "Kurd." Since both words mean "hero" and "courageous," they are the most persuasive evidence that these are innate qualities of the Kurds that they have inherited [from their ancestors].[179]

First, the author discursively mapped Kurdistan by invoking its major cities, regions, rivers, and mountains. Second, he described the location of Kurdistan using ancient references, that is, Media and Assyria, which subtly implies that the history of the Kurds can be traced back to the time of the ancient Medes (the Median Empire) and the Assyrians, which serves as a myth of common origin or ancestry. References to the Assyrian and Chaldean sources further consolidated his argument about the ancient roots of the Kurds. Exploring the origins of the term "Kurd" in ancient languages once again added an ancient or primordial quality to the root of the Kurdish community, establishing it as an "ancient nation." The link between Kurdish, Sanskrit, and Zend[180] might be read as a subtle reference to the pre-Islamic, Indo-European roots of the Kurds, which distinguishes and dis-identifies the Kurds from the Ottomans, particularly the Turks and Arabs, and reminds the reader of the "original" Kurdish national identity prior to the arrival of the Ottoman Turks and Arabs. Noteworthily, Abdurrahman Bedir Khan was in close contact with such orientalists as Martin Hartman and Hugo Makas, who were interested in the ancient past of the "orient."[181]

The Journal Kurdistan's Pantheon of Kurdish Heroes

Scholars of nationalism see nationalism and religion as two analogous phenomena. One such similarity pertains to the fact that nationalism has its own gods as nationalists treat its patriotic heroes as prophets and messiah-saviors.[182] Correspondingly, *Kurdistan* created what might be called the pantheon of Kurdish national heroes by making references to ethnic ancestry and personage. One prominent historical figure promoted by *Kurdistan* was Saladin, the Kurdish commander and founder of the Ayyubid dynasty. An article entitled "Selahedînê Eyûbî" [Saladin Ayyubi] narrated the glory of the Ayyubid Sultanate of Egypt, Syria, and Kurdistan under Saladin. The article concluded with Saladin's just administration, his role as the protector of Muslims, and his contribution to Islamic civilization. In the following sections of the article, the author stated: "The founder of the Ayyubid state was Saladin Ayyubi. He himself was Kurdish from the Ruwadiye clan. His father and ancestors were from Dwin [. . .] I pray to God that a few more people like this sultan rise among Kurds so that he [*sic*] can liberate Kurds and all Muslims from this danger."[183] Although the article promotes Saladin as a great Muslim warrior and a sultan within the context of Islam, the significance of Saladin for the editor was his Kurdish identity, which was reclaimed in the immediate outset of the article by wresting Saladin's Kurdish identity from Islamic history. The editor also designated him as the savior and protector of the Muslim world. Despite this nationalization practice, the significance of Kurdish identity to Saladin himself is debatable, as he was wholly assimilated into the Arabo-Islamic culture in a milieu where the dominant social identity marker was religion, not ethnicity.[184]

Two other Kurdish rulers promoted in the pages of *Kurdistan* were Bad, the founder of the Marwanid dynasty, and Abu Said, who also ruled the Marwanids. Abdurrahman Bedir Khan wrote:

> The courageous commander Bad, who established the Marwanid or Humeydiye dynasty with Diyarbekir as its capital city, provided a great service to Islamic civilization. Especially during the reign of Abu Said, this dynasty brought up many well-known scholars and people of merit. In fact, as if out of longing for its glamorous success of the good old days, Amed, that is Diyarbekir city,[185] seems as though it has wrapped itself up in a black robe of mourning; while back it was a centre of science and art, today it is just like the other Ottoman provinces; it is destroyed day by day under the cruelty of Abdulhamid's administration.[186]

The first thing to notice in this extract is the metaphorical use of "Amed" as a synecdoche for Kurdistan. Second, the author nostalgically celebrated the glorious days of Abu Said's administration and the Marwanids's contribution to Islamic culture. It seems that the implicit yet underlying message is about the prosperity of *Amed*, or Kurdistan, under a Kurdish ruler—suggestively before the arrival of the Turks in the region. Now that it is destroyed under "Abdulhamid," a Turkish ruler, Amed is "in grief as the outward expression of the loss of its Kurdish king." The editor's narrative revolved around present humiliation and oppression as opposed to a favorable and glorious past under Kurdish rulers.[187]

Naming practices are important because names become part of the subject's nature in collective remembering. If we are to imagine ourselves as unique, we need distinctive names as national labels.[188] Comparably, in the excerpt above, "Amed" as the original Kurdish nomenclature is foregrounded while "Diyarbekir," the official name of the city, is backgrounded as an act of semantic cleansing to foster the Kurdish identity of that city against the Arabo-Islamic or Ottoman Turks' claims. This discursive act is reinforced when the editor used "Amed" as a synecdoche for "Kurdistan." Finally, although the pantheon of *Kurdistan* consists of figures from different historical periods, the most dominant figures came, not surprisingly, from the house of the Bedir Khans, in which the father of the two editors received the most attention.

Classical Literature as an Element of Kurdish National Culture

The editors of *Kurdistan* were also engaged in the cultivation of Kurdish classical literature as a component of a common Kurdish culture that would demonstrate the capacity of Kurdish as a language of literature and high culture, which in turn would imbue the Kurds with a sense of national pride. However, the journal's use of Kurdish literature remained limited because although Kurds possessed a rich body of oral literature, a considerable portion of this heritage was not written due to social, economic, and political limitations.[189] Therefore, only a few written works of literature existed and even fewer were accessible, as most of these works were manuscripts held in scattered private collections.[190] As a result, *Kurdistan* heavily drew on Ahmad Khani's *Mem û Zîn* and the nationalist poetry of Haji Qadir Koyi.

Aware of the nation-forming power of language and literature, the Bedir Khan Brothers took great national pride in *Mem û Zîn* and pushed it to the foreground. From the 2nd issue onward, they began to publish *Mem û Zîn* in a piecemeal fashion, turning it into printed material and a monumental piece of Kurdish national literature. The editors of *Kurdistan* saw these samples of Kurdish literature "as the hallmark of a civilised and sovereign people."[191] In this context, the discursive act of publishing *Mem û Zîn* became a sample of Kurdish vernacular literature that served *Kurdistan* as an ideological and intellectual program, while it served the Kurdish masses as an emotional, intellectual, and ideological link between language and national identity and instilled the Kurds with a sense of national pride. It also validated Kurdish as a vibrant and colorful language of high literature. The editors intended to show Khani's learning and the articulation of this wisdom in Kurdish to revive the past, transform its cultural products into elements of everyday reality, and establish a link to the glorious past. What is more, the journal wished to demonstrate that Kurdish, "which was powerful enough to allow Ahmad Khani to become a great poet, could once again sustain a great culture."[192]

However, the significance of the language of *Mem û Zîn* for *Kurdistan* does not mean that the journal did not take interest in its content. On the contrary, *Kurdistan* exploited *Mem û Zîn*'s content as well as its form. As we saw earlier, the Bedir Khan Brothers did not hesitate to cite patriotic verses from Khani's *Mem û Zîn* to convey their own nationalist and sometime secessionist messages. When announcing the publication of *Mem û Zîn* in serial form, M. M. Bedir Khan wrote: "On the surface, it is the story of two young lovers, but many *hidden meanings*, accounts, and wisdom can be inferred from it. That is why one should read [it] carefully (my emphasis)."[193] Presumably, the "hidden meaning" of *Mem û Zîn* implies the view that the romantic aspect of this epic, the impossible love between Mem and Zîn, was just an allegoric reflection of the Kurdish society that was divided between the Ottoman and Safavid Empires at the time of its composition. While *Mem* and *Zîn* represented the two parts of divided Kurdistan, the third character, Bekir or Beko, represented the discord and disunity among Kurdish rulers.[194] Yet, instead of explicitly elaborating on this political allegory due to the unfavorable social and political circumstances of the period, the editor contented himself with giving only a *hint* and let the reader fill in the gaps and infer the "true" meaning of this love story.[195]

Since they believe that a nation is as old as its language, nationalists frequently appeal to classic literature in order to add the *image of antiquity* to their respective nations. In other words, if the language has always existed, so has the nation. From this perspective, it can be argued that the sections of *Mem û Zîn* in the pages of *Kurdistan* had implications other than lending authenticity, validity, prestige, and credibility to the Kurdish language or helping the editors to forms and express their nationalist narrative. The publication of *Mem û Zîn* also helped to demonstrate the retrospective pattern of the Kurdish language. In that *Mem û Zîn* served the journal's *strategy of perpetuation*,[196] emphasizing the uninterrupted historical continuity, or *la longue durée* of Kurdish national identity. Introducing *Mem û Zîn* to the reader, M. M. Bedir Khan proudly said: "In the year 1105 (1695),[197] Ahmad Khani, in Jazeera, wrote a poetic book. . . This book was written two hundred and ten years ago [berî du sed û deh sala]."[198] Having already provided the date, it was not a crucial piece of information to indicate how much time had passed since the time Khani wrote his *Mem û Zîn*. Perhaps the author added this "redundant" but crucial piece of information purposefully and with a particular goal in mind: to underline how old this monumental Kurdish book was and to emphasize the existence of the Kurds as an identifiable *national* community in history. By presenting *Mem û Zîn* as a piece of classical Kurdish national literature, *Kurdistan* transformed a literary tradition into a national legacy and a "usable past."

Lastly, national character is an indispensable element of nationalist narratives. Thus, "the first rule which we have to follow is that of national character: every people has, or must have, a character; if it lacks one, we must start by endowing it with one."[199] Discussing the rhetoric of identification, Billig asserts that when addressing the imagined national audience, national leaders identify themselves with the praised audience, which is described as the greatest on earth. "They dress it in rhetoric finery, then, these speakers-as-outfitters hold a mirror so the nation can admire itself."[200] Correspondingly, the editors of *Kurdistan*, in an attempt to "rediscover" the unique cultural genius of the Kurds, manufactured and fostered a collective Kurdish character, mentality, and behavior through *the strategy of positive self-representation* by using the lexemes of bravery, wisdom, generosity, and common positive attributions, which distinguished the Kurds from other ethnic communities of the empire.[201] Below are some relevant excerpts from *Kurdistan*:

Kurds are more hard-working and benevolent than all other nations [qewm].[202]
Kurds are generous and talented by nature.[203]

Although Kurds possess the most distinguished human traits such as intelligence, comprehension, courage, assiduousness, generosity, devotion, and
worshipful love of freedom, one does not come across their name in world
history.[204]

Knowing the importance of the authenticity, purity, and nobility of the
beliefs, values, and behaviors in ethno-cultural characterization, the editors
of *Kurdistan* portrayed Kurds as brave, intelligent, patriotic, strong, kind, and
generous people in their discourse of cultural-nationalism.[205]

Evolution of Kurdistan from a Geo-Ethnic
Land to a National Homeland

One of the conditions of modernity was a fundamental shift in ideas about
the significance of territory, which transformed from a geographical expression of cultural identity into an essential basis for defining group identity
in *national* terms.[206] In other words, since the social construction of one's
national homeland as an object of primordial attachment creates emotional
ties akin to that of kinship, territory as *locus amoenus* became a primary
factor in defining national identity.[207] Consequently, nations as products of
modernity usually claim a recognized territory with which they are associated
as *the homeland* beyond its physical and practical function. It follows that,
because "a nation without its homeland is unthinkable," every nation should
have a home[land], the way a family should have a home.[208] That is, in the age
of nationalism, "every inhabitant is expected to be tied to one national soil. . .
or to be an outcast."[209] Therefore, in nationalist narratives, territory acquires
a *perceptual unity* and becomes a *national territory* or *homeland* connecting
society and space in a profoundly new way that did not previously exist.[210]

Under the Ottoman Empire, the term "Kurdistan" referred to a geographical
area without any clearly defined boundaries. Nonetheless, given the essential
role of national territory in the national imagination, the journal *Kurdistan*, in
its discourse of *territorial nationalism*, presented Kurdistan as a well-defined
homogeneous geo-ethnic territory and the historical national homeland of the
Kurds. To begin with, the name of the journal, that is, *Kurdistan*, is significant
because the notion of the Kurdish national homeland was embedded in the
very fabric of the journal's name, which was flagged discursively in bold-
faced fonts at the top of the front page of every issue. As such, it turned into
an everyday representation and constant affirmation of the Kurdish national
homeland. What is more, starting from the 16th issue, the name of the journal
also appeared in the Latin script, though in smaller fonts right beneath the
Arabic (Figure 2.3). Reproducing the name of the journal *Kurdistan* in Latin
script itself was a major discursive act in that while the Arabic script was

Figure 2.3   The Folio Section of Journal *Kurdistan*.

associated with the Ottoman Empire and Islamic community and culture, the
Roman alphabet was associated with the West and Western modernity.

The folio section of the journal also reinforced the idea of Kurdistan as a
national territory. A notice on the right-hand side of the folio section read:
"Each time I will send two thousand [copies of the] newspapers to Kurdistan
to be distributed to people free of charge." On the left-hand side of the folio
section, another notice read: "Yearly subscription fee for everywhere outside Kurdistan [Kurdistan haricinde] is 80 pennies; it is free of charge for
special requests from within Kurdistan [Kurdistan dahilinde]." In both of
these *homeland-making* notes, the editors utilized the powerful dichotomy
of *particular homeland* versus *general elsewhere* with clear-cut imaginary
boundaries: Kurdistan is discursively constructed as a *particular territory*
as the Kurdish homeland in the phrase "within Kurdistan." This *particularity* is further consolidated with the construction of a *generalized elsewhere*
or *the unspecified world of foreigners and others* in the phrase "outside
Kurdistan." Although in the Ottoman administrative system, Kurdistan had
been divided into different provincial administrations under different names,
this discursive act disregarded this division and naming practice by presenting Kurdistan as a unified Kurdish national homeland.

Besides, although neither of the notes in the folio section mentions the
word "Kurd" explicitly, Kurds are inscribed in those notices through powerful presuppositions. In the first, the deictic word "people" refers to *us Kurds*
or to *the people of Kurdistan*, who would receive the paper free of charge,
which elevates the Kurds to a privileged position, while the second notice

further reinforces this unique and privileged status by repeating that the paper waives the subscription fee for "people from within Kurdistan." Given the fact that in modern politics "the people" is a discursive construct that is synonymous with "the nation," it is safe to assume that the word "people" in the first notice should be understood as "nation."[211] Needless to say, not everyone in Kurdistan was an ethnic Kurd. Nevertheless, offering a "Kurdish" paper free of charge to only those residing in what is presented as "Kurdistan" creates the impression that all people in Kurdistan *are* Kurdish. In any case, the name *Kurd-istan* (the place/home of the Kurds) inevitably reinforces this assumption.

Another powerful discursive act that strengthens this presupposition is the use of collocation. The proximity of the word "people" to the word "Kurdistan" determines the meaning of word "people" contextually as "nation."[212] The same practice of collocation can be observed in many other texts in the corpus of the journal *Kurdistan*. Consider the following extract: "we should take care of [all] Kurdish [Kurmanc] children as if they are our own children. Therefore, whoever among the people of Kurdistan wishes to send their child to Istanbul for education, they should send them to my brothers."[213] It is remarkable how the editor M. M. Bedir Khan in his excerpt equated the Kurds [Kurmanc] in the first sentence with *the people of Kurdistan* in the second sentence by implying through a supposition that *Kurds* and the *people of Kurdistan* are one and the same entity. Moreover, using *Kurds* and *the people of Kurdistan* interchangeably creates a new bond between the Kurds and their land, turning the territory into a common homeland and a primary element of identification. It is important to note that the word "Kurdistan" appears six times in the folio section of each issue alone. This high frequency further intensifies the familiar assumption among readers that the village, neighborhood, town, city, or region they live in might be different, but they are still a part of a larger (home)land called "Kurdistan."

A typical newspaper appears in a standard format where it is divided into sections such as domestic/national news, international news, opinion, and so on. This division also contributes to imagining the national homeland versus elsewhere as a form of *banal nationalism*. Owing to the lack of professionalism and the scarcity of resources, early Kurdish journals did not come out in such a standard format. Nonetheless, the discursive inference that corresponded to home versus abroad was achieved through the preponderance of news items from or about Kurdistan vis-à-vis news about *other* places, for example, the rest of the Ottoman Empire. In a *homocentric* sense,[214] roughly more than 60 percent of all texts in journal *Kurdistan* were exclusively about Kurds and Kurdistan, while around 21 percent were about issues pertinent to all Ottoman communities, including Kurds. Only 17 percent of the news

Table 2.2   Distribution of the Content of the News in Journal *Kurdistan*

News concerning Kurds	News concerning Kurds and other Ottomans	News not directly concerning Kurds
60%	21%	17%

pertained to issues that were not exclusively Kurdish concerns, but even those issues were presented from a Kurdish nationalist perspective (see, table 2.2).

Equally important is that the content of news items and articles in the journal also contributed to imagining Kurdistan as the Kurdish homeland. In an article, M. M. Bedir Khan wrote: "Likewise, his Excellency the Prophet said: 'Love of one's country is a part of faith,' that is . . . a true believer would also love his homeland [weten]."[215] Using religious intertextuality based on a hadith from the Prophet of Islam, the author articulated "love of country" as an indispensable strand of religion. In an open letter to Sultan Abdulhamid, the editor M. M. Bedir Khan requested the lifting of the ban on the circulation of his journal in Kurdistan: "Believing in the sanctity of the land on which you, the Padishah, to whom we turned for help, have set foot, I humbly request your orders that the journal *Kurdistan* be allowed in Kurdistan and other places where Kurds live [Kurdistan'la Kürdlerin bulundukları mahâll-ı saireye]."[216] The clause "in Kurdistan and other places where Kurds live," assumes that Kurdistan is an exclusive Kurdish homeland inhabited by Kurds, while there are also Kurds who do not live in their native homeland but *elsewhere*. In an article that condemns the Sultan for his mistreatment of the Bedir Khans, the editor Abdurrahman Bedir Khan wrote: "Five of my brothers who wanted to leave Istanbul for Kurdistan, which is their *ancient* sanctuary and their *original homeland* [vatan-ı aslîleri]."[217] Once again, the editor imagined Kurdistan as the ancient and the "original" [aslî] homeland of Kurds. In all these excerpts, the term "Kurdistan" acquired a political connotation as a national homeland and a unifying political entity.

After the French Revolution, the nation became the *patria* (homeland) and the goddess of the modern world, a new divinity and sacred: "The patria as sacred; blood shed for it as sanctified."[218] In a similar manner, the journal *Kurdistan* evoked the sacrifices using the rhetoric of blood and soil turning Kurdistan into a *patria* as illustrated in the following extract: "Now, Kurdistan is also under the Turks, under the control of Abdulhamid, like other countries [welat]. Abdulhamid sends the state officials who rule over you. But the Kurds are the owners of Kurdistan. For instance, if an enemy attacks Kurdistan, Kurds will die for it. Kurds cultivate the soil of that place; Kurds plant the trees of that place . . . Therefore, Kurdistan is yours."[219] Clearly, Kurdistan is portrayed as the Kurdish national homeland "exclusively" inhabited by Kurds, its "true owners," who would shed their blood for it. The extract evokes patriotic feelings by exploiting the emotional attachments to the folk, the agrarian lifestyle, and customs of the peasantry. However, the most politically out-standing assertion is in the first three lines, where Abdurrahman Bedir Khan portrayed Kurdistan as a colonized homeland under the rule of a non-Kurdish colonizer, that is, the Ottoman Turks, which is crystallized in the person of Sultan Abdulhamid and his officers, the unstated "foreign colonizers."

The Semantic Shift in the Term "Welat" (Homeland)

As far as the journal *Kurdistan*'s construction of the national homeland is concerned, it is important to discuss the semantic shift that the term "welat/wilat" underwent in early Kurdish journalistic discourse. In the premodern period, the term "welat/wilat," derived from the Arabic word "wilāyah," from which the Ottoman word "vilayet" (province) comes, generally referred to "region" or "province." In Kurdish, it had a similar connotation as evident from three oral versions of Khani's *Mem û Zîn*.[220] Likewise, the use of "welat/wilat" as a "native district, region or town" can be found in the Baban school of poetry, particularly in the poems of Nalî, Salim, and Kurdî, written in the Sorani variety of Kurdish, where the term "wilat" refers to the Kurdish province of Suleymaniye. The first major semantic shift in the meaning of "wilat" from "native province" to "native homeland" took place in the Sorani-Kurdish poetry of Haji Qadir Koyî, who used the term "wilat" in reference to the entire Kurdish land. In his famous qasida *Xakî Cezîr û Botan* (the Land of Jazira and Botan), Koyi said:

O the land of Jazira and Botan, which is the homeland of [willatî] the Kurds,
Thousands of shame that they will make you into Armenia.[221]

Remarkably, in these verses, Jazira and Botan, two distinct "wilats" (home-land), are combined into one large Kurdish national "wilat." What is more, analogous to Khani's use of the term, the editors of *Kurdistan* used "welat" to denote "native region" or "native district"[222] on a few occasions, which indicates that there was still a certain ambiguity around the term and that it was still being negotiated in the discourse of the journal. Nonetheless, on all other occasions, the editors of the journal *Kurdistan* used the term "welat" to denote the entire Kurdish national homeland. Of its 118 occurrences (in addition to 36 occurrences of the Arabic term "weten" [homeland]), the term "welat" predominantly signified the notion of a national homeland, similar to the French term *la patrie*. One such instance can be observed in the follow-ing lines by Abdurrahman Bedir Khan: "The homeland of the Kurds [welatê Kurdan] is weak like a wounded body."[223] Here, the term "welat" univocally refers to one unified Kurdish national homeland in its singular form (i.e., welatê).[224] Interestingly, in the title of the same article, the author uses both "welat" and "weten"—both of which denote "national homeland"—as if he wanted to ensure that he conveyed the meaning of the term "welat" with its new nationalist and political connotation. It is important to note that Ottoman public discourse was already familiar with the term "weten" or "watan" since the mid-nineteenth century, when Namik Kemal introduced this term with its modern connotations in his work *Vatan yahut Silistre* (Homeland or Silistra) in 1860.[225]

The Discursive Map of Kurdistan

Another discursive act the journal adopted to imagine Kurdistan as the Kurdish national homeland was by drawing a discursive map of Kurdistan. One such article, significantly entitled "Kurdistan and Kurds," appeared in the 24th issue of *Kurdistan*: "Although the political borders [hudud-i sîyas-îye] of Kurdistan are not clearly defined, today they dwell in Media and parts of ancient Assyria. The region that includes Erzurum, Diyarbekir, Mosul. . . Ardalan region and Kermanshah territory, Lower Zab, Bitlis, and Batman cities, as well as the Lake Van vicinity, are the ancient territory [cevelângâh] of this courageous nation [millet]."[226] Although the author was not particularly concerned with drawing a cartographic map of Kurdistan, with its precise borders, his discursive map still helped to create an assumption that Kurdistan, with its people, cities, rivers, lakes, and regions, forms a coherent geo-ethnic/territorial unit.[227] The fact that this discursive map was fashioned as a part of the journal's nationalist narrative in the age of nationalism means that it had an unambiguous symbolic function and political connotations, which is explicitly expressed in the phrase "although the *political borders* of Kurdistan." Equally important is the use of the conjunction "although" (ise de) at the beginning of the sentence, which might refer not only to the "lack of" but also "the necessity of" demarcating such "political borders." Finally, it is noteworthy that the author constructed "Greater Kurdistan" by including both parts of Kurdistan divided between the Qajar and Ottoman Empires. The same discursive act would be repeated later on by Babanzade Ismail Hakkı in the 4th issue of *KTTG* and by Kerküklü Necmeddin in the 1st issue of *Rojî Kurd*. This and similar discursive maps as an abstraction of the reality transcended the division of Kurdistan between two non-Kurdish empires and the fragmented reality of the Kurds along tribal, regional, linguistic, and sectarian lines. This practice perhaps meant to enable readers to add a spatial perception to their sense of an intact national homeland, identity, and unity. Nonetheless, it should be noted that on a few occasions, the term "welat" referred to the Ottoman homeland, making the term's referent rather vague, as illustrated in the following extract where the referent of "homeland" is not Kurdistan but the wider Ottoman homeland: "We know that recently many villages and cities of the homeland [weten] have fallen into the hands of other states."[228]

Kurdish Women and the Motherland

First and foremost, the journal *Kurdistan* lacked female contributors, as did the *KTTG* and *Rojî Kurd*. Although *Kurdistan* did not take a particular interest in gender relations, it promoted a gendered nationalist discourse where women were portrayed as innocent, pure, and chaste mothers of the nation that should be protected by the sons of the nation. This was a common feature of various incipient nationalisms.[229] Mojab has observed that "in the case of women. . . sexuality is inseparable from the project of nation-building. The purity of the nation, and its strength, is inseparable from the chastity. . . of its women. If the motherland should be cleared from foreign domination, the ideal woman, too, should be virgin and legally possessed."[230] Comparably, *Kurdistan* made extensive use of women's sexuality by endorsing the narrative around the chastity of women as the "women and wives of the nation."[231] This can be most visibly observed in articles concerning the enslavement of Kurdish women by Christian men, both in the context of the invasion of Crete and in the fear over a possible Russian invasion of Kurdistan.[232] A remarkable recurring imagined theme is Muslim Kurdish women being forced to serve wine to Russian soldiers in the event the Russians occupied Kurdistan. There is a strong link between serving wine and eroticism, and its erotic or sexual connotations were perhaps taken from a common theme in classical Persian literature and reproduced in *Kurdistan*. In those articles, the editors' arguments revolved around the use of Muslim Kurdish women as sex-slaves, prostitutes, or non-marital partners by Christian men. From a male-gendered perspective, the Bedir Khan Brothers drew on discourses of family, women's honor, the discourse of sexuality, and religious nationalism to emphasize that the emancipation of the motherland was synonymous with the emancipation of the woman and her honor.

Education was another domain through which women entered *Kurdistan*'s discourse. Being aware of the improvement to the status of women in the West and their contribution to their societies, the editors of *Kurdistan* endorsed the education of Kurdish girls along with boys. In this way, the European secular, modern, and democratic logic of the nationalist blueprint found its expression in the pages of *Kurdistan* through the virtue of women's right to education. To mitigate their modernist and secular tone regarding the educa-tion of women, they frequently drew on Islamic religious discourse to back up their arguments.[233] Finally, there is a discernible discursive shift in ensuing Kurdish journals about the role of women in Kurdish society. For instance, *KTTG*, *Rojî Kurd*, and *Jîn* emphasized the contribution of Kurdish women to Kurdish society as the treasure and true guardians of the purity of the Kurdish language, as warriors, and as a part of the workforce, reflecting their role in the public sphere from the perspective of the narrative of modernity.

Interpersonal Metafunctions in Journal *Kurdistan*

Language produces three types of meanings simultaneously in its multi-functional feature or semantic complexity, namely *ideational, textual,* and *interpersonal metafunctions.* This section specifically deals with the latter metafunction where linguistic choices made in a text entail not only particular types of relations between the participants of a communicative event, but also enact social identities.[234] As far as an interpersonal metafunction in a media outlet is concerned, a writer/speaker might adopt the position of a reporter who simply informs the audience by reporting the facts of a matter; might assume an expert attitude by offering his or her opinion; or alternatively, he or she might adopt an authoritative tone, making suggestions, assertions and giving commands through the use of particular linguistic choices and various sets of linguistic features including such modalities and moods as declarative, imperative, interrogative, desiderative, and subjunctive clauses and sentences.[235] Each approach, in turn, articulates quite different social relations and identities between the text producer and the audience. For instance, an assertion made through a declarative sentence might sound authoritative and as such suggests an unequal social status and relationship between the text producer and the reader, positioning the text's producer as an authority and the reader as a layperson. *Interpersonal metafunction* is an essential part of discourse analysis in the corpus of *Kurdistan* because it reveals the relations of power and dominance enacted between the Kurdish elite, Kurdish commoners, and other participants, such as other nationalist movements, the CUP, and the Sultan Caliph.[236]

Leaders by definition are not only the custodians of the future of their nations, but also the custodians of their own personal careers. They continuously allude to common problems and common enemies, as well as to common present and future aims in order to stimulate national solidarity and unity among their audience, which might be more advantageous for their own personal politics. Thus, in what follows, I discuss how the Kurdish nobility, in the person of the Bedir Khan Brothers, made the nationalist argument the basis of their claims to power and produced identities and relations between themselves and the Kurdish commoners in accordance with their politics. The Bedir Khan Brothers created a specific relationship and assigned particular identities to themselves and their readership in which they presented themselves as figures of authority or national leaders. As such, they were capable of identifying problems and proposing the right solutions. The reader, on the other hand, was presented as part of a receptive national community in need of guidance, waiting to be told, waiting to know. This approach is evident in the mission statement of the journal that appeared in its very first issue: "In this newspaper, I will discuss the merits of science and skills; I will show Kurds where one can receive education [and] where there are good schools and medreses; [also] I will tell you all about places where there are quarrels; what the great powers are doing; how they conduct a war; how business is done; I will narrate them all."[237] Notice how M. M. Bedir Khan positioned himself as the "educator" and "modernizer" by using the pedagogic and authoritative voice of an expert, while he presented the readership as the "learner." In a similar manner, Abdurrahman Bedir Khan did not shy away from creating a hierarchy between himself—as a member of a Kurdish nobility—and the reader: "Leave the advising up to me; I leave its execution to you."[238] This authoritative discursive expression is the combination of two clauses: (a) "what I say goes"; and (b) "yours is not to reason why, rather it is to do."

From the same authoritative point of view, the editors of *Kurdistan* felt that the Kurdish notables, that is, people from their own social background, for example, other mîrs, aghas, and ulema, were the only effective class that could educate and modernize Kurds and thus should be entrusted with the protection and education of the "weak" and "ignorant" Kurdish masses. Consider the following extract taken from an article by Abdurrahman Bedir Khan: "O ulema, mîr, and aghas of Kurds! As the Prophet has commanded: 'all of you are shepherds and all of you are responsible for your flock; on Judgment Day, God will hold the dignitary accountable for [the situation of] Kurds."[239] Another article by M. M. Bedir Khan read:

O mîrs and aghas! You are mîrs and aghas thanks to Kurds [Kurmanc]. Therefore, you should be considerate of them, help them study [and] learn the sciences and skills. Who would you rule over as mîrs and aghas if Kurds [Kurmanc] vanished? The more Kurds [Kurmanc] become strong and rich; the more their mîrs and aghas become honourable and famous. Therefore, O dignitaries of the Kurds! You should care for the Kurds [Kurmanc] as if they are your children.[240]

Here, a reciprocal relationship and dependency between the Kurdish notables and the commoners is emphasized around a nationalist rhetoric of solidarity as well as religious intertextuality. What is more, the metaphorical application of the paternalistic authoritative discourse of family positioned the Kurdish commoners as the children of the Kurdish nobility. Another point that should be highlighted in the construction of relations and identities concerns the way the Bedir Khan Brothers articulated their identities vis-à-vis the "other participants," for example, tribal leaders, ulama, literati, and professionals. In one of his articles, M. M. Bedir Khan wrote: "O ulema and mîr and aghas of Kurds! You all know my origin and descent. My ancestor is Khalid ibn al-Walid, may God be pleased with him, *our* tribe is Botan, *we* are known as the Eziz [Azîzan] (my emphasis)."[241] Although the Bedir Khan Brothers delegated to Kurdish dignitaries the duty to protect, inform, and educate Kurds, as evident in the proceeding extract above, they still reserved the "actual" role of supreme leadership for themselves and their princely family, presenting the other Kurdish dignitaries as their auxiliaries.

In a predominantly Sunni Muslim Kurdish community of the late Ottoman period, some sort of religious background in the form of Islamic lineage or at least the expectation of piety in political leaders was vital for an individual or a group to acquire and justify their leadership position. This is because authority is seen as legitimate when it is supplemented by religious rhetoric. Starting from the very first issue of *Kurdistan*, M. M. Bedir Khan proclaimed his and his family's religious authority by evoking his ancestors' religious backgrounds to establish authority over both Kurdish religious elites as well as Kurdish commoners. To that end, in the second sentence of the extract above, the author foregrounded the religious (Islamic) aspect of his tribe in the first clause. As I discussed above, for the Bedir Khans, tracing their gene-alogy back to an Arab commander may seem to contradict and undermine their claim to the leadership of a nation in the making, given the fact that Khalid ibn al-Walid[242] was an *Arab* military general. However, in such narra-tives, the general trajectory of the story overshadows the factual details; what is important here, from the author's perspective, is that this divine descent serves as a way of framing the Bedir Khan's political claims and legitimizing their authority.[243] This point was reinforced in subsequent issues of the jour-nal as the editors projected their ancestors—and themselves by default—as the only legitimate leaders of all Kurds. Consider the following extracts:

> In 680,[244] Prince Suleiman established his dynasty around Jazira. Prince Suleiman was a Kurd. This Prince Suleiman, may he rest in peace, *is the ances-tor of Bedir Khan Beg and all emirs of Kurdistan* (my emphasis).[245]

> Since the time of *our* ancestors, *we* have been the princes of Botan; we are the dignitaries of the Kurds [Kurmanca]. Therefore, it is our obligation to work for the wellbeing of the Kurds [Kurmanca] (my emphasis).[246]

After establishing Prince Suleiman's Kurdish identity at the outset, Abdurrahman Bedir Khan presented him not only as the ancestor of the Bedir Khans, but of all princes of Kurdistan. This inevitably designated the Bedir

Khans as the progenitor of all Kurdish rulers, lending further legitimacy to the family's aspirations to the supreme national leadership position.[247] With similar familial concerns, Abdurrahman Bedir Khan wrote: "You know that I am the son of that person who made great efforts with his sword for your wellbeing. Today, as a requirement of this era, I am providing that [same] service with my pen."[248] In the first sentence, by invoking the former leadership position of his aristocratic family, the editor aspired to the same position implicitly through presumptions: first, the reader is *expected* to know who the writer's father was—even though his name is not directly mentioned—and what he had done for the Kurds, an ostensibly unified community. Then, the editor presented his publication activities as an extension of his family's political and national legacy in an uninterrupted continuity to convey that his leadership is no less important than his father's: "the pen is mightier than the sword."

As briefly mentioned above, one of the main characteristics of *Kurdistan* is its authoritative and paternalistic attitude toward Kurdish commoners. In one article, Abdurrahman Bedir Khan wrote:

> Why are Kurds, who are so brave and hardworking, becoming unworthy and dishonourable like a herd in the hands of cruel officials? Aren't you human beings? Are you inferior to other people? [. . .
>
> Enough is enough; open your eyes, raise your hands, draw your swords. . . Go rally around your leaders; go rally around your ulema and unite. Rid yourselves of this cruelty of the officials. Shame on you.[249]

Utilizing the authoritarian discourse of family discipline or the disciplinary discourse of "scolding" in his criticism of his readership, the editor positioned himself as a figure of authority. He is bestowed with social and political superiority who knows and hence has the right to teach, discipline, and lead the readership, which is projected as an inferior "naughty child" that needs to be disciplined.[250] This harsh paternalistic discourse has manifested itself in the commanding tone of the editor through the use of the imperative mood, that is, "open!" "raise!," "draw!," "go!" "rally!" "unite!", and through tag question clauses such as "Aren't you human being?" and "Are you inferior?"[251] The editor further reinforced this authoritative tone and contempt with a phrase of scolding in line with the authoritative discourse of feudalism, i.e., "shame on you!"[252] Another source of this authoritarian attitude was what could be called "internal orientalism," "oriental orientalism"[253] or "Kurdish orientalism," an intra-ethnic civilizing project that took place between the self-appointed Kurdish modernizing elite and the "unreformed" and "backward" Kurdish commoners."[254]

Addressivity and Convocation of a New Audience

A text needs an audience to realize its potential to constitute meaning, because a writer writes "to" an imagined audience and expects them to play their "co-constitutive" role in the realization of the meaning.[255] In his discussion of the Victorian novel, Henry James argued that "in every novel the work is divided between the writer and the reader; but the writer makes the reader very much as he makes his characters."[256] Thus, an author does not only make the reader as part of this fictional world, but also tells the reader how to participate in this fiction by "offering a standpoint from which to secure uptake of the utterance."[257] Similarly, a study by Klancher on early nineteenth-century English periodicals shows that after the ideological chaos caused by the French Revolution, periodicals became a paradigm of audience-making, as they carved out a new audience and transformed old ones.[258] In this context, the formation of genres takes place in the realm of "addressivity" that is constituted by the mutual orientation of the text to the audience and vice versa.

Insofar as media studies are concerned, the audience is viewed from two perspectives: audience as potential consumer, and audience as composed of "citizens who must be reformed, educated [and] informed"[259] *Kurdistan*, which introduced the newspaper genre to the Kurds, adopted the latter standpoint, producing and convoking a new public not only as an audience that needs to be informed, educated, and reformed, but also an audience of a particular kind: a national audience whose members shared a common language, history, culture, ethnicity, concerns, political aspirations, and so forth. In *Kurdistan*, the convocation of the new audience as a new collectivity is most obvious in the forms of particular types of addressivity. In so doing, instead of an arid monological conception, the editors of *Kurdistan* formed a specific relational matrix through a dialogic exchange between themselves and their readers. To this end, as a strategy of emphasis on intranational sameness or national singularity, *Kurdistan* often addressed its readers in nationalist terms.[260] For example, the most frequently used term was *Gelî Kurdino!* (O Kurds!), which appears thirty-four times in the corpus of *Kurdistan* and aimed to downplay the tribal, linguistic, sectarian, and regional differences among Kurds and persuade them to imagine themselves as a homogeneous and horizontal national community.[261]

Following is a list of forms of addressivity and their frequency followed by brief analysis:

- O Kurds [Gelî Kurdino!] (thirty-four times)
- O mîrs and aghas and Kurds [Kurmancno]!) (one time)
- O Kurds, O mîrs and aghas! (one time)
- O mîrs and aghas [and] Kurds! (two times)

- O ulema of the Kurds! (thirteen times)
- O mîrs and aghas of Kurds! (two times)
- O mîrs and aghas of Kurds [Kurmanca]!) (two times)
- O ulema and mîrs and aghas of Kurds! (one time)
- O ulema and mîrs and aghas of Kurds! [Kurmanca] (three times)
- O ulema and pashas and mîr and aghas of Kurds! (one time)
- O wealthy Kurds! (one time)
- O Kurdish notables! (one time)

Through these various forms of addressivity, the editors forged a new type of audience as the members of an ethno-national community. Furthermore, in these forms of addressivity, the journal *Kurdistan* used the terms "Kurd" and "Kurmanc" interchangeably, lifting the concept of *Kurmanc* from its parochial context, that is, landless non-tribal peasants, and inserting it into a broader context of a national group: Kurds. As a result of this discursive act, the semantic difference between the term *Kurd* and *Kurmanc* was blurred as both terms came to signify the same entity as a national phenomenon. Consequently, instead of the previously dominant narrow elitist view that did not consider non-tribal *Kurmanjs* to be dignified enough to be called Kurds,[262] *Kurdistan* redefined Kurdishness through a semantic shift in the meaning of the term *Kurmanc*.

Another discursive act is embedded in the editors attempt to bring different strata of Kurdish society together in a new semantic context by using the possessive structures in possessive determiners mostly visible in such forms as "ulamas of Kurds/Kurmancs (Gelî ulemayên Kurda/Kurmanca)"; "aghas and mîrs of Kurds/Kurmancs" (Gelî mîr û axayên Kurmanca), and so forth. In these possessive structures, everybody is "of" Kurdish extraction, a discursive act that obscures class differences between the elite and non-elite as well as other social stratifications such as occupation, gender, religion, region, and language. By using these particular forms of addressivity, the journal found a new way to frame, channel, and organize social relations by creating a sense of belonging, interdependency, and solidarity among different strata that glossed over class differences.

NOTES

1. Kendal, *The Kurds under the Ottoman Empire*, 5; Olson, Robert. *The Emergence of Kurdish Nationalism and Sheikh Said Rebellion, 1880–1925*. (Austin: University of Texas Press, 1989), 7; van Bruinessen, *Agha, Shaikh and State*, 175–176.

2. Silopî, *Doza Kurdistan*; Klein, *Claiming the Nation; Klein, Kurdish Nationalists and Non-nationalist Kurds*, 135–153.

3. Cf. Breuilly, *Reflections on Nationalism*; Breuilly, John. *Nationalism and the State*. (Chicago: The University of Chicago Press, 1993); Brass, *Elite Groups, Symbol Manipulation*.

4. Zürcher, *Turkey: A Modern History*, 72–76; Akşin, Sina. *Turkey from Empire to Revolutionary Republic: The Emergence of Turkish Nation from 1789 to Present*. (London: Hurts & Company, 2007), 41.

5. Seton-Watson, Robert William. *The Rise of Nationality in the Balkans*. (New York: E. P. Dutton and Company, 1918). (Accessed January 6, 2011: http://www .promacedonia.org/en/pdf/setton-watson_the_rise_of_nationality_in_the_balkans_19 18.pdf), 135–136; Zürcher, *Turkey: A Modern History*, 86.

6. Klein, *Claiming the Nation*, 17; Zeine, *The Emergence of Arab Nationalism*, 85–86.

7. See, *Kurdistan*, No. 31, April 14, 1902.

8. Hanioğlu, M. Şükrü. *The Young Turks in Opposition*. (New York: Oxford University Press, 1995), 78–84; Göçek, Fatma Müge. *Rise of Bourgeoisie, Demise of Empire: Ottoman Westernization and Social Change*. (New York: Oxford University Press, 1996), 117; Tütengil, Cavit Orhan. *Yeni Osmanlılar'dan Bu Yana İngiltere'de Türk Gazeteciliği (1867–1967) [Turkish Journalism in England since the New Ottomans (1867–1967)]*. (Istanbul: Belge Yayınları, 1969), 1; Celîl, *Kürt Aydınlanması*, 14.

9. Fairclough, *Media Discourse*; Sheyholislami, *Kurdish Identity, Discourse, and New Media*.

10. Klein, *Kurdish Nationalists and Non-nationalist Kurds*, 141; Olson, *The Emergence of Kurdish Nationalism*, 7–8; Gelvin, *The Modern Middle East*, 54–55; Özoğlu. "Nationalism and Kurdish Notables in the Late Ottoman-Early Republican Era," *International Journal of Middle East Studies*, Vol. 33, (February 2001): 383–409, 384.

11. Malmîsanij, *Cızira Botanlı Bedirhaniler [The Bedirkhans' of Jazira Botan]*. (Istanbul: Avesta, 2000), 187–190.

12. Ibid.

13. See: Abdurrahman Bedir Khan's open letter to the Sultan entitled, "This Is My Humble Petition to the Majestic and Magnificent, His Excellence Sultan Abdulhamid Khan the Second" [Şevketlu Azametlu Sultan Abdulhamid Han-i Sanî Hazretlerine Arzihal-i Abidanemdir], *Kurdistan*, No. 6, October 11, 1898. The letter goes to great length to complain how the Sultan's advisors were unjustly punishing his brother in order to intimidate and discourage Abdurrahman Bedir Khan from publishing *Kurdistan*. The editor's brothers, including Emin Ali Bedir Khan, were indeed being harassed, beaten up, and arrested by the Ottoman authorities.

14. Malmîsanij, *Cızira Botanlı Bedirhaniler*, 188.

15. Malmîsanij, Mehemed. *Kürd Teavün ve Terakkî Cemiyeti ve Gazetesi [The Kurdish Society and Gazette for Mutual Aid and Progress]*. (Istanbul: Avesta Yayınları, 1999), 37; Jwaideh, *The Kurdish National Movement*, 298.

16. Malmîsanij, *Cızira Botanlı Bedirhaniler*; Dersimi, Nuri. *Hatıratım [My Memoire]*. (Ankara: Öz-Ge Yayınları, 1992).

17. See, Özoğlu, *Kurdish Notables and the Ottoman State*.

18. Malmîsanij, Mehemed. *İlk Kürt Gazetesi Kurdistan'ı Yayımlayan Abdurrahman Bedirhan: 1868–1936 [Abdurrahman Bedir Khan, the Publisher of the First Kurdish Journal Kurdistan: 1868–1936].* (Istanbul: Vate Yayın Dağıtım, 2009), 13.

19. Cited in Celîl, *Kürt Aydınlanması,* 45.

20. For instance, see, *Kurdistan,* No. 22, February 2, 1900.

21. See, *Kurdistan,* No. 31, April 14, 1902.

22. Cf. Breuilly, *Reflections on Nationalism;* Breuilly, *Nationalism and the State.*

23. Khoury, Philips. *Urban Notables and Arab Nationalism: The Politics of Damascus 1880–1920.* (New York: Cambridge University Press, 1983), 96.

24. Smith, *Nationalism: Theory, Ideology, History,* 56; Breuilly, *Reflections on Nationalism,* 138.

25. van Bruinessen, Martin. "Ehmedî Xanî's Mem û Zîn and Its Role in the Emergence of Kurdish National Awareness," in *Essays on the Origins of Kurdish Nationalism,* edited by Abbas Vali. (California: Mazda Publishers, Inc., 2003), 41–57, 48, 51.

26. See, Bozarslan, M. Emin. *Kurdistan (1898–1902).* (Uppsala: Weşanxana Deng, 1991), Vol. 1, 13; Malmîsanij, *İlk Kürt Gazetesi,* 121; Tütengil, *Yeni Osmanlılar'dan Bu Yana Türk Gazeteciliği,* 92.

27. Tütengil, *Yeni Osmanlılar'dan Bu Yana Türk Gazeteciliği,* 111.

28. Technical problems faced by the CUP printing presses affected the publication of *Kurdistan* too. According to an article published in *Osmanlı,* the long delay in the publication of the forthcoming issue of *Kurdistan* was due to a technical problem at the printing house belonging to journal *Osmanlı. See,* Malmisanij, *İlk Kürt Gazetesi,* 121.

29. In the 25th–31st issues, this phrase changed to "Monthly [published] Kurdish and Turkish Newspaper" [Ayda bir neşrolunur Kürdçe ve Türkçe gazetedir].

30. This was a CUP printing house. Abdurrahman Bedir Khan translated *İttihat ve Terakki Cemiyeti'nin Matbaası* (The Printing House of the Committee of Union and Progress) into Kurdish as *Metbea Cem'îyeta Tefaq û Qencîya Musulmana* (The Printing House of the Society for the Union and Well-being of Muslims). See: Malmîsanij, *Yüzyılımızın,*16; Tütengil, *Yeni Osmanlılar,* 92.

31. In an announcement on the cover page of the journal, the editor stated that he had to move the journal from Geneva to London. However, he did not specify where the journal was printed.

32. Or the "İntikam Printing House," which probably belonged to the İntikamcı Yeni Osmanlılar Cemiyeti (The Committee for Avenging Young Ottomans), an offshoot of the CUP established by Ali Fahri, a key figure in the Egyptian branch of the CUP. For more details see: Hanioğlu, *The Young Turks,* 159–160.

33. Seyid Tahirê Botî, 'Ji bo Cerîdeya *Kurdistanê'* [To *Kurdistan* Newspaper], *Kurdistan,* No. 5, June 17, 1898.

34. Lewis, *The Emergence of Modern Turkey,* 187–188.

35. Celîl, *Kürt, Aydınlanması,* 26.

36. The Ottoman state had around 1,700 postal stations. *See,* Mardin, Şerif. *Religion, Society and Modernity in Turkey.* (New York: Syracuse University Press, 2006), 106.

37. Malmîsanij, *İlk Kürt Gazetesi*, 128–130; Hanioğlu, M. Şükrü. *Bir Siyasal Düşünür Olarak Doktor Abdullah Cevdet ve Dönemi [A Political Thinker Doctor Abdullah Cevdet and His Era]*. (Istanbul: Üçdal Neşriyat, 1981), 211.

38. Diyarbekir Eşrafından Ş. M., 'Kurdistan'dan Gelen Bir Mektup' [A Letter from Kurdistan], *Kurdistan*, No. 13, p. 3, April 2, 1899.

39. Hassanpour, Amir. "The Creation of Kurdish Media Culture," in *Kurdish Culture and Identity*, edited by Philip Kreyenbroek and Christine Allison. (London: Zed Book Ltd., 1996), 48–84, 56.

40. Tütengil, *Yeni Osmanlılar'dan Bu Yana Türk Gazeteciliği*, 56.

41. Klein, *Claiming the Nation*, 123.

42. For an interesting discussion on Ottoman coffee house culture and its sociopolitical implications *see*, Karababa, Eminegül and Ger, Güliz. "Early Modern Ottoman Coffeehouse Culture and the Formation of the Consumer Subject," *Journal of Consumer Research*, Vol. 37, No. 5, (February 2011): 737–760.

43. Hassanpour, Amir. *Nationalism and Language in Kurdistan*. (San Francisco: Mellon Press, 1992), 77–81; Hassanpour, *The Creation of Kurdish Media Culture*, 51, 67; Klein, *Claiming the Nation*, 122–126; Strohmeier, *Crucial Images*, 21.

44. Habermas, Jürgen. *The Structural Transformation of Public Sphere: An Inquiry into a Category of Bourgeois Society*. (Cambridge: MIT Press, 1989).

45. Cf. Wodak et al., *The Discursive Construction of National Identity*.

46. Klein, *Claiming the Nation*.

47. M. M. Bedir Khan, 'Open Letter', *Kurdistan*, No. 4, June 3, 1898.

48. M. M. Bedir Khan, 'Open Letter', *Kurdistan*, No. 5, June 17, 1898.

49. Cf. van Dijk, *Principles of Critical Discourse Analysis*, 302.

50. Abdurrahman Bedir Khan, 'Al Mu'minun Ikhwatun' [All Believers Are Brothers], *Kurdistan*, No. 7, November 5,1898.

51. M. M. Bedir Khan, 'Untitled', *Kurdistan*, No. 1, April 22, 1898.

52. Abdurrahman Bedir Khan, 'Welat-Weten' [Homeland], *Kurdistan*, No. 9, December 16, 1898.

53. Abdurrahman Bedir Khan, 'Untitled', *Kurdistan*, No. 11, February 10, 1899.

54. In analyzing texts' intertextual relations, Fairclough distinguishes between two types of intertextuality: (i) manifest intertextuality; and (ii) constitutive intertextuality. In the former, other texts are overtly present in the text in the form of, for instance, quotation marks. Whereas in the latter, other texts are so integrated into the text that no trace of them can be explicitly seen. *See*: Fairclough, *Discourse and Social Change*, 104.

55. Razi, G. Hossein. "Legitimacy, Religion, and Nationalism in the Middle East," *The American Political Science Review*, Vol. 84, No. 1, (March 1990): 69–91; Akhmajian, et al., *Linguistics: An Introduction to Language and Communication*. (Massachusetts: MIT Press, 1995).

56. Bazerman, Charles. "Intertextuality: How Texts Rely on Other Texts," in *What Writing Does and How It Does It: An Introduction to Analysing Texts and Textual Practices*, edited by Charles Bazerman and Paul Prior. (New York: LEA, 2004), 83–86, 94.

57. *See*: Malmîsanij, *İlk Kürt Gazetesi*, 105.

58. The journal *Kurdistan* published six open letters to the Sultan in the 4th, 5th, 6th, 7th, 10th and 13th issues.

59. The letters also warn the Sultan against Shia Iran, though to a lesser extent.

60. M. M. Bedir Khan Bedir Khan, 'Open Letter', No. 1. *Kurdistan*, No. 4, June 3, 1898.

61. The Ottoman Empire had been wary, since the seventeenth century, of Russia's expansionist policy of Pan-Slavism in the Balkans, their search for access to the Mediterranean Sea and the Indian Ocean, as well as their desire to have control over the Holy Land of Palestine. Abdurrahman Bedir Khan in another lengthy article explained Russian intentions on the Balkans and the Mediterranean. *See*, Abdurrahman Bedir Khan, "Hamidian Cavalry Regiments" [Hamidiye Suvari Alaylari], *Kurdistan*, No. 28, September 14, 1901.

62. Kurds had bitter memories of the Russo-Turkish war of 1877–1878, also known as the "93 War" in Turkish, which caused destruction and great human losses. *See*, Akşin, *Turkey from Empire*, 41; Kendal, *The Kurds under the Ottoman Empire*, 23. Also, Abdurrahman Bedir Khan mentioned the destructive results of this war in more detail in the 28th issue of *Kurdistan*.

63. M. M. Bedir Khan, 'Open Letter', *Kurdistan*, No. 4, June 3, 1898.

64. Abdurrahman Bedir Khan, 'Welat-Weten' [Homeland], *Kurdistan*, No. 9, December 16, 1898.

65. M. M. Bedir Khan, 'Untitled', *Kurdistan*, No. 3, May 20, 1898.

66. Klein, Janet. *The Margins of Empire: Kurdish Militias in the Ottoman Tribal Zone*. (California: Stanford University Press, 2011); Zürcher, *Turkey: A Modern History*.

67. See, Abdurrahman Bedir Khan, 'Hamidian Cavalry Regiments' [Alayên Siwarên Hemîdî], *Kurdistan*, No. 28, September 14, 1901.

68. M. M. Bedir Khan, 'Untitled', *Kurdistan*, No. 4, June 3, 1898.

69. Reproduced in M. M. Bedir Khan, 'Untitled', *Kurdistan*, No. 4, June 3, 1898.

70. Hassanpour, *Nationalism and Language in Kurdistan*, 87; Hassanpour, Amir. "The Making of Kurdish Identity: Pre-20th Century Historical and Literary Sources," in *Essays on the Origins of Kurdish Nationalism*, edited by Abbas Vali. (California: Mazda Publishers Inc., 2003), 107–162, 123; M. M. Bedir Khan, 'Untitled', *Kurdistan*, No. 2, May 6, 1898; O'Shea, Maria T. *Trapped Between the Map and Reality: Geography and Perception of Kurdistan*. (New York: Routledge, 2004), 146.

71. Abdurrahman Bedir Khan, 'Untitled', *Kurdistan*, No. 8, December 1, 1898.

72. Reproduced in *Kurdistan*, No. 8, December 1, 1898.

73. Hassanpour, *The Making of Kurdish Identity*, 129.

74. Later on, for the same purpose, M. Salih Bedir Khan would reproduce the same verses in one of his articles published in *Rojî Kurd*.

75. It is noteworthy that Kurdish prose writing started with Kurdish journalistic activities. *See*, Blau, *Kurdish Written Literature*, 23.

76. Cf. Wodak et al., *The Discursive Construction of National Identity*.

77. The Ottoman Empire, under the Hamidian regime, suffered another wave of territorial loss as a result of the Greco-Turkish War of 1897, which included the loss of Crete. Hanioğlu, M. Şükrü, *The Young Turks in Opposition*, 64; Zürcher, Eric J.

The Ottoman Empire 1850–1922: Unavoidable Failure, Turkology Update Leiden Project Working Papers Achieve (Department of Turkish Studies, Leiden University, 2004b). (Accessed March 21, 2010 http://www.tulp.leidenuniv.nl/content_docs/wap/ejz20.pdf), 1.

78. In support of his argument, in the 14th issue of *Kurdistan* the editor expressed his concerns about the Italian intentions to annex Tripolitania. He concluded that the Sultan would once again abandon Muslim subjects of Tripolitania to their fate.

79. For an evocative discussion on the close nexus between masculinity and nationalism, *see*: Enloe, Cynthia. *Bananas, Beaches, and Bases: Making Feminist Sense of International Politics*. (Berkeley: University of California Press, 1990).

80. Abdurrahman Bedir Khan, 'Girîd' [Crete], *Kurdistan*, No. 7, December 5, 1898.

81. Cf. Wodak et al., *The Discursive Construction of National Identity*.

82. Abdurrahman Bedir Khan, 'Kurdçe Kısım' [Kurdish Section], *Kurdistan*, No. 27, March 13, 1901.

83. Abdurrahaman Bedir Khan, 'Untitled', *Kurdistan*, No. 6, October 11, 1898.

84. The same is true of the Turkish language, as Abdurrahman Bedir Khan in another article referred to Turkish as "Romî" (the language of the Rom, i.e., Turkish). Abdurrhaman Bedir Khan, 'Untitled', *Kurdistan*, No. 6, October 11, 1898.

85. Abdurrhaman Bedir Khan, 'Untitled', *Kurdistan*, No. 6, October 11, 1898.

86. Hourani, Albert. "How Should We Write the History of the Middle East," *International Journal of Middle Eastern Studies*, Vol. 23 (1991): 125–136.

87. Abdurrahman Bedir Khan, 'Kurdçe Kısım' [Kurdish Section], *Kurdistan*, No. 27, March 13, 1901.

88. Cf. Billig, Michael. *Banal Nationalism*. (London: Sage Publications, 1995), 79; Kristeva, Julia. *Strangers to Ourselves*. (New York: Columbia University Press, 1991), 96.

89. Firro, *Metamorphosis of the Nation (al-Umma)*, 30–32.

90. Fairclough, *Language and Power*, 120.

91. Billig, *Banal Nationalism*, 70.

92. Ibid., 78, 93–94.

93. Kurdish is a pro-drop language, that is, a Kurdish sentence requires no expressed subject because the suffix (personal ending) attached to the verb signifies the subject in person and number. Since the conjugated verb forms have an implied subject, Kurds tend to drop the subject from the sentence. As a consequence, the number of subject pronouns in this text—and the other Kurdish texts for that matter—is not as high as it should be. *See*, Ekici, Deniz. *Kurmanji Kurdish Reader*. (Maryland: Dunwoody Press, 2007).

94. Volmert 1989, 123, cited in Wodak et al., *The Discursive Construction of National Identity*, 45.

95. Cf. Fairclough, *Language and Power*, 127–128; Benwell, Bethan, and Stokoe, Elizabeth. *Discourse and Identity*. (Edinburg: Edinburg University Press, 2006), 115.

96. Cf. Fowler at al., *Language and Control*. (London: Routledge & Kegan Paul, 1979), 204.

97. *See, Kurdistan*, No. 26, December 14, 1900.

98. See, *Kurdistan*, No. 29, October 14, 1901; *Kurdistan*, No. 26, December 14, 1900.

99. Deringil, *They Live in a State of Nomadism*, 313.

100. Makdisi, *Ottoman Orientalism*.

101. Ibid.

102. In his theory of colonial discourse, Homi Bhabha uses the term "ambivalence" to describe the continual complicity and resistance that characterizes the fluctuating feelings of the colonized towards the colonizer. Bhabha, Homi, "Of Mimicry and Man: The Ambivalence of Colonial Discourse," October, Vol. 28, (Spring 1984): 125–133.

103. Khalidi, Rashid. *Palestinian Identity: The Construction of Modern National Consciousness*. (New York: Columbia University Press, 1997), 76–89.

104. Cf. Deringil, *They Live in a State of Nomadism*.

105. M. M. Bedir Khan, 'Untitled', *Kurdistan*, No. 1, April 22, 1898.

106. Abdrurrahman Bedir Khan, 'Untitled', *Kurdistan*, No. 17, August 27, 1899.

107. Abdurhaman Bedir Khan, 'Alayên Siwarên Hemîdî' [Hamidian Cavalier Regiments], *Kurdistan*, No. 28, September 14, 1901.

108. Abdurrahman Bedir Khan, 'Untitled', *Kurdistan*, No. 16, August 6, 1899.

109. Abdurrahman Bedir Khan, 'Wezîyeta Hazir û Musteqbel a Kurdistanê' [The Present and the Future Situation of Kurdistan], *Kurdistan*, No. 29, October 14, 1901. It is important to note that this text was translated into Ottoman Turkish and was published side by side with its original Kurdish version.

110. Armenians had two nationalist organizations called *Henchak* (the Bell), founded in 1887, and *Dashnakzoutiun* (Armenian Revolutionary Federation), founded in 1890, which sought Armenian independence. *See,* Zürcher, *Turkey: A Modern History*, 83.

111. Hassanpour, *Nationalism and Language in Kurdistan*; Sheyholislami, *Kurdish Identity, Discourse, and New Media*; van Bruinessen, *Ehmedî Xanî's Mem û Zîn*.

112. Cf. Chatterjee, Partha. *The Nation and Its Fragments: Colonial and Postcolonial Histories*. (New Jersey: Princeton University Press, 1993), 6–7.

113. *Kurdistan*, in the 1st–3rd, 8th–12th and the 15th issues, came out exclusively in Kurdish. From the 4th issue on, only a few articles, for example, letters addressed to the Sultan, appeared in Ottoman Turkish. Furthermore, from the 1st issue on it was indicated on the cover page of each issue that *Kurdistan* was a fortnightly "Kurdish" newspaper in the "Kurdish" language. Although articles in Ottoman Turkish started to appear from the 4th issue on, only from the 25th issue onwards did this note on the cover page change to "A Kurdish newspaper in Kurdish and Turkish languages."

114. It is noteworthy that Khani significantly wrote his masterpiece in Kurdish due to the inferior status of Kurdish vis-à-vis the more prestigious Arabic, Persian, and Turkish languages. For Khani, what made Kurdish inferior or less prestigious was the

lack of a written literature in that language. He expressed these feelings in *Mem û Zîn*, see, *Kurdistan*, No. 9, December 16, 1898.

115. Cf. Wodak et al., *The Discursive Construction of National Identity*.

116. Cf. Anderson, *Imagined Communities*, 34–35.

117. This phrase appeared in the 3rd through 25th issues.

118. It should be noted that in some issues the editors made insignificant changes in the wordings of this phrase.

119. However, from the 25th issue on, the following phrase appeared on the first pages of each issue: "Monthly Kurdish and Turkish Newspaper."

120. *See, Kurdistan*, No. 13, April 2, 1899.

121. *See*, Abdurrahman Bedir Khan, 'Teblig' [Notice], *Kurdistan*, No. 18, October 3, 1899.

122. M. M. Bedir Khan, 'Untitled', *Kurdistan*, No. 4, June 3, 1898.

123. Abdurrhaman Bedir Khan, 'Untitled', *Kurdistan*, No. 6, October 11, 1898.

124. Ş. M., A notable from Diyarbekir, *Kurdistan*, No. 13, April 2, 1899.

125. Soleimani, Kamal. *Islam and Competing Nationalisms in the Middle East: 1876–1926*. (New York: Palgrave, 2016).

126. Klein argues that both history and literature promoted in the Kurdish journals of the period were those of the elite, leaving the Kurdish language as the only and the most crucial cultural trait that the elite and the Kurdish masses had in common. Klein, *Claiming the Nation*, 107.

127. Ibid.

128. The issue of illiteracy and its consequences will be discussed later.

129. Anderson, *Imagined Communities*; Hastings, *The Construction of Nationhood Ethnicity*.

130. Hassanpour, *Nationalism and Language in Kurdistan*, 84; Hassanpour, *The Making of Kurdish Identity*, 121.

131. Fatani, Afnan H. "Translation and the Qur'an," in *The Qur'an: An Encyclopaedia*, edited by Oliver Leaman. (London: Routledge, 2006), 657–669, 57; Zadeh, Travis. *The Vernacular Qur'an: Translation and the Rise of Persian Exegesis*. (London: Oxford University Press, 2012), 6, 214, 216.

132. Hastings, *The Construction of Nationhood Ethnicity*, 200.

133. The first printed complete-translation of the Qur'an into Kurdish was made by Muhammad Koyi Galizadeh in 1968. Galizadeh's three volumes were published under the title "Tafsira Kurdî" (Kurdish Interpretation) in Baghdad, *see*, Binark, Ismet and Eren, Halit. *World Bibliography of Translations of the Meanings of the Holy Qur'an: Printed Translations, 1515–1980*. (Istanbul: Research Centre for Islamic History, Art, and Culture, 1986).

134. Meyrowitz, Joshua. "Shifting Worlds of Strangers: Medium Theory and Changes in 'Them' versus 'Us'," *Sociological Inquiry*, Vol. 67, No. 1, (January 1997): 59–71, 60.

135. Later on, Urdu also started to enjoy a similar prestige thanks to the translation of the Qur'an and other works of Islamic literature into this language, nevertheless to a much further extent. For a comprehensive discussion on translation/interpretation of the Qur'an and religious nationalism, *see*, van der Veer, Peter. *Religious*

Nationalism: Hindus and Muslims in India. (California: University of California Press, 1994).

136. Cf. Anderson, *Imagined Communities*, 71; Hastings, *The Construction of Nationhood Ethnicity*, 12.

137. Anderson, *Imagined Communities*, 70–71.

138. It is important to note that Khani's *Nûbihara Biçûkan* (*The Spring of the Children*) (1684) was also an Arabic-Kurdish lexicon promoting the Kurdish language. Although *Kurdistan* makes no mention of Khani's *Nûbihara Biçûkan*, later in its 19th issue, the journal *Jîn* would proudly draw attention to that lexicon.

139. Malmîsanij, *İlk Kürt Gazetesi*, 87–90.

140. Soleimani, *Islam and Competing Nationalisms*.

141. Deringil, *They Live in a State of Nomadism*, 327; Makdisi, *Ottoman Orientalism*, 780.

142. Chatterjee, *The Nation and Its Fragments*, 120.

143. Ibid.

144. Stewart, William A. "A Sociolinguistic Typology for Describing National Multilingualism," in *Readings in the Sociology of Language*, edited by Joshua A. Fishman. (The Hague: De Gruyter Mouton, 1968), 531–545.

145. Kloss, Heinz. "Abstand Languages and Ausbau Languages." *Anthropological Linguistic*, Vol. No. 7, (October 1967): 29–41, 29.

146. Today, many Kurdish media outlets have adopted the same strategy as they mix Sorani words with Kurmanji texts and vice versa as another step in the unification of the two varieties. This practice is endorsed not only by nationalists but also by linguists and academics. Furthermore, mixing the two varieties has become a common practice today among Kurds both in Kurdistan and the diaspora, which has come to be humorously called "Sormanji," similar to Spanglish.

147. Abdurrhaman Bedir Khan, 'Untitled', *Kurdistan*, No. 6, October 11, 1898.

148. Abdurrahman Bedir Khan, 'Al Mu'minun Ekhwatun' [All Believers Are Brothers], *Kurdistan*, No. 7, November 5, 1898.

149. Abdurrhaman Bedir Khan, 'Untitled', *Kurdistan*, No. 6, October 11, 1898.

150. Abdurrahman Bedir Khan, 'Ulemayên Kurda re Xîtabek' [An Address to the Kurdish Ulema], *Kurdistan*, No. 13, April 2, 1899.

151. Kloss, *Abstand Languages and Ausbau Languages*, 33.

152. Cf. Muljačić, Zarko. "Standardization in Romance," in *Trends in Romance Linguistics and Philology*, edited by Rebecca Posner et al. (Berlin: Walter de Gruyter, 1993), 77–116.

153. Haji Qadirê Koyî (1817–1897), who according to Hassanpour was the second exponent of Kurdish nationalism after Khani, composed his poetry in his native Sorani variety. Following in the steps of Khani, he attached great importance to the vernacularization of the Kurdish language. *See*: Hassanpour, Amir. The Kurdish Experience, *Middle East Report*, (No. 189, (July/August 1994) 2–7+23.), 4; Hassanpoour, *Nationalism and Language in Kurdistan*, 57; van Bruinessen, *Ehmedî Xanî's Mem û Zîn*, 45–50.

154. M. M. Bedir Khan, 'Untitled', *Kurdistan*, No. 3, May 20, 1898. It is remarkable to see here that M. M. Bedir Khan used the word *Sora* in reference to Koyi's

dialect long before the term *Sorani* was known by scholars and linguists as a reference to the *Central Kurdish* dialect.

155. Billig, *Banal Nationalism*, 32.

156. Renan, Ernest. "What Is a Nation?" in *Nation and Narration*, edited by Homi Bhabha. (London: Routledge, 1990), 8–22, 19.

157. The word "history" (tarîx) occurs only ten times in the entire corpus of *Kurdistan*, three of which occur in contexts not directly linked to the Kurds and one in reference to Ottoman history. The search for the word "ancestor" and its variations (ecdad, cedde, bapîr, etc.) revealed twenty-nine occurrences, of which only fifteen were directly linked to the Kurds. Of these fifteen words, five were used in the articles where the editor provided an account of his princely family. The search also revealed twelve occurrences of the word "Ezîz/Ezîzan," the name of the editor's princely family.

158. M. M. Bedir Khan, 'Bismillah al-Rahman al-Rahim' [In the Name of Allah, the Compassionate, the Merciful], *Kurdistan*, No. 2, May 6, 1898.

159. Abdurrahman Bedir Khan, '*Laysa lil-insani illa masaa*' [Man Can Have Nothing but What He Strives For], *Kurdistan*, No. 7, November 5, 1898.

160. Fairclough, *Language and Power*; Fairclough, *Discourse and Social Change*; Fairclough, *Critical Discourse Analysis*; Fairclough, *Media Discourse*.

161. Shryock, Andrew. *Nationalism and the Genealogical Imagination: Oral History and Textual Authority in Tribal Jordan*. (Los Angeles: University of California Press, 1997).

162. Renan, *What Is a Nation?*, 11.

163. Abdurrahman Bedir Khan, 'Untitled', *Kurdistan*, No. 8, December 1, 1898.

164. Baker, Paul. *Using Corpora in Discourse Analysis*. (London: Continuum, 2007).

165. The monopoly of the elite in Kurdish history is also evident in Sharaf al-Din [Sharaf Khan] Bitlisi's (1543–1598/99) *Sharafname* (1596), the first written account of "Pan-Kurdish history." Hassanpour indicates that *Sharafname* was written as the history of the rulers of Kurdistan rather than the history of the Kurdish people or tribes because "Sharaf Khan tried to demonstrate that the Kurds were a people with a tradition of governing. Therefore, Sharaf Khan significantly called his work 'The story of the rulers (hokkam) of Kurdistan.' " Hassanpour, *The Making of Kurdish Identity*, 111–112.

166. Bozarslan asserts that this is an inaccurate point because according to *Sharafname*, the founder of Jazir was Omar bin Abdulaziz of Umayyads. *See*, Bozarslan, M. Emin. *Kurdistan (1898–1902)*, Vol. 1. (Uppsala: Weşanxana Deng, 1991), 213.

167. 1281 according to the Gregorian calendar.

168. Abdurrahman Bedir Khan, '*Hukkamên Cezîretu îbnî Umer*' [The Rulers of the Jazirat ibn Omar], *Kurdistan*, No. 8, December 1, 1898.

169. There are minor discrepancies between the list of rulers in the *Sharafname* and in *Kurdistan*.

170. He introduced him with the following words: "Alimek xweyfedil, navê wî Şeref bîn Şemsedîn. . . . . . ." [(there was) a scholar of merit, his name was Sharaf bin

Shemseddin. . .], *see*, Abdurrahman Bedir Khan, '*Mîr Silêman bîn Xalid*' [Prince Suleiman bin Khalid], *Kurdistan*, No. 8, December 1, 1898.

171. *See*: Allison, Christine. *The Yezidi Oral Tradition in Iraqi Kurdistan.* (Richmond: Curzon Press, 2001); Kreyenbroek, Philip. "Religion and Religions in Kurdistan," in *Kurdish Culture and Identity*, edited by Philip Kreyenbroek and Christine Allison. (London: Zed Book Ltd., 1996), 85–110; Şengül Birgül Açıkyıldız. "Ezidîlik Dininde Melek Tavus İnancı ve İkonografisi" [The Belief and Iconography of the Peacock Angel in Yezidi Religion], *Kürt Tarihi Dergisi* [Journal of Kurdish History] No. 5, (October 2014): 7–17.

172. M. M. Bedir Khan, 'Untitled', *Kurdistan*, No. 1, April 22, 1898.

173. Abdurrahman Bedir Khan, 'Mîr Silêman bîn Xalid' [Prince Suleiman bin Khalid], *Kurdistan*, No. 8, December 1, 1898.

174. In the *Sharafname* the lineage of many Kurdish princely families was traced to Arabo-Islamic origins. In the 3rd issue of *Kürd Teavün ve Terakki Gazetesi (KTTG)*, the author V.H. claimed that Sayyid Abdulkadir, the son of the legendary Shaikh Ubeydullah, was a descendant of the Prophet Muhammad. *KTTG*, No. 3, December 19, 1908.

175. Hassanpour, *The Making of Kurdish Identity*, 114; Özoğlu, *Kurdish Notables and the Ottoman State*, 28.

176. Abdurrahman Bedir Khan, 'Bedirxan Beg' [Bedir Khan Beg], *Kurdistan*, No. 13, April 2, 1899.

177. Bozarslan, Hamid. "Kürd Milliyetçiliği ve Kürd Hareketi (1898–2000)/ Kurdish Nationalism and Kurdish Movement," in *Milliyetçilik*, edited by Tanıl Bora. *Modern Türkiye'de Siyasi Düşünce.* (Istanbul: Iletişim Yayınevi, 2002), 841–870, 844; Kendal, *The Kurds under the Ottoman Empire*, 17.

178. Abdurrahman Bedir Khan, 'Bedirxan Bey' [Bedir Khan Beg], *Kurdistan*, No. 14, April 20, 1899.

179. Abdurrahman Bedir Khan, '*Kurdistan ve Kürdler*' [Kurdistan and Kurds], *Kurdistan*, No. 24, September 1, 1900.

180. The use of Zend as the name of a language or script is a misnomer because the term *Zend* means "interpretation" and as such it refers to the language commentaries of the verbatim translation of the manuscripts of Avesta, the most ancient scriptures of Zoroastrianism, into Middle Persian. *See*: Opengin, Ergin. "Tevatür ve Temellük Kıskacında Kürt Kültür Tarihçiliği" [Kurdish Cultural Historiography Caught between Hearsay and Appropriation], *Kürt Tarihi Dergisi* [Journal of Kurdish History], No. 11, (February/March, 2014): 17–29, 19.

181. Malmîsanij, *İlk Kürt Gazetesi*, 20.

182. Hayes, Carlton J. H. *Essays on Nationalism.* (New York: Russell, 1966); Smith, *Nationalism: Theory, Ideology, History.*

183. Abdurrahman Bedir Khan, '*Selahedînê Eyûbî*' [Saladin Ayyubid], *Kurdistan*, No. 15, May 5, 1899.

184. It is said that when the Mufti of Jerusalem praised "the Kurdish swords which defeated the Crusaders and liberated the Holy Land," in his reply Saladin emphasized his Islamic identity rather than his Kurdish identity, *see*, Kreyenbroek, *Religion and Religions in Kurdistan*, 107; Nezan, Kendal. "The Current Position and Historical

Background," in *Kurdish Culture and Identity*, edited by Philip Kreyenbroek and Christine Allison. (London: Zed Book Ltd., 1996), 7–19, 10.

185. It should be noted that although Amed was also under the rule of the Marwanids, the capital city of the Marwanids was not Amed but Farqîn (Silvan). *See*, Bozarslan, *Kurdistan*, Vol. 2, p. 427, fn. 53. Bozarslan further stated that the Marwanid dynasty was never known as the Humeydiye dynasty.

186. Abdurrahman Bedir Khan, 'Kurdistan ve Kürdler' [Kurdistan and Kurds], *Kurdistan*, No. 24, September 1, 1900.

187. Cf. Chatterjee, *The Nation and Its Fragments*, 97.

188. Halbwachs, Maurice. *On Collective Memory*. (Chicago: University of Chicago Press, 1992), 72; Billig, *Banal Nationalism*, 73.

189. Allison, Christine. "Old and New Oral Traditions in Badinan," in *Kurdish Culture and Identity*, edited by Philip Kreyenbroek and Christine Allison. (London: Zed Book Ltd., 1996), 29–47; Hassanpour, *Nationalism and Language in Kurdistan*.

190. For a discussion on challenges related to lost or inaccessible manuscripts of classic Kurdish literature, *see*, Ghaderi, Farangis. "The challenges of writing Kurdish literary history: Representation, classification, periodization." *Kurdish Studies*, Vol. 3/1, (January 2015): 3–25.

191. Hassanpour, *The Creation of Kurdish Media Culture*, 49.

192. Strohmeier, *Crucial Images*, 23.

193. M. M. Bedir Khan, 'Untitled', *Kurdistan*, No. 2, May 6, 1898.

194. Hassanpour, *Nationalism and Language in Kurdistan*, 87; Hassanpour, *The Making of Kurdish Identity*, 123; O'Shea, *Trapped Between the Map and Reality*, 146; Chyet, Michael L. "And a Thornbush Sprang up between them: Studies on Mem û Zîn, a Kurdish Romance." PhD diss. (University of California, Berkeley, 1991), 33.

195. See a fascinating discussion between Hassanpour and Vali about whether Khani's *Mem û Zîn* was the first manifestation of Kurdish nationalism, Hassanpour, *The Making of Kurdish Identity*; Vali, Abbas. "Introduction: Nationalism and the Question of Origins," in *Essays on the Origins of Kurdish Nationalism*, edited by Abbas Vali. (California: Mazda Publishers, Inc., 2003), 1–13.

196. Cf. Wodak et al., *The Discursive Construction of National Identity*.

197. 1105 according to Hijri calendar, which corresponds to 1675 in Gregorian calendar.

198. M. M. Bedir Khan, 'Untitled', *Kurdistan*, No. 2, May 6, 1898.

199. Cited in Smith, *Nationalism: Theory, Ideology, History*, 27.

200. Billig, *Banal Nationalism*, 98.

201. Cf. Wodak et al., *The Discursive Construction of National Identity*, 39.

202. M. M. Bedir Khan, 'Untitled', *Kurdistan*, No. 4, June 3, 1898.

203. Abdurrahman Bedir Khan, 'Laysa lil-insani illa masaa' [Man Can Have Nothing But What He Strives For], *Kurdistan*, No. 7, November 5, 1898.

204. Abdurrahman Bedir Khan, 'Kurdistan ve Kürdler' [Kurdistan and Kurds], *Kurdistan*, No. 24, September 1, 1900.

205. Bozarslan describes the pre-World War I era as the period of Kurdish cultural-nationalism. Bozarslan, *Kürd Milliyetçiliği ve Kürd Hareketi*.

206. Penrose, Jan. "Nations, States and Homelands: Territory and Territoriality in Nationalist Thought," *Nations and Nationalism*, Vol. 8, No. 3, (January 2002): 277–297, 283.

207. Cf. Wodak et al., *The Discursive Construction of National Identity*, 150.

208. Smith, *The Ethnic Revival*, 63.

209. Harris, Nigel. *National Liberation*. (London: I.B. Tauris, 1990), 257–258.

210. Penrose, *Nations, States and Homelands*, 278–279.

211. Hall, Stuart and Held, David. "Citizens and Citizenship," in *New Times: The Changing Face of Politics in the 1990s*, edited by Stuart Hall and Martin Jacques. (London: Lawrence and Wishart, 1989), 173–188.

212. Cf. Baker, *Using Corpora in Discourse Analysis*, 95–96.

213. M. M. Bedir Khan, 'Untitled', *Kurdistan*, No. 3, May 20, 1898.

214. Cf. Fowler, Roger. *Language in the News: Discourse and Ideology in the Press*. (London & New York: Routledge, 1991), 16.

215. M. M. Bedir Khan, 'Untitled', *Kurdistan*, No. 2, May 6, 1898.

216. M. M. Bedir Khan, 'Open Letter No. 1', *Kurdistan*, No. 4, June 3, 1898.

217. Abdurrahman Bedir Khan, 'Open Letter No. 4', *Kurdistan*, No. 7, November 5, 1898.

218. Chabod, Federico. "The Idea of Nation," in *Nationalism in Europe: from 1815 to the Present*, edited by Stuart Woolf. (London: Routledge, 1996), 124–136, 125.

219. Abdurrahman Bedir Khan, *'Thabat Al-Mulk Bel 'Adl'* [Justice is the Foundation of the Authority], *Kurdistan*, No. 9, December 16, 1898.

220. Chyet, *And a Thornbush Sprang Up*.

221. Koyî, Haji Qadir. *Dîwanî Hacî Qadirî Koyî [Collected Poems of Haji Qadir Koyî]*, edited by Sardar. H. Mîran and Karim. M. Şareza. (Stockholm: Nefel, 2004), 83. http://www.pertwk.com/pdf/haciqadikoye.pdf.

222. This meaning of the term "welat" has lingered into present day Kurmanji-Kurdish in the northern (Turkish part of) Kurdistan. On a personal note: When I was a child, one of our neighbors raised cattle for a living. In summers, they would go to the uplands of their native village to graze their animals. When I asked my mother their whereabouts, she would say: "Ew çûne welatê xwe" (They have gone to their "welat" [hometown/home-region]). The same is true of Sorani Kurdish, especially in its Mukriyani variety. For example, in parts of eastern (the Iranian part of) Kurdistan, Kurds use the term "welat/wilat" to refer to a space, place, area, or the interior of a house, for example, "wilatim xawên kirdewe" (I cleaned the house); "hemu wilatyan pis kird" (they made a mess here/there), (personal correspondence with Michael Chyet, Jaffar Sheyholislami and Ergin Opengin).

223. Abdurrahman Bedir Khan, 'Welat-Weten' [Homeland], *Kurdistan*, No. 9, December 16 , 1898.

224. The singular suffix–*ê* in "welatê" is one of the Kurdish possessive endings attached to a noun when that noun receives a modifier.

225. For the evolution of the term "weten/watan" in the context of Arab nationalism, *see*: Firro, *Metamorphosis of the Nation (al-Umma)*, 26–27; Hudson, Michael C. *Arab Politics: The Search for Legitimacy*. (New Haven: Yale University Press, 1977), 36–37.

226. Abdurrahman Bedir Khan, 'Kurdistan ve Kürdler' [Kurdistan and Kurds], *Kurdistan*, No. 24, September 1, 1900.

227. It is important to note that the journal *Kurdistan* never produced a cartographic map of Kurdistan. Except for the map presented to the Paris Peace Conference, formal attempts by Kurds to map Kurdistan appeared only in the 1930s. All previous cartographic maps of Kurdistan were drawn by non-Kurds. Cf. O'Shea, *Trapped Between the Map and Reality*, 143.

228. Abdurrahman Bedir Khan 'Hewadis' [News], *Kurdistan*, No. 16, August 6, 1899.

229. Cf. Mojab, Shahrzad. "Women and Nationalism in the Kurdish Republic of 1946," in *Women of a Non-State Nation: The Kurds*, edited by Shahrzad Mojab. (California: Mazda Publishers, Inc., 2001), 71–91, 76; Najmabadi, Afsaneh. *Women with Mustaches and Men Without Beards: Gender and Sexual Anxieties of Iranian Modernity*. (California: University of California Press, 2005), 97.

230. Mojab, *Women and Nationalism*, 76.

231. Najmabadi, *Women with Mustaches*, 207.

232. For relevant articles, *see*, Abdurrahman Bedir Khan, 'Maqaleê Mexsûse' [Special Article], *Kurdistan*, No. 20, December 29, 1899; M. M. Bedir Khan, 'Untitled', *Kurdistan*, No. 1, April 22, 1898; Abdurrahman Bedir Khan, 'Girîd' [Crete], *Kurdistan*, No. 7, November 5, 1898; Abdurrahman Bedir Khan, 'Welat-Weten' [Homeland], *Kurdistan*, No. 9, December 16, 1898; Abdurrahman Bedir Khan, 'Untitled', *Kurdistan*, No. 9, December 16, 1898; Abdurrahman Bedir Khan, 'Hirka-i Saadet' [The Cloak of the Prophet Muhammed], *Kurdistan*, No. 12, March 2, 1899.

233. For example, *see*, M. M Bedir Khan, 'Kullukum Ra'in Wa Kullu Ra' in Mas'ulun 'An Ra'iyyatihi' [All of You Are Guardians (in Trust of Something or Someone) And Are Accountable for Your Flock], *Kurdistan*, No. 3, May 20, 1898; and Abdurrahman Bedir Khan, 'Hel Yestewî'llezîne Ye'lemûne We'llezîne La Ye'lemûne' [Those who know are not the same as those who do not know], *Kurdistan*, No. 9, December 16, 1898.

234. Halliday, *An Introduction to Functional Grammar*; Fairclough, *Critical Discourse Analysis*, 133; Fairclough, *Media Discourse*, 5, 25; Wodak, *The Discourse-Historical Approach*, 8.

235. Fairclough, *Media Discourse*, 128.

236. Cf. Halliday, *An Introduction to Functional Grammar*; Fairclough, *Critical Discourse Analysis*; Fairclough, *Media Discourse*; Wodak, at al., *The Discursive Construction of National Identity*; Kress, *From Saussure to Critical Sociolinguistics*.

237. M. M. Bedir Khan, 'Bismillah al-Rahman al-Rahim' [In the Name of God; The Compassionate, The Merciful] *Kurdistan*, No. 1, April 22, 1898.

238. Abdurrahman Bedir Khan, 'Untitled', *Kurdistan*, No. 6, October 11, 1898.

239. Abdurrahman Bedir Khan, 'Untitled', *Kurdistan*, No. 6, October 11, 1898.

240. M. M. Bedir Khan, 'Untitled', *Kurdistan*, No. 4, June 3, 1898.

241. M. M. Bedir Khan, 'Untitled', *Kurdistan*, No. 1, April 22, 1898.

242. Later, the same practice was repeated in an anonymous article in *Rojî Kurd* (1913), where the author in his eulogy for Hüseyin Pasha Bedir Khan traced the genealogy of the Bedir Khans back to Khalid ibn al-Walid.

243. Cf. Halbwachs, *On Collective Memory*, 47; Brubaker, *Religion and Nationalism: Four Approaches*, 4.

244. 1281 according to the Gregorian calendar.

245. Abdurrahman Bedir Khan, 'Hukkamên Cezîretu îbnî Umer' [The Rulers of the Jazirat ibn Omar], *Kurdistan*, No. 8, December 1, 1898.

246. M. M. Bedir Khan, 'Untitled', *Kurdistan*, No. 3, May 20, 1898.

247. It is important to note that in May 1920 the Bedir Khans established their own familial association. *See*, Malmîsanij, *Cizira Botanlı Bedirhaniler*, 15–43.

248. Abdurrahman Bedir Khan, 'Kurda re' [To the Kurds], *Kurdistan*, No. 26, December 14, 1900.

249. Abdurrahman Bedir Khan, '*Welat-Weten*' [Homeland], *Kurdistan*, No. 9, December 16, 1898.

250. Cf. Fairclough, *Media Discourse*, 4, 95.

251. Cf. Ibid., 72.

252. This is similar to Makdisi's notion of "Ottoman Orientalism, *see*, Deringil, *They Live in a State of Nomadism*, 317.

253. Alles, Elisabeth. "Minority Nationalities in China: Internal Orientalism," in *After Orientalism*, edited by François Pouillon and Jean-Claude Vatin. (Laden: Brill, 2014), 134–141.

254. Makdisi, *Ottoman Orientalism*.

255. Hanes, Philip J. *The Advantages and Limitations of a Focus on Audience in Media Studies*. (Cambridge: MIT Press, 2000), 1; Barber, Karin. *The Anthropology of Texts, Persons and Publics*. (Cambridge: Cambridge University Press, 2007), 137.

256. Cited in Stewart, Garrett. *Dear Reader: The Conscripted Audience in Nineteenth-Century British Fiction*. (Maryland: John Hopkins University Pres, 1996), 6.

257. Barber, *The Anthropology of Texts*, 138.

258. Klancher, Jon P. *The Making of English Reading Audiences, 1790–1832*. (Madison: University of Wisconsin Press, 1987), 3–4.

259. Ang, Ien. *Desperately Seeking the Audience*. (London: Routledge, 1991), 28–29.

260. Cf. Wodak et al., *The Discursive Construction of National Identity*, 37.

261. Anderson, *Imagined Communities*; Brennan, Timothy. "The National Longing for Form," in *Nation and Narration*, edited by Homi K. Bhabha. (London: Routledge, 1990), 44–71.

262. van Bruinessen, *Agha, Shaikh and State*, 120–121; van Bruinessen, *Ehmedî Xanî's Mem û Zîn*, 54–55.

Chapter 3

The Journal *Kürd Teavün ve Terakkî Gazetesî (KTTG)* and Its Ottomanist Rhetoric

KURDISH JOURNALISTIC ACTIVITIES AFTER THE 1908 YOUNG TURK REVOLUTION

To situate the journalistic activities of *KTTG* in its historical context, I offer an account of the new sociocultural and political environment in which *KTTG* and its parent organization, the *KTTC*, operated. In the rest of this section, I conduct a close textual analysis of excerpts taken from the journal following six semantic macro-areas for content analysis. By the time *KTTG* came out, the Ottoman political context had changed drastically as a result of the 1908 Young Turk Revolution, which had ushered in the Second Constitutional Period and put an end to the despotic regime of Sultan Abdulhamid II. It also brought an end to the Sultan's Islamic Ottomanism and the Turkish form of Pan-Islamism, replacing them with a constitutional regime dominated by the CUP and a more secular form of Ottomanism. The new regime promised to embrace all *citizens* of the empire as equal partners regardless of their ethnic, religious, or confessional background by granting them political and civil rights and liberties. The new circumstances and promises brought great joy to all Ottoman subjects who responded to the new regime with festivities, receptions, and public meetings. In this burst of universal rejoicing, everyone was convinced that the tyrannical Hamidian period was gone and that the CUP would initiate large-scale reforms that would grant liberties to confessional and ethnic communities.[1] During the first year of the revolution and under its pseudo-liberal atmosphere, the CUP approved the establishment of 200 new newspapers in Istanbul, which raised the number of papers in Istanbul to 353.[2] The Young Turks felt that newspaper publication was an ideal medium to disseminate state reforms among Ottoman subjects and thus politicize Ottoman society in favor of the CUP's leadership and politics.[3]

As a result of this relatively liberal climate, not only dissident Ottoman Turks but also intellectuals from ethnic and confessional communities returned to Istanbul from exile. They engaged in social, cultural, and political activities to find a niche for their respective minority communities in the new Ottoman political landscape. Similarly, the Kurdish elite, now composed of both aristocratic and nonaristocratic self-appointed Kurdish leaders, seized the opportunity to set up the first legal Kurdish association (*KTTC*) and an eponymous newspaper (*KTTG*) at the turn of the century in Istanbul.

Figure 3.1   The First Issue of the KTTG.

The period leading up to the Second Constitutional Period featured a range of intellectual and ideological currents. In his *Üç Tarzi Siyaset* (*Three Types of Policies*) published in episodic fashion in the 23rd to 34th issues of *Turk*, a Young Turk publication in Cairo, Yusuf Akçura discussed the pros and cons of three possible policies the Ottoman state could adopt.[4] These were: (1) Ottomanism, the formation of a state based on the notion of an Ottoman nation that would embrace the empire's non-Muslim population, akin to the *Tanzimat* version of *secular* Ottomanism; (2) Pan-Islamism, the formation of an Islamic state that would incorporate all non-Turkish Muslims, which corresponded to Sultan Abdulhamid II's policy of Pan-Islamism or Islamic Ottomanism; and (3) Turkism or Turanism, the formation of a nation-state solely based on the dominance of the Turkish race.[5] Akçura found Turkism or Turanism as the only viable option that reflected the reality on the ground, given that long before the Balkan Wars, Turkism had taken root among prominent Ottoman intellectuals as well as the CUP leadership, first as a cultural concept and later on as a political program.[6] However, the CUP leadership did not find it wise to adopt Turkism as the state ideology yet, because they felt that the unabated constraints imposed by circumstances both at home and abroad would not allow for such an impractical dream to come true. Instead, they found it wise, for the time being, to opt for a more secular and inclusivist form of Ottomanism to appeal to both non-Turkish and non-Muslim communities. This policy would give the Young Turks time to keep the empire intact until they felt ready to oppose secessionist inclinations and more openly favor Turkish racial domination.

After the July revolution, the Kurdish intelligentsia in Istanbul hoped that under the banner of secular Ottomanism the Kurds' social, cultural, and political demands would be taken into consideration and eventually met. Thus, *KTTG* authors enthusiastically advocated CUP's notions of an Ottomanist and constitutional revolution. To that end, they presented Ottomanism as an integral part of Kurdish collective identity in their discourse and sought the future of the Kurds within this liberal Ottoman political framework. There are a few possible reasons for this enthusiastic Ottomanist attitude on the part of *KTTG*. First, Ottomanism was the hegemonic ideology of the period. Although the majority of Kurdish intellectuals were not convinced of the CUP's rhetoric of secular Ottomanism and its liberal promises, they still felt compelled to incorporate Ottomanism into their nationalist discourse. They used it, from a pragmatic point of view, as a rhetorical tool to disguise their ethno-nationalist inclinations. The Young Turks, however, were aware that "the non-Turkish communities of the empire inclined towards separatism; demand for cultural rights and recognition were mere pretexts for dangerous nationalist agendas."[7] Second, by remaining on the good side of the Young Turks, the Kurdish intelligentsia would have a chance to participate in the

Ottoman political scene by representing Kurdish national interests. Kurds, like Arabs, Armenians, Greeks, and others, were represented in the Ottoman parliament and other imperial institutions, including the central as well as provincial bureaucracy.[8] Third, *KTTG* used the concept of Ottomanism as a practical concept to curb growing Turkish nationalism, keep it in check, and prevent it from turning into a chauvinistic and oppressive state ideology at the expense of non-Turkish populations.[9] Fourth, ironically, the Young Turks and the CUP also were exploiting the idea of Ottomanism against rising ethno-nationalist feelings among non-Turkish constituencies to keep the empire intact.[10] Although it is hard to pin down one particular reason for this ostensibly strong commitment to Ottomanism, the empirical evidence presented in this chapter suggests that it was the interplay of all these factors that led *KTTG* to adopt a dense form of Ottomanism for *tactical* or *strategic* purposes.

This seemingly fervent Ottomanist attitude toward the notion of Ottomanism has obscured the connection between Kurdish nationalists and Ottomanism. It has led most of the relevant scholarship—particularly in the West—to believe that the *KTTG* and *KTTC* were genuine Ottomanists or even Ottoman nationalists. One might wonder how non-Turkish groups such as Kurds and Arabs could be considered Ottoman nationalists, while Turks themselves who fashioned the very idea of Ottomanism never genuinely believed in the ideal of this concept but instead used it as a disguise for their ultimate political ends: the subjugation of non-Turkish elements under the Turks.

The Proprietors of *KTTG*: Patterns of Ownership and the Control of Media

Kurdish intellectuals and notables, many of whom from Kurdish dynastic families that were excluded from the power structure after the demise of the Kurdish Emirates in the mid-nineteenth century, took advantage of the relatively liberal climate to resume their activities. They established the first legal Kurdish nationalist organizations and periodicals, mainly in the capital city Istanbul. The first such organization was *Kürd Teavün ve Terakki Cemiyeti* (KTTC), or the Kurdish Society for Mutual Aid and Progress, founded on September 19, 1908, in the Vezneciler district of Istanbul.[11]

The *KTTC* leadership remained, for the most part, in the hands of the former Kurdish feudal nobility and dominated by rival Kurdish families, namely the Şemdinans and Bedir Khans. The founding members of this first legal organization included Sayyid Abdulkadir, Emin Ali Bedir Khan, Halil Hayali, Ferik Şerif Paşa, Damat Ahmet Zülkif Paşa, and Şükrü Mehmet Sekban.[12] The *KTTC* elected Sayyid Abdulkadir as its president for life and Ahmet Zülkif Paşa as its vice president. Shortly after its foundation, the *KTTC* started publishing its eponymous weekly journal, *Kürd Teavün ve Terakki Gazetesi*[13] (KTTG), whose first issue appeared on December 5, 1908, in a bilingual Kurdish and Ottoman Turkish form. Prominent authors of *KTTG* included Halil Hayali, Babanzade Ismail Hakkı , Molla Saîd-î Kurdî, Diyarbekirli Ahmed Cemil, Suleyman Nazif, Suleymaniyeli M. Tevfik (aka Pîremêrd), and Ercişli Seyyah Ahmet Şewqi.

Since media ownership and its relations with the state and with its readership are effective in shaping media discourse, one should look into the background of *KTTG/KTTC* members to understand fully *KTTG*'s politics and identity discourse. Noteworthily, most Kurdish intellectuals involved in *KTTG* had received an education in the empire's institutions and were integrated into the Ottoman state machinery. They were on the state payroll and serving as prosecutors, MPs, local administrators, civil servants, military officers, and so forth.[14]

Sayyid Abdulkadir (1851–1925)

Sayyid Abdulkadir, the second son of the legendary Sheikh Ubeydullah, the leader of the Naqşibendi Şemdinan Family, was born in 1851 in Şemdinan. Educated in the Naqşibendi tradition, he took part in the famous Kurdish rebellion led by his father in 1880 as a commander. In 1896, he became an active member of the CUP, which commissioned him to visit Kurdistan in order to secure Kurdish support for the CUP program and the constitution.[15] After the Young Turk revolution, Sayyid Abdulkadir was appointed president of the Ottoman Senate and remained in this post until 1920. In 1919, he was elected president of *Kurdistan Teali Cemiyeti* (KTC) or the *Society for the Rise of Kurdistan* (1918). Although he remained an autonomist as opposed to those within the *KTC* ranks who sought Kurdish independence, the Turkish Republic sent Sayyid Abdulkadir to the gallows after the Sheikh Said rebellion in 1925.

Emin Ali Bedir Khan (1851–1926)

Emin Ali Bedir Khan, one of Bedir Khan Bey's sons, was born in Crete in 1851. Upon graduation from law school, he became a public prosecutor and served in Adana, Konya, Salonica, and Ankara. He joined the decentralist *Ahrar Fırkası* (Party of Ottoman Liberals) and then *Hürriyet ve Itilaf Fırkası* (Freedom and Accord Party), both of which opposed the CUP. In 1918, he was elected vice president of the *KTC*. Later on, he became president of the *Teşkilat-i Içtimaiye Cemiyeti* (TIC), or *the Society of Social Organization* (1920), the result of a split in the *KTC*, in which the *TIC* adopted a secessionist line against Sayyid Abdulkadir's autonomist policy. Before the establishment of the Turkish Republic in 1923, Emin Ali Bedir Khan left Turkey for Egypt, where he died in 1926.

Suleymaniyeli M. Tevfik (aka Pîremêrd) (1867–1950)

Pîremêrd, the publisher and the director of *KTTG*, was born in Suleymaniye in 1867. He is one of the most important figures of modern Kurdish literature and journalism. Pîremêrd, who came from a less prestigious background, received his education at traditional Kurdish medreses. After working as a public servant for several years in Kurdistan, he went to Istanbul along with Sheikh Said Barzinji in 1899. He wrote extensively for both Kurdish and Ottoman journals. Pîremêrd was appointed to the Ottoman parliament upon the order of Sultan Abdulhamid in 1899. He later studied law and worked as an attorney. He married a Turkish woman and both before and after the Young Turk revolution served as a *qaymaqam* (district governor) for many years in such places as Hakkari, Beytüşşebap, and Adapazarı. Having been at odds with the CUP regime, he was imprisoned after the 31 March incident.[16] He settled in Suleymaniye in 1924, where he continued his intellectual activities until his death in 1950.[17]

Xelîl Xeyalî (1864–1946)

Xelîl Xeyalî or Halil Hayali was born in the Mutki district of Bitlis in 1864, where he received education from an early age at Kurdish medreses. He spoke Zazaki, Kurmanji, Turkish, Arabic, Persian, and French. From a modest background, Xeyalî was the most active member of *KTTG/KTTC*. He became a civil servant in 1882 in Bitlis, then moved to Istanbul in 1890 and lived there until his death in 1946. He actively took part in Kurdish cultural and political activities in Istanbul. In addition to *KTTG*, he wrote extensively for such Kurdish journals as *Yekbûn*, *Rojî Kurd*, *Hetawî Kurd*, and *Jîn*. The dominant themes in his writings were language cultivation, Kurdish national literature, and national history. Hayali prepared a grammar book and a dictionary with Ziya Efendi (Gökalp), but the latter burned them after he became the founding father of Turkish nationalism. Later on, Hayali worked on rewriting both works.[18] In Kurdish journals, he signed his articles with such (pen) names as Xelîl Xeyalî, Halîl Hayalî, M. X., Modanî X.

Babanzade Ismail Hakkı (1876–1913)

Babanzade Ismail Hakkı, son of Zihni Paşa from the aristocratic Baban family, was born in Baghdad in 1876. After studying law, he began to teach at Mektebi Mülkiye (School of Political Science) in Istanbul in 1909. As an active member of the CUP, Babanzade became a deputy for Divaniye (Baghdad) on the CUP ticket and, in 1911, served as the Minister of Education under the Kamil Paşa government. Babanzade wrote a few articles for *KTTG* as well as *Rojî Kurd*. He is the author of *Letters from Iraq*, *The Political Life of Bismarck*, and the coauthor of *The Dreyfus Incident*. He died of a brain hemorrhage in 1913.

Molla Saîd-î Kurdî (1876–1960)

Molla Saîd-î Kurdî, also known as Molla Saîd Nursî or *Bediuzzaman* (Marvel of the Time), was a Kurdish theologian born in the Nurs district of Bitlis Province in 1876. As a poor cleric from a nonaristocratic background, he received a traditional religious education at Kurdish medreses of the Nakşibendi *derviş* order. He went to Istanbul in 1896, where he was involved in Kurdish intellectual circles and wrote Kurdish and Turkish articles for *KTTG*. In his articles, he highlighted the importance of education and promoted Kurdish national identity within the political framework of Ottomanism and Islam. He was imprisoned for his involvement in the *Muhammedian Union* during the March 31 incident. During World War I, he served in the *Teşkilat-i Mahsusa* (the Special Organization), which functioned as the CUP's intelligence apparatus and was involved in the Armenian genocide. Since he was at odds with the newly established Turkish Republic and Mustafa Kemal's policies, he was arrested and put on trial many times for his political use of religion. His writings are collectively known as *Risale-i Nur* (Message of Light), a body of Qur'anic commentary, which acquired a large following that later on turned into a movement called *Nurculuk* or *Enlightenment*.[19]

Diyarbekirli Ahmed Cemil (1872–1941)

Ahmed Cemil, the editor-in-chief of *KTTG*, was born in Diyarbakir in 1872. He studied at the Aşiret Mektebi (Tribal School), then at the Schools of Political Science. He was a relative and close friend of Ziya Efendi (Gökalp) and one of the first members of the CUP branch in Diyarbakir. He was involved in the establishment of the *Kurd Neşr-i Maarif Cemiyeti* (Kurdish Society for the Diffusion of Education). Ahmed Cemil served as *qaymaqam* (district governor) in Siverek, Midyat, Cizre, Nusaybin, and Dersim, then as the deputy mayor of Diyarbakir. He broke away from the Kurdish movement after the establishment of the Turkish Republic.

Production and Distribution of *KTTG*

On the cover page of each issue, it was indicated that the owner and chief director of this first legally circulated Kurdish newspaper was Suleymaniyeli M. Tevfik and the editor-in-chief was Diyarbekirli Ahmed Cemil. Although only the first nine issues of *KTTG* have survived, it is not clear whether more issues are waiting to be discovered. In any case, it is believed that after the journal dropped the ideal of Ottomanism and started to pursue a Kurdish nationalist policy, the CUP shut down both the *KTTG* and *KTTC* based on Article 3 of "Cemiyetler Kanunu" (Associations Law). This law provided a legal basis for further curtailing civil liberties, including the closure of all ethnic associations after the 31 March incident.[20] The issue numbers and the publication dates of nine extant issues are as follows (Table 3.1):

Table 3.1   *KTTG*'s Publication Dates and Places

Issue Number	Publication Date	Printing House	Place
1st	December 5, 1908	Selanik Printing House	Istanbul
2nd	December 12, 1908	Selanik Printing House	Istanbul
3rd	December 19, 1908	Merkez Printing House	Istanbul
4th	December 26, 1908	Merkez Printing House	Istanbul
5th	January 2, 1909	Merkez Printing House	Istanbul
6th	January 9, 1909	Merkez Printing House	Istanbul
7th	January 16, 1909	Merkez Printing House	Istanbul
8th	January 23, 1909	Merkez Printing House	Istanbul
9th	January 30, 1909	Merkez Printing House	Istanbul

Given that the *KTTG*, unlike *Kurdistan*, was published and circulated legally, and since its parent organization *KTTC* had several branches in Kurdistan, including Bitlis, Diyarbakir, Erzurum, Muş, Mosul, and Baghdad, the paper probably reached a larger readership in the far-flung regions of Kurdistan.

DISCOURSE PRACTICES AND TEXTUAL ANALYSIS OF JOURNAL *KTTG*

More Royalist than the King

At this level of analysis, the primary concern will revolve around the problematization of the new political circumstances, including social and political crises, common worries, and their future consequences for the Kurds. This will reveal the politics of *KTTG*, how they perceived and tried to tackle contemporary issues from a Kurdish viewpoint, and how they envisaged a political future for themselves and the Kurdish masses. As was saw, after the July 1908 revolution, under the banner of the CUP, the Young Turks started promoting the constitutional monarchy and a more secular form of *Ottoman official nationalism* or *Osmanlılık* (Ottomanism). With this new form of secular Ottomanism, which resembled the Ottomanism of the *Tanzimat* period, the CUP appealed to non-Turkish and non-Muslim minorities to foster a notion of *civic nationalism* and a political community made up of equal *Ottoman citizens* bound together by their commitment to a common set of legal norms. This, in its turn, would help preserve the integrity of the empire.

Given the new social, political, and ideological circumstances, the formation of a common political present and future in *KTTG* was remarkably different from that found in *Kurdistan*. While *Kurdistan* promoted Kurdish nationalism against a backdrop of the dominant ideology of Islamic Ottomanism or Pan-Islamism, in *KTTG*'s era, the common political present and future of the Kurds were constructed against the backdrop of the hegemonic ideology of secular Ottomanism. Consequently, in the process of a power struggle, the nationalism developed in *KTTG* discourse was a complex type. While it promoted Kurds as a separate ethnic group that deserved a certain amount of political autonomy, it had to ensure that its national demands remained in line with hegemonic Ottomanist and religious discourses. This position was articulated in the founding declaration of the *KTTC* published in the inaugural issue of *KTTG*:[21]

> As has been declared in its bylaws, the purpose for founding the Kurdish Society for Mutual Aid and Progress is to advance and hence find happiness for the noble Kurdish nation [Kürd kavm-i necibi] following modern principles.
>
> The Protection of the constitution [Kanun-i Esasi] from any infringement and the territorial unity of the Ottoman state is tied to such important matters as the permanent consolidation of national and religious values and willpower with integrity. Moreover, the transformation of these associations into political parties [fırak-ı siyasiyeye] after the opening of the parliament [Meclis-i Meb'usan] should not violate the legal rights of the office of the Great Caliph of Islam and the Great Ottoman throne as determined in the constitution. Based on [the principle of] not privileging [imtiyaz] one community over another, and bestowing provinces with broader power, the state should make changes following the constitution when considered necessary by the parliament. Since the society [*KTTC*] accepts and supports all ideas and initiatives that entail the advancement and glory of the Ottoman state [. . .] it subscribes to the provisions of the CUP's political program that takes upon itself the well-being and progress of the homeland; the position of the society regarding other issues is based on the provisions [of CUP's political program] in question.[22]

The declaration is the manifestation of the political program of the *KTTC* regarding the present and future of the Kurds. The first paragraph explicitly specifies that the *KTTC* is a Kurdish association working for the rights of "the noble Kurdish nation" by improving their position within an Ottomanist political framework. As foregrounded in the second paragraph, the constitutional law, the territorial integrity of the empire, and loyalty to the Sultan Caliph indicate that the society was not in favor of secessionism, at least not openly. However, the *KTTC* perceived the idea of *Ottomanism* or *Ottoman official nationalism* not as a melting pot into which Kurds should be assimilated but rather as a concept and a political contract that would guarantee Kurdish ethno-national rights. Therefore, the *KTTC* explicitly argued that as stipulated in the constitution, no community should be favored over another, a point specifically made to express the Kurdish intelligentsia's concerns about Turkish racial dominance over other ethnic groups. In any case, the society expresses its commitment to Ottomanism and the CUP's political program within the framework of the Ottomanist principles of ethnic equality.[23] Equally important is the *KTTC*'s demand to give broader power to the provinces, which subtly advocates a form of Kurdish political and administrative autonomy. Finally, it is also striking that the founding declaration mentions the possibility of associations, especially their own, turning into political parties. Apparently, if the Young Turks had not shut down the *KTTC*, the Kurdish leadership had every intention of transforming this association into a Kurdish political party. Some of these views were also echoed in the first article of the *KTTC*'s constitution, which stipulated:

> A beneficial association by the name of *KTTC* has been established to enlighten those Kurds who are not aware of the virtuous principles of the constitution, which are in accordance with the great provisions of Islam, and guarantee the well-being of the homeland and the happiness of the people; to consolidate strong Kurdish ties with the office of the highly esteemed Caliph and the great Sultan as long as the system of constitution [meşrutiyet] and consultation [meşveret] is protected; to consolidate the relations between Kurds and other Ottoman peoples such as Armenians and Nestorians; to solve the conflicts and hatred between [Kurdish] tribes and to find out the means and methods to unite them around a legitimate body; to promote education, industry, commerce, and agriculture.[24]

The passage foregrounds not only the protection of the constitution, which is a fundamental social and political contract meant to regulate the relations between the Ottoman state and the Kurds, but it also makes it clear that the *KTTC*, and by extension the Kurds, would remain loyal to the Ottoman State and the Caliph "as long as" the constitution, which ensures equality between different Ottoman ethnic communities, is protected. Moreover, the *KTTC* attached great importance to intertribal rivalries and suggested the unification and mobilization of the tribes around a "legitimate body." Needless to say, this "legitimate body" was none other than the *KTTC* itself, which would gain more legitimacy and political leverage in Istanbul as the representative of a unified ethno-national community. Taking up the issue of political autonomy, Suleymaniyeli Seyfullah reiterated the need to strengthen local governance capacities:

> Since not every Ottoman region has the same capacity—given that they all display differences following their ethnicity and character—and since the light

of education does not reach every corner [of the empire] equally, also since the administration of one region differs from that of other regions, the application of a centralized decision-making mechanism is not favourable.[25]

Through the use of the *strategy of rationalization*, the author put emphasis on the differences between regional subgroups, each composed of different ethno-national communities. He criticized the system of centralized government and instead advocated decentralization in the form of stronger local bodies or governance that could tend to divergent needs of each ethnicity.[26] It goes without saying that although the author's suggestion was for the entire Ottoman territory, his primary concern was self-governance for the Kurdish provinces. The extract contains enough evidence to refute claims in some of the relevant literature that tend to portray the *KTTC* as a truly Ottomanist or Ottoman nationalist "cultural club" and *KTTG* as a "cultural publication" that did not make any nationalist or political demands. However, close textual investigation of the *KTTG* corpus reveals that far from being a mere cultural club or cultural publication, the *KTTC* and *KTTG* were political centers for Kurdish intellectuals to formulate their nationalist political agenda.[27] In any case, just because a nationalist movement or its publication immerses itself in the rediscovery of history and the cultivation of the culture of the nation does not mean that it is a mere "cultural club" or "cultural publication" without a nationalist agenda. This is because nationalism, as a source and form of social and cultural identity and as a sociopolitical movement, inevitably entails immersion in the vernacular language, literature, history, and other cultural resources of the nation.

Nonetheless, for pragmatic reasons, the *KTTG* adopted a very dense Ottomanist tone in its discourse about Kurdish national identity. In what follows, I investigate actual instances of language use in the corpus of *KTTG*, whereby Ottomanism and Kurdish ethno-nationalism were interwoven. The extract below from an article by Babanzade Ismail Hakkı is typical:[28]

The Kurdish nation [Kurd kavmi], to whom I am proud to belong, is also showing signs of revival and restoration [. . .] This pure and virtuous nation, which constitutes the most fertile and eternal branch of the river of Islam as well as the strongest and most durable bastion and fortress of the great Ottoman masses [kitle-i muazzama-ı Osmaniye], is first of all Muslim. Second, without any dishonesty or hidden intent and within the framework of the constitutional monarchy, which is the source of life for nations, is a true Ottoman. And thirdly, it is Kurdish.[29]

Here, the author, a deputy in the Ottoman parliament, employed various discursive strategies to articulate the Kurds' Ottoman identity. First, employing *the strategy of positive self-representation* along with the lexemes of "purity" and "virtuousness," he created a sense of national pride in being a member of the Kurdish nation, which was presented as a part of the great Ottoman mass society (*kitle*). It is important to notice how Kurds were imagined as a nation (*kavim*), while Ottomans were presented as a mass society (*kitle*) made up of nations. Second, via *the strategy of cohesivation*, he emphasized the collective history of the Kurds as a Muslim Ottoman community and their will to stay as such in solidarity with other Ottomans. The most striking part of the author's argument is in lines 5–7. Following the journal's Ottomanist strategy, he significantly expressed the multilayered nature of Kurdish identity by degree of importance in which Islam (religion)[30] and Ottomanism were the first two primary components of Kurdishness, with Kurdish national identity coming in the third and last place. Apparently, the layers of Kurdish identity determined by Babanzade was a pivotal discursive act that aimed to consolidate the journal's overall Ottomanist rhetoric in order to assure the Young Turks of Kurdish loyalty to the idea of Ottomanism. However, although Kurdish identity came in third place, it was still foregrounded because the author disregarded the Kurds' parochial loyalties and identities such as tribal, denominational, dialectal, and provincial by presenting the Kurds as a unified and coherent national community. As Hobsbawm once said, "ideologies and identities are attributed to the commoners by the state or the elite, and for that reason, they do not reflect the true ideas or feelings of the people they supposedly represent."[31] What is more, the promotion of religious identity, unlike Ottoman identity, took nothing away from the author's Kurdish nationalist argument because religion can be and has been an integral part of national identities, as evident from many cases of religious nationalisms.[32]

In the next installment of his article Babanzade, further promoted the ethnic component of Kurdish national identity: "A Kurd is still a Kurd; he has not even slightly changed [neither] his nationality [milliyet], [nor] his physical appearance or his material and moral identity." From a primordialist point of view, and via the *strategy of singularization*, the author attributed an uninterrupted historical continuity and coherence to Kurdish national identity by citing the "inherent" moral, racial, and physical features of the Kurds to be shared characteristics of a national community that differentiated them from their discursive opposites: non-Kurdish Ottoman communities. The author added:

> Yet, the Kurd has been loyal to Ottomanism with a strong tie [. . .] Ottomanism has encompassed Kurdishness and Kurdishness in return has encompassed Ottomanism [. . .] God forbid, if Ottomanism is destroyed, Kurdishness will be

reduced to a shadow of its former self; God forbid, if Kurdishness is destroyed and loses its name and fame, [then], Ottomanism will become weak and miserable.

Nevertheless, the tyrannical period, which should be left in the frightening darkness of the past that we do not want to remember, has also crushed this strong component [Kurds] and maltreated it more cruelly even when compared to the other components [of the Empire].[33]

In the first paragraph, the *strategy of unification* and the rhetoric of *we are in the same boat*[34] helped the author to envisage a collective political future and destiny for the Kurds and other Ottomans. However, he emphasized the mutual dependency between the two entities in which the Ottoman state was in need of Kurdish support, a common theme in *KTTG* discourse. Parallel to the paper's general Ottomanist stance, in the second paragraph, the author made a distinction between the Hamidian regime and the new Young Turk government by utilizing the rhetoric of *then and now*.[35] He expressed his resentment of the past tyrannical period, while excepting the new CUP government from such criticism. A similar Ottomanist attitude can be observed in Halil Hayali's article entitled *The Homeland and the Unity of the Kurds [Kurmanc]*:

> With the benevolence of the CUP and the assistance of the army, the Constitution was declared and the troublesome cruelty vanished. The honourable deputies have gathered and [now] the [Ottoman] Parliament will discuss the situation of the homeland. May God give them all success.
>
> The Kurd [Kurmanc] is a significant component of the Ottoman nation [qewm]; [he] is religious, brave, and skillful [jêhatî].[36]

Praising the CUP and the new constitutional monarchy, Hayali designated the CUP and the Ottoman army as the saviors who liberated the Ottomans, including the Kurds, from the previous tyrannical period. However, using the *strategy of self-positive representation* in the second paragraph, he did not only distinguish the Kurds from other Ottomans, but he also glorified them as a significant element of the Ottoman community.

KTTG authors avoided criticizing Sultan Abdulhamid II by utilizing the rhetoric of *then and now* and the *strategy of shift of blame* or *scapegoating*. In this way, they defended the Sultan by portraying him as an "innocent perpetrator" and putting the blame on the malicious state officials from his former tyrannical period (*devr-i sabık-ı istibdad*). Because the glorification of the Sultan Caliph was a part of the Ottomanist narrative, this is hardly surprising.

A more radical form of Ottomanism, which I call *the extreme case of Ottomanism*, was another key rhetorical device used by the *KTTG* in its construction of a common political present and future for the Kurds. The anonymous article below is a good case in point:

> O Brothers!
>
> The name of our nation [millet] is Kurd [Kurmanc]. Kurds [Kurmanc] are united. Our cities are sacred. [. . .] Our country [memleket] is under the suzerainty of the government of the Sublime Ottoman state. We, too, are subjects of the Ottoman [state]. All the people living on the Ottoman lands, be it Turk, Kurd, Christian, Yezidi, and Nestorian, are together as one [body] with no differences. Our name and our nation's [milet] name is Ottoman and our homeland is the Ottoman homeland [memleketê Osmanli].
>
> We are proud of the name of Ottoman. This is how we have been feeling since the time of our forefathers [ji bav û kala].[37]

This is a perfect illustration of the constructive nature of national identities, showing how the production or fabrication of national identities could be heavily influenced by the political and ideological concerns of the period in which they were produced. The author of this extract, convinced of the hegemonic power of Ottomanist identity and the invincibility of the empire, was at pains to "prove" the loyalty of the Kurds to Ottoman identity and ideals through hyperbolic claims. To this end, he designated the Kurds as true Ottomans and Kurdistan as an extension of the Ottoman land.[38] Here and elsewhere,[39] Ottomanism was overtly *propagated* via rhetorical devices to persuade the readership, mainly the Young Turks, of the Kurdish dedication to Ottomanism. Yet, it is remarkable that the Kurdish ethno-nationalist undertone of this extract is louder than its explicit Ottomanism. In that, Ottomanism is present in the form of an explicit *persuasive discourse* of propaganda, while the presence of Kurds as a distinct and unified ethno-national community is embedded or interwoven in the texts as an *ideology* in the form of an *assumption* or *presupposition*. That is, while a *persuasive discourse* uses explicit rhetorical devices from a particular point of view to be more convincing, *ideologies* by contrast are not usually *adopted* but are instead *taken for granted common assumptions* without recourse to rhetorical devices.[40] For example, the word *Kurd* referred to a supposedly unified and homogeneous ethno-national group, ignoring the fragmented nature of Kurdish society. Although Kurds were designated as a part of the larger Ottoman body, they were imagined as Ottomans not as individuals, but as a cohesive ethno-national entity called *Kurds*. Then, it is fair to argue that the overall discourse of the paper, even when it ostensibly propagated an extreme form of Ottomanism, contributed to the construction of Kurds as a distinct (i.e., non-Turkish), unified, and recognizable national community.[41] What is more, the author astonishingly designated the Turks as a *mere* component of Ottomanism, just like the other components, for example, Kurds and Arabs. This was part of another significant discursive act that can be observed throughout the *KTTG* corpus, which persistently makes a distinction between *being a Turk* and *being an Ottoman* to refute the Young Turks' equation of Ottomanism with Turkish identity or Turkism.[42] However, later on, as the idea of Ottomanism diminished and Kurdish nationalism matured, Kurdish intellectuals gave prominence to Kurdish national identity at the expense of Ottomanism and Ottoman identity.

Education and Modernization as Core Elements of Nation-Building

KTTG authors were well aware that modernity and education were vital components in blueprints for nation building. As Klein has observed, "education was increasingly viewed as an institution to serve nationalist goals. Thus, it could, if institutionalized in a body run by the nationalists themselves, serve to teach their people, not only about technology and modern arts and science, but about their own Kurdishness."[43] Intellectual, industrial, commercial, and agricultural development became indispensable themes in *KTTG*'s narrative of "progress," which was embedded in the very name of the periodical, that is, the Kurdish Gazette for Mutual Aid and *Progress*. Saîd-î Kurdî, Halil Hayali, Babanzade Ismail Hakkı, and Suleymaniyeli Tevfik were the most prominent figures who advocated schooling, education, and wholesale modernization as a way to emerge from a state of backwardness and claim the status of nationhood.

As we saw, *Kurdistan* also promoted modernization and education of the Kurds within a hegemonic Pan-Islamist framework and as a means to counter perceived Russian/Christian threats to the Empire's eastern frontiers. *KTTG*, on the other hand, made use of the rhetoric of creating better Ottomans out of the Kurds as part of an argument to secure CUP support for the modernization, education, and, ultimately, the economic and "scientific" progress of the Kurds. Moreover, as I will discuss later in detail, while *Kurdistan* made no demands for the use of Kurdish as the language of instruction, *KTTG* did demand education in the Kurdish language. Furthermore, *Kurdistan* promoted education via a discourse that was profoundly affected by religious intertextuality and Pan-Islamism, while *KTTG*, in line with the CUP's secular and more inclusive form of Ottomanism, relied on a secular discourse, which often promoted education through Comptian positivism.[44] For instance, Malatyalı Bedri wrote:

Today the major shortage and the fault of the Kurds is ignorance and lack of education and schooling, even though they remain courageous [. . .] Nations [milletler] acquire great status and glorious ranks within their civilizational circle only after they combine the superior moral merits that they possess from birth with [skills] acquired from science and the arts.[45]

Bedri's primary concern was modern education without recourse to religious intertextuality. On the contrary, he felt that only modern scientific education—emphasized with the lexeme of *ilim* (science)—would help Kurds to achieve all the attributes and be recognized as a fully formed modern nation. What is more, he presented the Kurdish community as a nation-in-the-making when he pointed to the shortage of Kurds in comparison to other *nations*.

Saîd-î Kurdî was among those who attached great importance to education. In one article, he asserted that education and unity would liberate the Kurds from their "miserable" situation:[46] "Then, we have three enemies that destroy us. One of them is poverty, as 40,000 Kurdish porters in Istanbul prove. The second one is ignorance and lack of education [bêxwendinî], which is proved by the fact that not even one out of a thousand of us can read a newspaper. The third is our internal hostilities and conflicts, which weaken us."[47] It is remarkable to see that a religious figure like Saîdî Kurdî advocated education and literacy in modern terms and context rather than in religious intertextuality; Kurdî expressed the importance of education and literacy by noting the number of Kurds who could or could not read a *newspaper*, not the Qur'an. This was in stark contrast to the Bedir Khan Brothers, who lacked a religious background but still promoted education through a dense religious intertextuality—Kurds' inability to read the Qur'an or say their prayers—which was in line with the hegemonic Pan-Islamist discourse of the period in which *Kurdistan* appeared.

Saîd-î Kurdî also endorsed the Light Hamidian Cavalries, arguing that they constituted one of the vehicles for education through which Kurds could receive both religious, but more importantly, scientific education. He also saw the cavalries as an ideal mechanism for upward social mobility for Kurds through employment and high positions in the Ottoman administration. They eventually could defend Kurdish interests in the Ottoman political and administrative system. In an article, Kurdî wrote:

The first necessity is the national unity [of the Kurds]; the second is disseminating modern science that is essential besides religious science; Tribal Regiments can provide the basis for this progress. By virtue of this secret, I fearlessly say: those who are not already Tribal Regiments soldiers should become national soldiers [of Tribal Regiments] until the military, which resembles the rays of electricity that generates a chemical/magnetic connection between neighbouring tribes; so that it reconciles their differences; brings out their essence and true values; produces the light of education and schooling and brings out Kurds' true potential.[48]

Clearly, Kurdî had observed that the Tribal Regiments did not only provide the Kurds with modern education and science,[49] but they also played a unifying function by bringing together Kurds from different, perhaps even feuding, tribes and replaced feudal affiliations, titles, and enmities with modern military ranks, thus creating a new type of relation and connection.[50] It seems that Kurdî was aware of the homogenizing power of mass conscription in the sense that, like education, conscription into mass armies in the modern age had a unifying and homogenizing effect.[51] Therefore, the author considers the army (the Hamidian Regiments) as a key feature in the historical development of the Kurds into a unified nation. It is noteworthy how Kurdî expresses the unifying power of the army through the narrative of modern science, for example, lexemes from chemistry and electrical science.

Multimodality: KTTG's Photographic Images and the Folio Sections

For Fairclough, it is artificial to conceive of discourse in exclusively *verbal* terms, because discourses are interwoven with *visuals*, in that often *visuals* and *verbals* operate in mutually reinforcing ways in the meaning-making process.[52] Such multimodal texts, which constitute a particular type of intertextuality, include *visual/photographic images* that function as complementary meaning sources for *verbals*. In this regard, multimodality is another important dimension of intertextuality because in multimodal texts, the meaning of one mode depends on its relation with other modes.[53] Drawing on Halliday's concepts of *elaboration, extension,* and *enhancement*,[54] van Leeuwen identifies two types of connections between different modalities: *elaborative* and *extensive*.[55] The relationship between the modalities is elaborative when the content of one mode is repeated in another mode to provide the reader with further explanation or to reproduce the same discursive act through another mode; this relation is extensive when one mode contains an aspect of *extension* that would add a new but still related meaning to the general content of another mode.

The corpus of *KTTG* does not consist of mono-modal verbal texts, but rather multimodal texts due to the use of twelve images, only two of which can be regarded as examples of *elaboration*. One of the images is a magnificent portrait of Sultan Abdulhamid II on the front page of the 4th issue, right above a quote taken from the Sultan's inaugural address during the opening ceremony of the Ottoman parliament.[56] In the 6th issue of the journal, we see a panoramic image of Crete surrounded by an article that defends this island against Greek claims of aggression.[57] Both images serve to reinforce the Ottomanist content of the surrounding texts that they supplement. All other images can be regarded as examples of *extension*, as they are not directly related to the immediate surrounding texts but instead are "fragments of the more general syntagma" of the paper, that is, the paper's overall Ottomanist discourse. These images include the interior of the Ottoman Senate (Meclis-i Ayan),[58] the parliament building,[59] the Sultan's private chamber,[60] and an image of MPs,[61] which together reproduce and consolidate the paper's Ottomanist position.

As far as the folio sections of the *KTTG* are concerned, Van Leeuwen argues that the *reading path* is another dimension of multimodality. Particular textual elements can capture readers' attention over others when a range of visual features, such as their position, framing, font size, tonal construct, color, and so forth, are arranged in a particular way.[62] In the folio sections of *KTTG*, the word *Kürd* (Kurd) in the name of *Kürd Teavün ve Terakki Gazetesi* is in large and bold typography in the middle-top of the page with its own line, commanding a differential salience to the remaining parts of the journal's name (Figure 3.2). This differential salience affects the reader's attention in favor of this element, that is, *Kurd*, marked with bold typography, which reinforces a particular reading path and hence foregrounds the ethno-centric or Kurdish nationalist coloring of the journal.

Figure 3.2   The Word "Kurd" Marked with Large and Bold Typography in KTTG's Folio Section.

This Language Is Our National Honor: Articulation of the First Kurdish Language Policy

The Kurdish language remained the most important marker of Kurdish national identity in the discourse of *KTTG*. Nevertheless, the journal's approach to the use of Kurdish differed from that of *Kurdistan*. Unlike *Kurdistan*, *KTTG* adopted Ottoman Turkish as its dominant medium of communication because Turkish had both a powerful politico-symbolic and pragmatic communicative function. The dominance of Turkish reproduced *KTTG*'s ostensibly dense Ottomanist policy and showed Kurdish intellectuals' loyalty to the state. In this context, language preference rendered a two-way *strategy of inclusion*: in pragmatic terms, the Kurdish intellectuals of the period attempted to make the content of their journal accessible to non-Kurds, for example, Armenians, Arabs, but most importantly to Ottoman Turks, because *KTTG* felt compelled to convince the Ottoman Turks of their commitment to the state. To the same end, *KTTG* also translated some Kurdish articles and poems from their original Kurdish into Turkish. In any case, despite the pluralist rhetoric of the 1908 Revolution, Young Turks were openly intolerant of other languages; for them, those who did not use Turkish or did not speak it fluently were considered unpatriotic and potential traitors responsive to alien influences.[63] Preferring the Turkish language perhaps helped *KTTG* to circumvent the Young Turks' accusations and antagonism.[64]

As previously discussed, Kurdish is not a unified standard language as it consists of multiple dialects that are not necessarily mutually intelligible. Therefore, another possible reason behind *KTTG*'s language preference was that, unlike *Kurdistan*, which was owned by two Kurmanji-speaking brothers and was predominantly meant for Kurmanji-speaking reader, *KTTG* brought together Kurdish intellectuals from different Kurdish speech varieties. This probably caused communication problems among the members of the leadership as well as between the leadership and the audience who spoke different varieties of Kurdish. Perhaps, *KTTG* publishers felt that they could solve this obstacle by adopting Turkish, the *lingua franca* of the empire, as the dominant language of their journal. Finally, it is also possible that Kurdish intellectuals refrained from publishing in multiple Kurdish dialects as this might have revealed or highlighted the linguistic differences between Kurdish dialectal communities, causing further fragmentation and undermining the notion of Kurdish unity against the backdrop of the nation-state premise of *one nation, one language*.[65] Nevertheless, despite this linguistic choice, one can surmise that *KTTG*, like *Kurdistan*, perceived the Kurdish language as the most vital resource available to mark the Kurds off from other Ottomans, particularly the Turks.

KTTG promoted Kurdish in an innovative and fundamental way that had not been seen in the discourse of *Kurdistan*: the *KTTG* demanded the use of Kurdish as the language of instruction in public schools. This demand perhaps was a reaction to the declaration of the official status of Turkish, which had been made compulsory at schools by Sultan Abdulhamid II.[66] One of the figures who championed the use of Kurdish as the language of instruction in public schools was surprisingly Babanzade Ismail Hakkı, a modern Islamist and a seemingly zealous supporter of Ottomanism. He presented the Kurdish language as a central component of the collective Kurdish identity and referred to it as the "national honor" (*namus-i milliye*) of the Kurds. The extract from two articles by Babanzade epitomize his—and *KTTG*'s—stance on the language issue:

> The previous government, while the enemy of [free] thought, when it came to the Kurdish nation [Kürd kavmi] it was the enemy of both thought and language.
>
> Kurds were about to lose not only their nationality [kavmiyet] but also their religious denomination [mezhep] due to their "languagelessness" [lisansızlık]. A great ignorance was widespread in many places [and] many Kurds almost lost their humanity. Due to the lack of civilizational progress and ignorance [coupled with] the lack of religious principles, not only the life of the miserable Kurds but also their dignity and honour, their national honour [namus-ı millîleri], which is the dearest to them, was on the point of becoming besmirched.[67]

The author created a unique Kurdish identity based on the Kurdish language by placing language at the emotional, spiritual, and intellectual heart of Kurdish national identity. As a result of their "languagelessness," that is, the ban on the use of Kurdish, "Kurds were about to lose their nationality, national honour, dignity, and religion." In this context, Babanzade not only transformed the Kurdish language from an everyday thing to an essential national value and cultural patrimony, but he also elevated it to the level of *national honor* parallel to the German Romantic view of the nation and the concept of the *Volk* (national spirit), which revolved around national language.

Moreover, religious nationalism in the form of religious intertextuality was also significant. First, the hegemonic power of religion provided the author with the perfect reason or excuse to defend the Kurdish language: Kurds should be able to keep their native language for the sake of religion because if there is no language, there is no religion. Further, the wording of the sentence pertaining to religion in the second paragraph also deserves attention as a discursive act for the nationalization of religion. Significantly, the author preferred the word *mezhep* (religious denomination/sect) to *din or diyanet* (religion) when referring to the religion of the Kurds. Through this discursive act, perhaps he meant to underline the fact that Kurds, *unlike* the *Hanafi* Turks or the *Hanbali* Arabs, adhere to the Shafi'i school of Sunni Islam. It is important to note that nowhere else in the corpus of *KTTG* are the words *mezhep* and *din* used interchangeably, which indicates that this was most probably a deliberate discursive act to distinguish Shafi'i Kurds from other Muslims, particularly the Hanafi Turks. Next, when the author said, "Kurds were about to lose not only their nationality [kavmiyet] but also their religious denomination [mezhep] due to their 'languagelessness' [lisansızlık]", he established a special link between the Kurdish language and Shafi'i Islam, which constituted another discursive act in the nationalization of religion.

In short, this religio-national symbiosis as a major diacritical marker was instrumental in evoking yet another unique aspect of Kurdish national culture and, as such, an exclusive Kurdish national identity around a distinct religious sect closely connected to the Kurdish language. For the author, the waning power of the Shafi'i school of Islam—the religious tradition of the Kurds—and Kurdish language, which are closely connected, was detrimental to the very existence of the Kurds as an ethnic community. In reality, not all Kurds were Muslim, and not all Muslim Kurds adhered to the Shafi'i school. It should be noted that under the reign of Sultan Abulhamid II, the Ottoman state had begun a systematic program of forced conversion to Sunni Hanafi orthodoxy, particularly among the Shi'ite, the Nusayri, and the Yezidi Kurds, thereby declaring the Turkish brand of Sunni Hanafi school the official belief (mezheb-i resmiye) of the empire.

The journal *Kurdistan* never problematized this religious peculiarity of the Kurds. Only a reader letter published in the 5th issue of *Kurdistan* from Adana, a city outside of the historical Kurdish territories, touched on this problem, complaining about the lack of mullahs from the Shafi'i School in Adana as well as the lack of Shafi'i religious books. However, almost three decades previously, Sheikh Ubeydullah of Nehri,[68] in his theo-political campaign against the Hanafi Ottoman Turks and the Shi'a Qajar Empire, exploited this very same religious peculiarity of Kurdish identity to differentiate Kurds from other Muslim communities.[69]

Modernization and progress in the empire in order to catch up to the Western powers had been a state-sponsored project since the *Tanzimat* period. Intellectuals and leaders of non-Turkish or non-Muslim Ottoman groups were able to advocate for the modernization and progress of their own respective communities within the Ottomanist framework without sounding too pro-Western or ethno-nationalist, which might have otherwise provoked state retaliation. Similarly, *KTTG* authors demanded modern education for the Kurds, arguing that thanks to schooling, Kurds would become better Ottomans and better able to serve the Ottoman state. In an article that draws attention to repressive Ottoman policies against the use of the Kurdish language, Babanzade discusses the need to use Kurdish as the language of instruction:

> Among the Ottoman nations [akvam-ı Osmaniye], the Turks are more advanced in science and technology than the Kurds [Kürdler], Albanians, Laz, and Circassians, because Turkish is the official language, and that they possess schools and [other] state institutions. . . . If a Circassian, a Laz, a Kurd [or] an Albanian intends to receive education in science and technology, he has to speak Turkish or Arabic, to say nothing of foreign languages.
>
> A community that lacks a written language and rich written literature would also be bereft of the ability to speak properly and express its ideas. . . Because their tongue has been cut off, Kurds, as one of the Ottoman communities, lack progress due to their languagelessness. Kurds do not have grammar books, Kurds do not possess a printing press or published books, Kurds are deprived of literature, science, and modern technologies. . . If the speech functions in the brain cells of this important Ottoman component become rusty as a result of this cruel oppression, then it goes without saying how much Ottomanism would be affected and damaged. . . . Power and authority are embedded in education, and education is tied to language. If the Kurds, who constitute the most important pillar of Ottomanism, remain in such a rusty and decayed condition, then Ottomanism, which relies upon the Kurds, will, God forbid, collapse.
>
> Although the possibility of the Turkification or Arabization of the Kurds, the Laz, and the Albanians might come to mind, such a cruel and shocking method that would wipe out the language of a community has not been seen since the dawn of time; therefore, such attempts produce nothing because they are meaningless and absurd.
>
> Let's assume that there is a Kurdish child. In his village, no language is spoken other than his mother tongue [lisan-ı maderzadından]. If we open a Turkish school in that village and educate this child step by step in Turkish, he will still grow up to be a responsible member of the society and will have a great career, too, if he is astute. However, he would have to lose quite a few precious years of his life for the sake of learning a new language, which is the instrument that provides access to science. If this Kurd goes to a Kurdish school and obtains books on science in his own language, he will, without any doubt, learn thoroughly and much faster and will become a more valuable member of the Ottoman family.
>
> Therefore, first and foremost, I strongly recommend that my fellow Kurdish countrymen acquire a strong command of [Kurdish] language. First, there should be a grammar book and a dictionary. Then, Kurdish history should be written down. And finally, all scattered and unwritten poems and other works of literature should be collected and written down. Once the foundation of language is laid down in this way, the bird of development and progress will open up its benevolent wings for us with great enthusiasm.[70]

First, the author described the dominant position of the two more privileged and advanced languages, that is, Turkish, the official language of the empire, and Arabic, the divine language of Muslim Ottomans, which posed an existential threat to the languages of Ottoman minorities such as Kurds, Albanians, Laz, and Circassians. Although we do not come across a history of *systematic* linguistic oppression in the late nineteenth-century Ottoman Empire, it seems that the Ottoman state, since the ascension of Sultan Abdulhamid II to the throne and particularly under the CUP, started a systematic language policy. They promoted the use of the Turkish language in schools and gradually imposed it on non-Turkish Ottoman communities, including Arabs. As we saw earlier, Sultan Abdulhamid II banned Sheikh Yusuf Zîyaeddîn Pasha's Kurdish-Arabic dictionary and had its copies confiscated from booksellers in June 1906. From the German Romantic view of language, which places language at the emotional and intellectual center of the nation, the author referred to Kurdish as a mother tongue, a term of nationalism and modernity. He further argued that the oppression of the Kurdish language resulted not only in the absence of social, economic, and political progress but also in the lack of self-expression and social decay among Kurds.

As discussed, *KTTG* authors always mitigated their nationalist tone so as not to be accused of ethno-nationalism or secessionism by the Young Turks. Although the author Babanzade was obviously against the education of Kurds in Turkish language, he softened his argument through the *strategy of rationalization* in a carefully worded and well-balanced narrative. He painstakingly tried to convince the Young Turks to provide Kurds with mother tongue education. He argued that if Turkish remains the only language of instruction, then a Kurdish child would be disadvantaged in the sense that he would have to sacrifice "a few precious years of his life" to learn a "new" language to receive education. He further reinforced this rational argument via an Ottomanist rhetoric by invoking the empire's civilizing mission or the project of modernity: Kurds would fail to serve the Ottoman Empire in full capacity if they were not educated in Kurdish language.[71] As we will see later in an article published in *Rojî Kurd*, Babanzade completely dismissed this Ottomanist rhetoric and replaced it with an argument around Kurds as an active agent in Islamic modernism. If the author's primary concern were the lack of education among Kurds, he could have suggested that Kurds master Turkish to gain access to education because it would have taken less time for a pupil to learn Turkish in the textbooks that were already available.[72] As a matter of fact, Erzincanlı Hamdi Süleyman, in the 8th issue of *KTTG*, challenged Babanzade's point by asserting that Kurdish children should be educated in Turkish because: first, the language of the bureaucracy and military was Turkish; second, there were no teaching materials in Kurdish; and third, the language of the Ottomans was Turkish and therefore all Ottoman communities should continue to speak

Turkish. In any case, Babanzade's argument contributed to the transformation of Kurdish language to a symbol of Kurdish national identity.

In addition, the author was aware of the gradual imposition of Turkish language onto the non-Turkish constituencies. Indeed, the Young Turks appeared to be pursuing the policy of Turkification to transform Turkism into an oppressive form of chauvinist Turkish nationalism. But instead of an overt accusation, the author used the ironic device of *paralipsis* as a part of the strategy of *confirmation through negation*, in which he problematized the Young Turk policy of Turkification by "denying" its existence. He accomplished this by using the conjunction "although" (*olabilirse de*) in "*although* it might occur to one the possibility of the Turkification . . .*" which allowed the author to distance himself from this "untrue" accusation by ostensibly dismissing it but simultaneously highlighting it. He reinforced this strategy when he said that even if what was claimed were true, such a "meaningless and absurd" attempt would be doomed to fail. What is more, using the *strategy of avoidance*,[73] the author never touched on the fragmented nature of the Kurdish language when he promoted Kurdish as the language of instruction. On the contrary, he created the assumption that Kurdish was a unified language. What was left unsaid, unthematized, or backgrounded was, in itself, a discursive strategy that attempted to avoid possible contradictions with what is actually said.[74] Although the author also brought up the possibility of Arabization, it seems that he mentioned this just to mitigate his tone and not to put the Turks on the spot. Due to Turkification, which had started during the reign of Sultan Abdulhamid II, the dominance of Turkish language in education and administration was also challenging Arabic. The diminishment of Arabic became a source of tension and the use of Arabic in education and state institutions were among the primary demands of Arab nationalists in the late nineteenth and the early twentieth centuries.[75]

The publication of grammar books, dictionaries, and works of literature became indispensable components of the national identity for *KTTG* in the age of nationalism. For instance, Babanzade encouraged Kurds to obtain printing presses for the vernacularization of the Kurdish language by producing grammar books, dictionaries, books on Kurdish history, and literature, thereby turning the Kurdish language and national literature into vehicles for national unification. Moreover, *KTTG* disseminated works of Kurdish literature on its pages, including poems by Suleymaniyeli Tevfik in the first three issues. It also advertised and praised intellectual works on the Kurdish language. For instance, in the 6th issue, the journal announced three books in progress:

We sincerely thank you for the good news about the works of Aktepeli Abdurrahman Efendi, one of the most virtuous Kurdish notables, on history in

Kurdish language; honourable Ziya Efendi's [Gökalp] research manuscript on Kurdish proverbs, grammar, and dictionary, which have been in the making for the past 10 years and will be published soon; and a similar work by Hanili Salih Bey, one of the honourable figures of the region; we congratulate them all.[76]

Evidently, *KTTG*, like *Kurdistan*, took great pride in Kurdish language and literature since scientific and literary works in Kurdish language would lend credence to Kurdish. What is more, this prestige bestowed recognition and respect onto Kurds as speakers of that language. In conclusion, compared to *Kurdistan*, *KTTG* followed a more radical path. While it did not make use of Kurdish as its medium of communication, it encouraged the publication of books in Kurdish and, more importantly, strove to convince the state to make Kurdish the language of instruction in Kurdish schools.[77]

Kurdish National Historiography: Kurds Since Time Immemorial

For *KTTG*, national historiography was a novelty that linked the past with the present, which was instrumental for instilling a sense of shared history and a collective political past. *KTTG* discourse often made references to ancient Kurdish history. For example, using the *strategy of unification and cohesivation*, as well as the *strategy of perpetuation,* Hüseyin Paşazade Suleyman designated the Kurds to be the descendants of the Medes:

> If there really were discord and animosity between the Kurds and Armenians, one of these two communities, who have lived in Kurdistan in perfect harmony since 2600 BC [Milâd-ı İsa'dan 2600 sene evvelinden] or as far as one could go back in history, would probably have annihilated the other over such a long period of time.
>
> . . . if Armenians are the ancient inhabitants of that piece of territory, so too are the Kurds, who are the descendants of the Medes [Medyalılar] and the ancient and primary inhabitants of that piece of territory as proven by historical evidence.[78]

Although the article revolved around the improvement of Kurdish-Armenian relations, the author used temporal and special references to historicize the Kurds as an ancient community whose past could be traced back to antiquity. He set the birth of the Kurds to the time of the "ancient Medes" or "2600 BC" to prove how Kurds were rooted in an uninterrupted historical continuity as an unchanged, coherent, and unified *national* community. Given *KTTG*'s audience profile, this text was also meant for the Young Turks and Armenians. While it implicitly told the Turks that the Kurds were the primordial inhabitants of the territory for the past three and half millennia, way before the Turkish presence, it also contested Armenians' claims by designating the Kurds as the *primary* inhabitants.

Saîd-î Kurdî also made reference to the Medes as the ancestors of the Kurds: "under the consultative governance that is known as the limited monarchy and constitution under the name of Shariah. . . what would you lose by connecting the Turan, the Aryan, and the Semites?. . . [On the contrary] you will make enormous gains."[79] Although the notion of coexistence in the context of Ottomanism and Ummahism was the dominant theme of the article, Saîd-î Kurdî distinguished Kurds from the Turks and Arabs by referring to the racial composition of the empire, that is, Turanians, Semites, and Aryans.

The narrative of shared sorrows is another effective strategy in the construction of a collective political past. Correspondingly, *KTTG* made frequent references to the situation of the Kurds under the tyrannical Hamidian regime, portraying the Kurds as a *community of victims* who were collectively oppressed. The extracts below taken from two articles by Halil Hayali and Babanzade epitomize this narrative:

> Oh, those tyrants, first prevented us Kurds [Kurmanca] from education, then from trade and agriculture.[80]
>
> Nevertheless, the tyrannical period, which should be left in the frightening darkness of the past that we do not want to remember, has also crushed this strong component [Kurds] and maltreated it even more cruelly compared to the other components [of the Empire].[81]

It is noteworthy that many Kurdish tribes, particularly the Hamidian Tribal Cavalry regiments, enjoyed extensive privileges under the Hamidian clientele system. However, *KTTG* dismissed this privileged segment of the Kurdish community in its narrative of common sorrow to further demonize the previous regime and emphasize the suffering of the Kurds.

KTTG authors also created narratives of a glorious past and the need for its restoration. They asked readers to take pride in their splendid common past and urged the Kurds to revive it. Suleymaniyeli Tevfik wrote the following lines in the very first issue of *KTTG*: "For years we have not been able to find a solution due to our painful sightlessness, flopping in a state of strangulation. Kurdistan, which in the past brought up geniuses in the fields of science and technology, today has left its children a book of religious sciences brought from India, duplicated and used in every class."[82] The author nostalgically celebrated the glorious "good old days" of Kurdish history and invited readers to a "collective act of remembering." Interestingly, Kurdistan was humanized as an entity "who" raised genius Kurds in the past. Such metaphors are powerful linguistic tools that encourage the addressees to identify with the personified collective subjects: the homeland.

Presuppositions, or taken-for-granted assumptions, constitute another underlying discursive act that presents a nation as a historical community. This discursive act was at work in the discourse of *KTTG*, as evident in the following short extracts from various *KTTG* texts:

> The high value of the history of Kurdistan for the Ottomans, but particularly for all Kurds, does not need to be explained.[83]
>
> The headquarters of the Kurdish Society for Mutual Aid and Progress in Istanbul . . . has decided to prepare an excellent history of Kurds and Kurdistan [and also] to compile and publish Kurdish national literature [edebiyat-ı milliye].[84]
>
> Therefore, first and foremost, I urge my Kurdish countrymen to have a proper language as a matter of the utmost importance . . . then let a history of the Kurdish nation [Kürd kavmi] be written.[85]
>
> Kurdish history, which has not been compiled and written so far, is transmitted in Kurdistan like many proverbs. It is passed down from father to son, from heart to heart by word of mouth.[86]

The common denominator in these extracts is their assumption that such a thing as *Kurdish history* exists, which consists of a series of linear and recurrent themes or coherent and meaningful events that pertain to all Kurds. This discursive act is expected to foster a collective identification with the past among the Kurds and produce a *collective memory*.

Not surprisingly, hegemonic notions of Ottomanism also permeated the narrative of Kurdish history. An article by Suleymaniyeli A. Hilmi is illustrative:

> Just think a little bit; those who established a gigantic state out of a tribe of a handful, yes, those who passed the Dardanelles with [only] 40 people, and shook all of Europe thanks to the success bestowed upon them by almighty God and the sword of valour, those who succeeded in putting the flag of pride on three vast continents of the globe were our ancestors [ecdad-ı kiramımız], just as those ancestors who went all the way to the gates of Vienna, withstanding the bullets of the enemy. They trusted us with that dear homeland, which they founded with their swords and their blood.[87]

In this instance of the *extreme form of Ottomanism*, the author tried, notably around the lexeme of "ecdad" or "ancestor/forefather," to reinforce the idea that Kurds are true Ottomans via the absurd implication that the Kurds are the descendants of *the house of Othman*, the Oğuz Turk founder of the Ottoman

Empire. In a similar way, the editor-in-chief Ahmed Cemil, celebrating the Second Constitutional Period, wrote:

> There have been many successive events and innovations until this 7th century of our existence, but it is impossible to come across such a bright and joyous national festival throughout our long national life.[88]

By "*our* long national life," the author refers to the national life of the Ottoman state, in which the inclusive historical deixis "our" also encompasses Kurds. This claim has been strengthened in the phrase, "this 7th century of *our* existence," in which the "7th century" refers to the establishment of the Ottoman Empire seven centuries earlier (1299 CE). The deictic word "our," on the other hand, implies that the Kurds have been part of the Ottoman state and society since its very foundation. This anachronism misplaces Ottoman-Kurdish relations in time, as Kurdistan's incorporation into the Ottoman Empire did not take place until 1517. In any case, the relations between the two were not as rosy as implied in the text, even after the incorporation of a part of Kurdistan into the Ottoman Empire. Amicable relations between the Ottomans and the Kurds deteriorated soon after the Safavid Empire ceased to pose a threat to the Ottomans. As a result, from 1650 until the demise of the Kurdish dynasties in the mid-nineteenth century, Kurdish emirates and the Ottoman state were in a constant battle for power. Therefore, such a historicization of Ottoman-Kurdish relations should be seen as a part of *KTTG*'s endeavor to conform with the hegemonic discourse of Ottomanism, which once again confirms that history is not an account of the past but a response to the requirements of the present.[89] As far as the pantheon of Kurdish heroes is concerned, *KTTG* does not make frequent references to historical Kurdish figures in the same way *Kurdistan* did. Only in the 9th issue does Ahmed mention *Sharaf Khan of Bitlis* and *Saladin Ayyubi*.

KTTG's Construction of Kurdish Common Culture

National identity implies "a complex of similar conceptions and perceptual schemata, of similar emotional dispositions and attitudes and of similar behavioural conventions, which bearers of a given 'national identity' share collectively."[90] In addition to emphasizing a common Kurdish language, literature, and history, the *KTTG* concerned itself with the production of a Kurdish collective identity on a historical-cultural basis. This Kurdish collective identity revolved around the concept of an ideal—occasionally superior—Kurdish national character when compared to other Ottoman communities, as well as to the West. *Kurdistan*, for example, attributed distinctive behavioral dispositions to its imagined national audience, describing the Kurds as the greatest people on earth. In a similar way, *KTTG*'s identity narrative functioned as a mirror through which the Kurds could admire themselves based on their allegedly inherent and superior qualities of mind and character, which were presented as integral or stereotypical parts of Kurdish national identity. This imagined national character was formulated via a stereotypical phantasmagoria that had no real counterpart outside of the minds of those who believed it. For instance, Malatyalı Bedri underlined the superior moral merits of the Kurds and warned other Muslims against the potential influence from "corrupt" moral principles of the West:

> Kurds disdain the moral degeneration spreading from the West to the East. Similarly, tribes and those living in the countryside disdain pretentious habits, moral values, and weak character spreading from the big [Ottoman] cities. . . However, this has not changed Kurds' moral merits and habits, which are blended with bravery and strength; and no force is capable of changing them.
>
> Since we Kurds have never been possessed by perverted absurdities either at the intellectual or practical levels, we keep away from that stain. This virtue stems not from ideas but from our nature. Today, our moral values have not been corrupted, since we were born as Muslims and live in the mountains, the countryside, and valleys that have not been contaminated by corrupt principles . . . These are our essential traits. Kurds will rise to the occasion to serve this land, this nation, and this Ottomanness. They will revive Islamic and Eastern civilization against the West.[91]

From a primordialist/essentialist perspective, the author listed the "superior" *moral merits* of the Kurds, such as bravery and integrity, as natural and inherent characteristics shared by all Kurds. These were the traits of their collective culture vis-à-vis the corrupt values of city dwellers, who had come under the influence of Western moral degeneration. These attributes contributed to the making of a Kurdish national moral code through the discourse of moral purity allegedly preserved by the rugged nature of Kurdistan's geography, that is, its mountains and valleys, which helped to prevent the penetration of "impure" foreign or Western influences. Islamic identity was also presented as a religious resource that complemented this well-preserved "superior" Kurdish character. This type of promotion and preservation of moral values correspond to what Chatterjee calls the "spiritual domain," a fundamental feature of anti-colonial nationalism.[92] This "inner domain" is supposed to be the site of resistance against intervention to protect traditional institutions, values, and customs. Notably, the author mentioned two sources of moral degeneration, Ottoman city dwellers and the West, which elevated the

Kurds above both the West and the city dwellers, who must be non-Kurdish Ottomans. Consequently, Kurds, who might be inferior to the West and city dwellers economically and technologically, were superior in the spiritual domain.[93]

Saîd-î Kurdî, who spared no effort to emphasize and promote Kurdish identity, was arrested and put in a mental hospital when he dared to petition the Sublime Porte for the establishment of a university in Kurdistan. He told the following to the doctor at the mental hospital:

> First of all, I grew up in Kurdistan. You should measure my rough nature on a Kurdish scale, not on a "civilized" Istanbulian one. If you do not [. . .] you will have to lock up most of the Kurds in mental hospitals, because the greatest moral merits in Kurdistan are bravery, honour, loyalty to religion and honesty. What is called "politeness" by the "civilized" is flattery to them [Kurds] . . .
>
> My strange appearance and "unsuitable" clothes show that I do not have earthly needs . . . it shows my genuineness as a natural human being and exalts my love for my nation. . .
>
> An untamed [and] free Kurd, who does not know Turkish well, can express himself only this much [in Turkish language].[94]

Apparently, Ottoman Orientalist minds depicted the Kurds as "untamed," "rough," and "unsophisticated" mountain people. To oppose this metropolitan arrogance toward Kurds as a people of the Ottoman periphery, the author romanticized Kurds' "uncultured" characteristics by turning what appears to be "inadequacy" into the "moral merits" and positive essential traits that made Kurds distinct from and superior to "high" Istanbulian culture.[95] In other words, Kurdî opposed Ottoman Orientalism through the politics of difference by exalting such Kurdish characteristics as being unspoiled, free, honest, rough, brave, vis-à-vis the "ingenious," "pretentious," "decadent" urbanite culture of Istanbul, the center of *Ottoman Orientalism*.[96] Thus, he equated urban politeness with hypocrisy and flattery. What is more, the author presented Turkish as a foreign language that is not necessarily known or mastered by Kurds, including himself, perhaps in comparison to Istanbulian Turks. Once again, he turned something that might be perceived as a shortcoming (not knowing "proper" or "high" Turkish) into a merit. Finally, he turned his "strange appearance" and "unsuitable outfit" into a Kurdish cultural symbol and a source of Kurdish national pride.

In another article, Saîd-î Kurdî reproduces a dialogue that took place between himself and the Minister of Security: "[. . .] The minister became upset. [Then], I said: I have lived [as a] free [man]; I have grown up in the mountains of Kurdistan, which are the site of boundless freedom. [Your] rage is useless. You are exhausting yourself to no avail."[97] Here too, the author put emphasis on the free nature of a Kurdish culture that was closely associated with the mountainous geography of Kurdistan. It should be noted that Khani was the first to express the rugged and mountainous nature of Kurdistan's geography as an essential part of Kurdish culture. In his *Mem û Zîn*, he wrote: "I am a Kurd from mountains and the peripheries / These are a few words of Kurdishness."[98] The theme of Kurds as free, unfettered inhabitants of rugged mountains has remained a central theme in present-day Kurdish identity narratives.

Although gender relations were never a significant theme or concern of *KTTG*, there were instances in which *KTTG* authors referred to the role of Kurdish women in Kurdish society as a part of Kurdish culture. Consider the following excerpt:

> one of the marvels of the Kurds -among the well-known fine qualities of all Ottomans, such as bravery, heroism, and noble morals- is that Kurdish women are capable of facing dangerous situations that do not [normally] fit into a typical women profile; [Kurdish woman] has never shown any sign of weakness, she has died and killed, she has taken part in wars and endured great difficulties side by side with her husband. We strongly feel that we should show how every single one of these qualities is the proof and embodiment of the Kurdish nation's endless [moments of] heroism [and] their national morals and traditions that have not changed for centuries.[99]

Using the *strategy of dissimilation*, the author foregrounded Kurdish women's "manly" abilities and extraordinary qualities as elements of Kurdish national character, which differentiated Kurds from other Ottoman communities. Conceivably, the author still felt compelled to mention the good qualities of other Ottomans to comply with the journal's overall Ottomanist rhetoric.

Although non-Muslim Kurds did not constitute a dominant theme in the discourse of *KTTG*, Sayyid Abdulkadir, the president of the *KTTC*, mentioned non-Muslim Kurds as a part of the Kurdish common culture. It was the first time the Kurdish intellectual elite incorporated non-Muslim Kurds into the broader Kurdish national community: "Kurds' innate abilities and their capacity for development and enlightenment are recognized and admitted by all men of reason. The previous regime, motivated by who knows what irrational policy, had sown discord and created an abyss among various Kurdish tribes, as well as Muslim and non-Muslim Kurds; and Kurdistan was harmed in the most destructive way by fracturing the ties of unity and mutual affection."[100]

An anonymous article stated: "O Brothers! [. . .] [We] the people living on the Ottoman lands, be it Turks, Kurds, Christians, Yezidis, or Nestorians, are together as one [body] with no differences between us."[101]

In this excerpt, the author cited both Kurds [Kurmancs] and Yezidis as if Yezidis belonged to a separate *ethnie*, even though most spoke Kurdish.[102] Given the importance of religion as an identity marker and the association of Sunni Islam with Kurdish identity during this historical period, perhaps Kurdish-speaking non-Muslims were not yet truly incorporated into the Kurdish identity discourse.[103] The excerpt illustrates how Kurdish intellectuals had just started to think in terms of ethnicity rather than religion, given that the inclusion of Kurdish-speaking non-Muslims into Kurdish identity was a new idea, a discursive novelty or a discursive quest, which was still being negotiated.

Between Kurdish National Homeland and Ottoman Homeland

As we saw, the idea of nationhood rests on the claim to a specific territorial area believed to be the exclusive historical and ancestral homeland of a particular nation. For that reason, every nationalist discourse engages in the articulation of a national homeland by exploiting its historical, cultural, symbolic, political, and economic dimensions simultaneously. First and foremost, *KTTG* regularly presented Kurdistan as a well-defined and virtually homogenous geo-ethnic Kurdish territory whose borders were demarcated by territories inhabited by non-Kurdish *others*. As far as the political aspect of these discursive maps is concerned, *KTTG* presented Kurdistan as the Kurdish homeland for a particular reason: to legitimize their political demands. As discussed in the previous chapter, the cartographic demarcation of territory is an indispensable modus operandi for the construction of a national homeland. Although the map of Kurdistan never took cartographic form, *KTTG* authors did not shy away from discursively drawing such maps utilizing spatial references. Babanzade Ismail Hakkı, in an article titled "The Geopolitical Position of the Kurds," defines the borders of Kurdistan roughly based on its inhabitants:

[I]n this article I am not going to discuss the geography of Kurdistan, its mountains and rivers, its cities and towns [. . .]

As is known, the eastern parts of the Ottoman Empire and the western parts of Iran [and] from the north to the south, nearly from Mount Ararat to the Persian Gulf, is inhabited by the Kurds. Although there are Armenians [living] in the Ottoman part [of Kurdistan] and Turks and Persians [Acem] in the Iranian part, there is no doubt that the population of the Kurds is much larger than the number of all the other components [unsur] combined in the crescent running through Erzurum, Tabriz, Shiraz, and Mosul. While, the Loristan region of Iran is inhabited by Kurds in its entirety, Orumieh and its suburbs are predominantly inhabited by these people.[104]

First, the author established Kurdistan as an identifiable ethnic territory and a national homeland by way of an assumption embedded in the phrase "the geography of Kurdistan." Second, he drew a discursive map of Kurdistan by identifying certain regions, cities, mountains, and seas that allegedly either constituted or demarcated the Kurdish homeland. Third, he mentioned the composition of the population in Kurdistan: In the first clause, even though the author recognized the existence of non-Kurds, he reduced the effect of this recognition through "although" (*ise de*), a sentence-linking contrastive conjunction, to assert that the Kurdish population in Kurdistan was much higher than the total number of all non-Kurds combined.[105] Hence, what made Kurdistan a Kurdish national homeland was its Kurdish majority vis-à-vis the "insignificant" number of *others*. This *strategy of avoidance* is a common tactic in nationalist narratives, whereby nationalists tend to dismiss or down-play the existence of ethnic groups other than their own within the national territory. It is also fascinating to see how the author referred to both parts of Kurdistan to highlight that the Kurdish homeland was partitioned between the Ottoman and Qajar Empires.

The eastern part of the Ottoman Empire was a disputed area between the Armenians and Kurds.[106] Therefore, *KTTG* invoked the ancient history of the region and made the Kurds its oldest inhabitants to justify its present claims. An extract from Hüseyin Paşazade Suleyman's article, which was discussed above, is a perfect case in point. Tracing the history of the Kurds back to 2600 BCE, Hüseyin Paşazade Suleyman stated:

> If there really were discord and animosity between the Kurds and Armenians, one of these two communities, who have lived in Kurdistan in perfect harmony since 2600 BC [Milâd-ı İsa'dan 2600 sene evvelinden] or as far as one could go back in history, would probably have annihilated the other over such a long period of time.
> . . . if the Armenians are the ancient inhabitants of that piece of territory, so too are the Kurds, who are the descendants of the Medes [Medyalılar] and the ancient and the primary [aslî] native inhabitants of that piece of territory as proven by historical evidence.[107]

Although the author traced the existence of both the Armenians and the Kurds to ancient history, that is, 2600 BCE, he still presented the Armenians as the inhabitants of "Kurdistan" and not of "Armenia." In fact, not once is the name "Armenia" as an ethnic territory used in *KTTG*. This discursive act has been further reinforced with the use of the adjective *primary* (*aslî*), which qualified

Kurds as the *primary* inhabitants, implying that Armenians were "secondary" *or* "not quite native" inhabitants. In an attempt to substantiate his argument, he evoked the *Medes*, an ancient empire whom Kurds see as their ancestors. This is a typical nationalist approach to territory, whereby only one ethnic group possesses intrinsic rights to a particular piece of land, while these rights are denied to others who inhabit the same land.

Kurdish ethno-national identity, as articulated on the pages of the *KTTG*, drew much of its appeal from common past experiences such as the collective joy and suffering in the homeland, which is depicted as the greatest on earth. Appealing to this emotive power of the homeland, Halil Hayali wrote:

> O homeland [weten]! How dear you are, how lovely you are! Your tulip gardens are from the blood of the martyrs. Your hyacinths and sweet basils are from the beauty of the eyes of your heroes. Once, you were prosperous, every corner of yours was a resting place for horsemen, your trees and woods were the destinations of the youth; embellished were your lowlands with farmers, your plateaus with tents, your valleys with flocks of sheep, your pastures with herds of horses [and] your hillsides and plains with milkmaids; every corner of you was a humanmade heaven. . . Suddenly, the storm of cruelty and tyranny pestered you, it killed your children, ruined every corner of you, leaving no trace of joy and fortune.
>
> O Kurds [Kurmancan]! Love your homeland! Because love of one's homeland is part of faith [îman].[108]

Clearly, the author made extensive use of the symbolic significance of the body metaphor by conceptualizing the homeland as a figure of attachment parallel to the family. He presented the homeland as a parental figure and Kurds as children. This anthropomorphism is particularly evident in the use of the vocative expression through which the author addressed the homeland, that is, *O homeland! (Weten!)*. He lends a human quality to a nonhuman object in order to endear the homeland to the reader and increase the level of relations between the two. Such metaphors of personification, as we saw, favor identification of the addressees with that of the personified collective subjects. Next, a strong link was established between the land and its inhabitants who shed their blood for the homeland. The use of religious intertextuality embedded in the term *martyr (şehîd)* was a discursive act in its own right, showing how nationalism assumes a religious quality by demanding strong religious piety and self-sacrifice from its "believers." In this glorification of death, sacrifice, and the promise of immortality to national martyrs, *KTTG* manipulated perennial human concerns about body, death, and mortality in much the same way as religion. It is this religious quality of nationalism that helps to create a strong emotional connection to the (home) land. Consequently, through the "political use of the language of sacredness" in the rhetoric of soil and blood, the author presented the homeland as something to die for. *Heaven* (*cennet*), another metaphysical term, reinforced this religious intertextuality. What made Kurdistan a *heaven* was its nurturing fertility, landscape,[109] rich plethora of plants and flowers, beauty, and a prosperous agrarian lifestyle. In this narrative, material resources are relevant only when they are used to strengthen what are fundamentally emotional bonds and claims to space. Therefore, when praising the beauty of the homeland, such narratives usually do not mention any particular location in the homeland but rather remain general and vague. That is, "in these hymns of praise the beauty is not localized: America is not beautiful because it offers a stunning waterfall near Buffalo or a canyon a couple of thousand miles away in Arizona. The country as a totality is praised as special, as 'the beautiful.' "[110] Finally, to strengthen Kurds' attachment to their homeland, the author evoked a hadith in which one's love for homeland was presented as a part of the Islamic faith.

As far as the term *welat* (homeland) is concerned, the process of its semantic shift in meaning from the "native region/province" to "native homeland" continued. Seyyah Ahmed Shewqî's article exemplified this process: "If you forgive the past misdeeds, your *homeland* [welat] will prosper day by day. Our objective is the welfare of *Kurdistan*."[111] Here, given the collocations of *welat* and *Kurdistan*, the term *welat* precisely referred to the entire *Kurdistan*, significantly presented as the *homeland*. It is noteworthy that *KTTG* made use of the term *welatî* (fellow countrymen) in its discourse of national homeland. However, the fact that only two authors utilized the term *welatî* is hardly surprising given the novelty of this term as a neologism in Kurdish political discourse.[112]

What is more, *KTTG* made extensive use of presuppositions, which afforded the depiction of Kurdistan as the exclusive homeland of the Kurds. Consider the following extracts:

> The paramount ideal of this association of us Kurds in Istanbul is the protection of the religion and the progress of Kurdistan.[113]

> The Kurdish Society for Mutual Aid and Progress, taking this point into consideration, has decided to prepare an excellent history of the Kurds [and] Kurdistan [and also] compile and publish [Kurdish] national literature.[114]

It is remarkable that in both articles, Kurdistan was presented as the unified Kurdish national homeland via assumptions about reality, which were taken for granted. Such presuppositions were widely used throughout the *KTTG* corpus.

However, following the journal's Ottomanist line, *KTTG* authors stretched their use of the term *homeland* (vatan/weten/welat) to encompass the whole Ottoman territory. Consequently, the existence of two referents, that is, Kurdistan and the entire Ottoman territory, made *vatan/weten/welat* an elusive term. For instance, Erzincanlı Hamdi Suleyman wrote: "I would also like to suggest that we appeal earnestly to those that are capable of translating this valuable history [of Kurdistan] . . . into Turkish so that our other citizens/compatriots [vatandaş] can also benefit and have an opinion about Kurdistan, which constitutes an important part of their homeland [vatan]."[115]

Additionally, *KTTG* often concerned itself with attacks on Ottoman sovereignty, lamenting independence movements in the Balkans and elsewhere. Protesting Crete's union with Greece, Huseyin Paşazade Suleyman said:

> If we talk statistically about the souls we have lost for that cause, the total loss of us Kurds alone, who are the furthest from Crete Island and hence the least affected, is a few times bigger than the current population of the island. . . . One cannot imagine a single Kurd, not even in the most remote and rugged part of Kurdistan, who would not sacrifice his life to save Crete, which is an inseparable part of the homeland.[116]

The extract used the term *homeland* in its broader sense, turning Kurdistan into a mere extension of the larger Ottoman homeland. However, it seems that the author was trying to highlight the Kurdish contribution to the war, rather than the war itself or the loss of Crete. By foregrounding the Kurdish contribution, perhaps he wanted to "prove" Kurdish loyalty to the CUP and Young Turks, who were wary of the *KTTC* and *KTTG*'s activities.[117]

Finally, KTTG, unlike *Kurdistan*, separately published hard news under the title *Havadis* (News), in which it distinguished domestic news from international news. The interesting aspect of this practice is that the domestic news *(Dahili)* included news from all over the Ottoman lands, rather than from Kurdistan alone, which constitutes another powerful discursive strategy that consolidated the idea of a greater Ottoman homeland.[118]

The Inception of a Discursive Shift from Elitist to a Populist Notion

In parallel with the corresponding section in the previous chapter, the analysis here focuses on how the identities and the interpersonal relations between the Kurdish elite and Kurdish commoners were reproduced in the pages of *KTTG*. This is done through an analysis of lexicogrammatical choices and various sets of linguistic features, including modalities and moods such as the declarative, imperative, optative, interrogative, desiderative, and subjunctive.[119]

In the discourse of *KTTG*, it was not a particular dynastic family but rather the Kurdish intellectual elite, including some members of the aristocratic elite, who were presented as the leaders of the Kurds. They had gathered under the banner of the Society for Mutual Aid and Progress (*KTTC*) and its publishing organ, *KTTG*. In the discourse of *KTTG*, this Kurdish intellectual elite was an authority capable of identifying the Kurds' common problems and the proper means to tackle them, while the readership was constructed as unaware, uninformed, and backward commoners, in need of education, modernization, and guidance. Suleymaniyeli Tevfik, the executive director of the journal, wrote the following in the inaugural issue:

> Thus the "Kurdish Society for Mutual Aid and Progress" [the KTTC] found the Kurdish nation [kavim], to whom it belongs, in awful darkness and bitter muteness, [. . .] The Society has promised to undertake the task of advancing and improving its Kurdish brethren in education, trade and industry; Kurds constitute a valuable organ of Ottomanism and were the first to enter into a covenant to be honoured by the title "Ottoman"—; in short, [it has promised to work] for their happiness following the honourable title of Ottomanism. Our journal is the [sign of] an exciting divine melody of our determination and good intentions for our Kurdistan.[120]

Here the *KTTC* members were presented as the self-appointed leaders, educators, and modernizers of the Kurds. This power relation was accomplished via the pedagogic voice of an expert, represented by the author, who knew the solution to the "awful darkness" that has plagued the Kurds, who were in need of modern education and guidance under the tutelage of the *KTTG* and *KTTC*. Further, the author presented the Kurdish masses as the *brethren* (*kardeş*) of the Kurdish intellectual elite, which served multiple purposes: first, as a common term in populist discourse it mitigated the patronizing voice of the author—and hence that of the journal—and approximated a relationship between equals; second, it implied kinship—brotherhood—between the Kurdish elite and the commoners by evoking a sense of solidarity and claiming co-membership in the same national group; third, it imagined Kurds as a unified body of equal members in an Andersonian sense of a cross-class "horizontal comradeship." This was a discursive shift in the Kurdish journalistic discourse vis-à-vis identities and relations between the Kurdish elite and commoners. This is because we still observe instances where the same Kurdish leadership takes an extremely paternalistic attitude toward Kurdish commoners, as illustrated in an article by Seyyah Ahmed Şewqî:

Hundreds [of] thousands [of] Alexanders[121] rose from among Kurds; they have
fallen martyr for the land of Kurdistan; [but] not even one of them is remem-
bered [today]. What a shame for those lions whose children you are. If you still
exist today, it is thanks to the fame of those ancestors. Aren't you men [mêr]?
Yes, you are men and noble; [but] unfortunately, you do not get along with each
other.[122]

First, through the *strategy of positive self-presentation*, the author referred to
an unspecified pantheon of Kurdish heroes in the past. By using the metaphor
of Alexander the Great, he reminded Kurdish commoners of the bravery of
their ancestors, who were "martyred" for Kurdistan. As we saw earlier, in
nationalist narratives, all past sacrifices, particularly death sacrifices, were
conceptualized in a more secular and nationalist sense: the ancestors of the
Kurds were martyred for the sake of the Kurdish homeland, not for religion.
It is also interesting that the author exemplified greatness in the personality of
Alexander the Great and not in a Kurdish or Muslim figure. Then, adopting a
paternalistic authoritarian discourse of family discipline, the author "scolded"
the readers, calling into question their manhood and claiming that they were
not worthy children of those "lions" to whom they owed their very existence
and homeland.[123] Next, as a self-appointed Kurdish leader, he positioned
himself as a father figure who knew best for his "ill-behaved children," who
could not get along with each other.

The *KTTG* leadership, similar to the editors of *Kurdistan*, delegated the
role of education, unification, and protection of the Kurds to local Kurdish
dignitaries such as the ulama and other influential leaders. Halil Hayali, in the
8th issue of *KTTG*, wrote:

O distinguished ulema, o powerful sheikhs, o influential Kurdish leaders of the
Kurds [Kurmanca]! You should know well that the future of our nation [qewm],
the salvation of our homeland, depends on your unity and hard work. Abandon
the past habits, unite the Kurds, and teach them right from wrong, because you
are the learned and they are ignorant. Guide them! This guidance is for the common interest of the homeland [weten], for the improvement of the nation [milet],
not for your personal ambitions. Remember the doomsday! In this mortal world,
try to achieve an immortal fame through kindness! Keep in mind the provision
that says: "Be kind the way God has been kind to you!"[124]

The author tried to create a bond of solidarity between the two strata by
invoking a collective identity where local dignitaries did not only belong
to, but were also responsible for, the same national community (*qawm*) as
the Kurdish commoners. Equally interesting is that the text also related the
KTTC/KTTG to local dignitaries in which these dignitaries were designated

as *auxiliaries* to the *KTTC/KTTG*, the embodiment of the "real" leaders of the Kurdish community. These identities and relations between the *KTTG*'s intellectual elite and the local dignitaries were achieved by: (1) the fact that a member of the elite who represented the *KTTC/KTTG* called on the dignitaries; (2) the authoritative and commanding tone of the text that was manifested in the imperative mood of several sentences and clauses, for example, *know that!, abandon!, unite!, tell!, guide!, keep in mind!, remember!*; (3) positioning the *KTTC/KTTG* as an authority even above the *ulama* (religious scholars), and daringly "reminding" them of their religious duties and the doomsday.

Although Hayali's article was published in its original Kurdish, each paragraph was followed by a Turkish translation. A fascinating aspect of this practice is the discrepancies between the original text and the translation. The most notable discrepancy occurred in the paragraph where the author Hayali addressed Kurdish dignitaries. While the original Kurdish read, "O distinguished ulema, O powerful sheikhs, O influential Kurdish leaders of the Kurds," the Turkish translation read, "O distinguished *Ottoman* ulama, O powerful sheikhs, O influential Kurdish leaders" (my emphasis). Notice how the word *Ottoman* is *inserted* or *added* to the Turkish translation. Perhaps the author himself or the editor found it necessary to add the word *Ottoman* to the Turkish translation in order to lessen the Kurdish ethno-nationalist tone of the text and give space to the general Ottomanist rhetoric of the paper. A similar discursive act is observable throughout *Kurdistan* due to similar concerns.

Going back to the call on dignitaries, it seems that these calls were effective, as they played a significant role in mitigating the tensions between rival tribes, as is evident from telegrams sent to *KTTC* headquarters in Istanbul. Below is one such telegram sent from the Siirt Sanjak district signed by several tribal leaders:

> We have abandoned the enmity and hostilities of the past tyrannical period, then we kissed each other in the presence of the Mutasarrıf [the governor] and took an oath on the Qur'an. We kindly wish to inform you that we—all the tribes—will sacrifice our lives for the sake of our just constitutional government, the constitution, and our sacred homeland. We appeal to your authority. [Signatories:] Abdullah, one of the leaders of the Pinçinar Tribe; Hasan, the leader of the Alikan Tribe; Bişarê Çeto, a leader of the tribes mentioned above; Mehmed Bişar, one of the leaders of the Pinçinar Tribe; Mehmed Yunus, one of the leaders of the Batun [Tribe]; Derviş, one of the leaders of the Pinçinar Tribe.[125]

Kurdish tribes, which after the demise of the Kurdish emirates tried to fill the power vacuum in Kurdistan, had turned into multiple centers of power and facilitated multiple opposition movements. *KTTG* proudly published such telegrams for political leverage because they could help consolidate the *KTTG*'s leadership position among these disorganized Kurdish tribal leaders[126] and also convey to the Young Turks that the *KTTG* deserved recognition as the legitimate leader of the Kurds.

Moreover, in some of their telegrams, the tribal leaders who had participated in the Hamidian Cavalries expressed their frustration with the unjust practices of corrupt local officials. The extract below, taken from a telegram sent to *KTTG* by Halil, the leader of the Karakeçi tribe, epitomizes such telegrams:

> In 320,[127] 5,000 houses in 120 villages belonging to our tribe were completely destroyed and our tribe members were left homeless on their own land. . . Nonetheless, in this era of restoration and progress, we were officially commissioned by the government to chase and capture Milli Ibrahim—who had revolted against the Sublime Porte—and [in the process] we sacrificed many young souls. Although we were expecting to be rewarded, on the contrary, without any warrant of arrest from a military or civil court and in violation of the constitution and military regulations reminiscent of the despotic period, I have been put in a civilian prison along with my brother by the governor [mutasarrif] of Siverek, who is a servant of Izzet, the traitor. As a result, the tribe has been agitated.[128]

In this telegram, Halil, the leader of the Karakeçi tribe from Siverek, calls upon the *KTTC/KTTG* in anticipation that the Society would *arbitrate* between his "agitated" tribe and the state.

Another telegram, this time from a local branch of the *KTTC* in Muş Province, read:

> From Muş, January 25, 1909
> Upon effective suggestions which grew out of the unifying ideals [of the *KTTC*] about providing our Kurdish brothers—who have somehow been deprived of friendly relations—with the benefits of the constitution, all of the tribes under the jurisdiction of the [provincial] governorate have come to the *[KTTC]* branch. . . and have become members of the Society by shaking hands with one another.
> Muş Branch of Kurdish Society for Mutual Aid and Progress.[129]

Evidently, by publishing this correspondence, *KTTG* not only created a field of communication in which Kurds had a chance to gather around a single political body, but it also designated itself and its parent organization, the *KTTC*, as the sole legitimate voice and representative of the Kurds. This and similar practices, in turn, not only reinforced the image of *KTTG/KTTC* members as the legitimate leaders of the Kurds in the eyes of both the Kurds, the

Young Turks, and the CUP, but it also provided them with political leverage in Istanbul as the representative of a supposedly unified national group.

The Murder of Sheikh Said Barzanji

One of these telegrams was particularly important as it revealed the *KTTC/ KTTG*'s stance vis-à-vis relations between the Kurdish masses and the Ottoman state. The telegram broke the news of Sheikh Said Barzinji's uprising against the new regime and his murder by Ottoman Turkish forces:

> From Simil, 31 December 324 (13 January 1909):
> To the Istanbul Kurdish Society for Mutual Aid and Progress:
> 16 cavalrymen were killed during a heated argument between the (local) people, joined by the local soldiers, and cavalry soldiers [state troops] coming from Kirkuk. The next day it was decided to collaborate in a holy war against the Kurds [cihad-i Ekrad] and they attacked the residence of the Sheikh. The Sheikh, who was holding the glorious Qur'an in his hands to disperse them, begged the soldiers to no avail; the holy Qur'an was trampled to pieces underfoot and [the Sheikh] was killed in front of the government.
> Kurdish Society for Mutual Aid and Progress, Mosul Branch[130]

It is important to note that the telegram stated that the local (most probably Kurdish) soldiers sided with the local Kurds against government forces. Equally important, the letter presented the quarrel as an *anti-Kurdish holy war* (cihad-i Ekrad), which indicates that the local *KTTG* branch adopted a more radical discourse compared to that of *KTTG* headquarters in Istanbul, as we shall see shortly.

What makes this uprising more interesting for the discourse of *KTTG* is the attitude the journal reflected in the hard-news *reporting* on the incident:

> Terrible Incident in Mosul
> Upon the bitter news of the martyrdom of Sheikh Said Efendi, the grandson of Ahmed Efendi from the house of the Barzinji Sayyids, may he rest in peace, we immediately appealed to His Excellency the Paşa, the interior minister, to investigate the matter and seek justice; it is clear that, aware of the gravity of the situation, His Excellency the minister attaches great importance to this tragedy, as he has given orders to the authorities and promised to find out the perpetrators along with possible instigators, and to punish them severely.
> Accordingly, thanks to the justice system, it is obvious that the perpetrators of this sad incident will be captured and the just government will restore the rights of individuals; our association has advised the concerned parties [the Kurds] not to arouse excitement, to stay away from any form of provocation, and also to strictly prevent any situation and behaviour that might disturb the

public order and instead wait for the solution and the deliverance of justice by the government.[131]

This telegraph is a good case in point that demonstrates how the media operate in power relations. As Hodge and Kress assert, "both text and message signify the specific social relations at the moment of their production or reproduction."[132] Hence, analysis of the contexts within which a text occurred helps us understand the social, economic, and political conditions as well as purposes, values, or motivations that might have been behind a particular way of producing a text in the construction of a particular "reality." As far as Sheikh Said Barzinji's uprising is concerned, the truth of the matter was that this "incident" was a Kurdish uprising that the Hamavand tribe, under Sheikh Said Barzinji's leadership, organized against the Young Turk regime, which kept a tight grip on Kurdish notables who had enjoyed extensive autonomy in the prerevolution period. Yet, the paper constructed this politically motivated uprising without its social, political, and historical contexts, presenting it as a mere "incident" (*hadise*), a legal, criminal, or personal matter between the Sheikh and the local state official. Such word choices as *investigation, government's justice, punishment, responsible agents, individuals, sad incident*, and *public order* further consolidated the presentation of the event as a legal or criminal matter. What is more, the paper appealed to the interior minister, asking him to bring the perpetrators to justice on the basis of the protection of *individual* rights. The noun "martyrdom" that describes the Sheikh's death remained too weak to add any substantial meaning to the incident in favor of the rebellion, except that it might have helped to mitigate the paper's pro-government attitude in the eyes of the Kurds. Furthermore, employing the *strategy of calming down*,[133] the text warned the Kurds *not to arouse excitement* among the locals and to strictly *stay away from any provocation* and instead wait for the government's justice.[134] It might seem that *KTTG* was trying to play the role of mediator between the concerned parties, that is, the local Kurds and the Ottoman state. However, in reality, it was leaning more toward the government side. In any case, it is not an unusual practice for a media narrative to create the allusion of siding with the disadvantaged by giving space to dissident voices in an intensely mediated and controlled way, but making sure that they do not pose any serious challenge to the dominant power structure.

An anonymous article went so far as to blame the Sheikh, implying that the Sheikh, his family, and his associates "provoked" this massacre:

We cannot think of anything that could go against the rightful defense of the person in question [Sheikh Barzinji] by his Excellency Sayyid Abdulkadir

Efendi, the president of our association. However, as a consequence of the weak and abusive administration in the region, the associates and the relatives of the Sheikh have lately been spoiled; we find the bothersome behaviours and actions of the Sheikh's brother and son worthy of complaint, and in this regard, we acknowledge the truth of the matter.[135]

Clearly, the article lent a degree of legitimacy to the action of local officials. The killings of Sheikh Said Barzinji and Ibrahim Paşa Milli by the state were the first manifestations of Kurdish resentment toward the new government in the first year of the Young Turk regime.[136] Due to conflicts between the Kurds and Ottoman state officials, the CUP commissioned some leading Kurdish figures, who were members of the *KTTC* headquarters in Istanbul, to strengthen the authority of the state in the Kurdish provinces by way of campaigns of persuasion. As a part of this plan, Sheikh Abdulkadir was sent to Kurdistan as an emissary. It seems that it was not Kurdish nationalists in Istanbul, but the formerly autonomous Kurdish nobility and tribal leaders in Kurdistan, that were seen as the major threat to the new Young Turk regime.[137] Given its attitude toward the anti-government Kurdish uprising, it is fair to presume that the policies of the Kurdish intelligentsia in Istanbul went so far as to prevent the development of a more radical and perhaps secessionist form of Kurdish nationalism in Kurdistan. Put differently, given the media's pacification function, the *KTTG* might have inadvertently hindered the emergence of a more radical form of Kurdish nationalism by insisting on an Ottomanist political framework in which Kurds would be granted some sort of political autonomy under the leadership of Kurdish intellectuals in Istanbul. Thus, *KTTC* centers in Kurdish provinces should not be seen as mere branches of the Istanbul *KTTC*, as their members came from different social and political backgrounds and pursued different agendas.[138] For example, while the *KTTC* center in Istanbul supported the new Young Turk regime and the constitutional monarchy, *KTTC* branches in Kurdistan had mixed feelings toward the new regime. The content of *KTTG* articles confirms this reality as nothing against the new regime managed to find its way onto the pages of *KTTG*. On the contrary, *KTTG* painted a rosy picture of Kurdish attitudes toward the new regime, as if all *KTTC* centers were in favor of the Young Turks and the CUP. Given that a substantial number of Kurdish leaders in Kurdistan were not happy with the new regime, the paper either censored articles/letters with such content or refused to publish them altogether, perhaps because the *KTTC* in Istanbul and *KTTG* were convinced that the Kurds could obtain some sort of political autonomy under their own leadership without resorting to confrontation or violence. It is fair to argue that the *KTTC* Istanbul and *KTTG* monopolized

Kurdish politics and marginalized alternative Kurdish voices. As Klein insightfully asserts:

> The nationalist elite, in speaking for the nation, in this way silenced other voices. They claimed the leadership roles and the tasks that went with them for themselves. In short, they claimed the nation for themselves. Through their discourse, they indicated, directly and indirectly, that should there ever exist an independent Kurdish identity, then the leadership would be in their hands.[139]

Addressing an Imagined Audience as Citizens-in-the-Making

In the previous chapter, I discussed in detail how novels and periodicals became paradigms of audience-making in the convocation of a new public. I also explained how journal publication contributed to the construction of a readership composed of "citizens who must be reformed, educated [and] informed."[140] *KTTG*, in a similar way, summoned a new audience as the recipient of its nationalist discourse. One of the effective means utilized by *KTTG* was the use of a particular type of addressivity aimed at imagining an ethno-national audience, as illustrated below:

O Kurds! (ten times)
O countrymen! (three times)
O Brothers! (one time)
O Dear Brothers (two times)
O Friends! (one time)
My Brothers! (two times)
O Kurdish masses! (one time)
To my fellow Kurdish compatriots (one time)
O distinguished ulema!; O powerful sheikhs!; O
    powerful Kurdish leaders! (two times)[141]

As we saw, the addressivity in *Kurdistan* was a mixture of calls on the Kurdish masses and local Kurdish notables, for example, the ulema, sheikhs, and aghas. *KTTG*, on the other hand, frequently called on Kurdish commoners. This perhaps indicated the beginning of a discursive shift from a feudal view toward a more liberal view of the commoners in line with the spirit of the July 1908 revolution and maturing Kurdish nationalist discourse. Moreover, *KTTG*'s forms of addressivity were often author-inclusive, claiming co-membership with the lay audience in the same national identity, for example, "O Brothers! O Countrymen! My Brothers! O Friends!" This inclusive and humbler tone served to balance the paper's otherwise authoritative, paternalistic, and patronizing tone.

NOTES

1. Kendal, *The Kurds under the Ottoman Empire*; Zeine, *The Emergence of Arab Nationalism*; Zeki Beg, Mihemed Emin. *Dîroka Kurd û Kurdistanê [The History of Kurds and Kurdistan]*. (Istanbul: Weşanên Avesta, 2002).

2. Firro, *Metamorphosis of the Nation (al-Umma)*, 45.

3. Nevertheless, soon after the revolution, the Young Turks felt that a free press harmed its centralist policies. *See*, Firro, *Metamorphosis of the Nation (al-Umma)*, 45.

4. Later on, Yusuf Akçura, a Volga Tatar by birth, became a driving force behind the Turkish Hearth movement. He was elected to the National Assembly and remained a member of the Turkish Parliament for sixteen consecutive years from 1923 to 1939. He also served as the president of the Turkish Historical Society and professor of Turkish history at Istanbul University in the 1930s. *See*, Zürcher, *Turkey: A Modern History*, 383.

5. Akçura, Yusuf. *'Üç Tarzi Siyaset' (Three Kinds of Policy)*. (Ankara: Turk Tarih Kurumu Basımevi, 1904[1976]), (Accessed May 25, 2012: http://aton.ttu.edu/pdf/Uc_Tarzi_Siyaset.pdf).

6. Hanioğlu, M. Şükrü. "Turkism and the Young Turks, 1889–1908," in *Turkey Beyond Nationalism: Towards Post-Nationalist Identities*. (London & New York: I.B. Tauris, 2006), 3–19, 19.

7. Ibid., 3–19.

8. Bozarslan, *Kürd Milliyetçiliği ve Kürd Hareketi*.

9. For an interesting discussion on the imperial character of the Ottoman Empire in the context of postcolonial studies, *see*: Türesay, *The Ottoman Empire*. Türesay takes up the issue whether the Ottoman Empire was a colonial empire despite its egalitarian notions of Ottomanism and Pan-Islamism policies.

10. Cf. Hanioğlu, *Bir Siyasal Düşünür Abdullah Cevdet*, 209–215; Azarian, *Nationalism in Turkey*, 79; Khalidi, *Palestinian Identity*, 86; Zürcher, *The Young Turk Legacy*, 215.

11. Malmîsanij, *Kürd Teavün ve Terakkî Cemiyeti ve Gazetesi*.

12. Other members included Süleymaniyeli M. Tevfik (a.k.a. Pîremêrd), Salih Hulusi Paşa, Naim Baban, Babanzade Zihni Paşa, Diyaberkirli Ahmet Cemil Bey and Liceli Ahmet Ramiz, *see*, Malmîsanij, *Kürd Teavün ve Terakkî Cemiyeti ve Gazetesi*, 23–25.

13. Celîl erroneously calls this newspaper *Kurd*, probably because the word "Kurd" in the first line has a larger font size than the second line that reads "Teavün ve Terakki Gazetesi." Another possibility is that he might have been referring to *Kurdistan*, a journal published simultaneously by the *KTTC*, *see*, Celîl *Kürt Aydınlanması*; Silopî, *Doza Kurdistan*.

14. Emin Ali Bedir Khan, as a retired Ottoman civil servant, was on the state payroll until 1923, *see*, Bedir Khan, Celadet Ali. *Günlük Notlar 1922–1925 [Diary 1922–1925]*. (Istanbul: Avesta, 1997), 32.

15. Klein, *Kurdish Nationalists and Non-nationalist Kurds*, 144; Hanioğlu, M. Şükrü. *Bir Siyasi Örgüt Olarak Osmanlı İttihad ve Terakki Cemiyeti ve Jön Türklük 1889–1902 [Ottoman Committee of Union and Progress and the Concept of Young*

Turks as a Political Organization 1889–1902], Vol. 1. (Istanbul: İletişm Yayınları, 1989), 188.

16. The 31 March incident was an attempted counter-revolutionary plot against the CUP. Since the July Revolution, two forms of opposition had challenged the Young Turk regime. One was "Ahrar Fırkası" (the Party of Ottoman Liberals), established by former Ottoman intellectuals dissatisfied with the CUP's authoritarianism; and the other was composed of conservative religious circles against the secularist policies of the CUP, and who wished to restore Islam and sharia law. However, the real instigator of the 31 March incident was the latter group, who had established "Ittihad-i Muhammedi" (the Muhammedan Union). The CUP used the rebellion to purge not only the members of Ittihad-i Muhammedi,' but also other dissidents, including the members of "Ahrar Fırkası." What is more, it provided the CUP with the opportunity to dethrone Sultan Abdulhamid and replace him with his brother Mehmet Reşit (Sultan Mehmet V), see, Zürcher, *Turkey: A Modern History*, 95–99, 382.

17. Cf. Malmîsanij, *Kürd Teavün ve Terakkî Cemiyeti ve Gazetesi*, 67–102.

18. Silopî, *Doza Kurdistan*, 29–30.

19. Zürcher, *Turkey: A Modern History*, 401–402; Kutlay, Naci. *21. Yüzyıla Girerken Kürtler [Kurds on the Eve of the 21st Century]*. (Istanbul: Pêrî Yayınları, 2002), 140.

20. Bayir, Derya. *Minorities and Nationalism in Turkish Law*. (Farnham: Ashgate Publishing Company, 2013); Minassian, Gaidz F. and Avagyan, Arsen. *Ermeniler ve Ittihat ve Terakki: Işbirliğinden Çatışmaya [Armenians and the Union and Progress: From Collaboration to Conflict]*. (Istanbul: Aras Yayınları, 2005). It is noteworthy that the second *Kurdistan* was also shut down and its publisher Sureyya Bedir Khan was imprisoned, *see*, Malmîsanij, *Kürd Teavün ve Terakkî Cemiyeti ve Gazetesi*, 64–65; Silopî, *Doza Kurdistan*, 23.

21. The founding declaration was published in Ottoman Turkish; however, a summary of the major points made in the declaration was also published in the Sorani variety in the same issue of the journal by Süleymaniyeli Tewfik a.k.a Pîremêrd.

22. Cem'iyet'in Beyannamesi [The Founding Declaration of the Association], *KTTG*, No. 1, December 5, 1908.

23. The same concerns were shared by Palestinian Arabs, *see* Khalidi, *Palestinian Identity*.

24. Cited in Malmîsanij, *Kürd Teavün ve Terakkî Cemiyeti ve Gazetesi*, 19–20.

25. Süleymaniyeli Seyfullah, 'Telhîs-î Sîyasî' [A Summary of the Political Situation], *KTTG*, No. 4, December 26, 1908.

26. Decentralization was also a defining characteristic of Arab political demands after the 1908 revolution. Arab leadership established a number of political parties during this period, one of which was the Ottoman Administrative Decentralization Party (Hizb al-Lamarkaziyyah al-Idariyyah al-'Uthmani), *see*, Zeine, *The Emergence of Arab Nationalism*, 94.

27. The same was true for the associations established by other ethnic groups such as the Albanians and Arabs, *see*, Sönmez, Banu İşlet. *Ikinci Mesrutiyette Arnavut Muhalefeti [The Albanian Opposition During the Second Constitutional*

Period]. (Istanbul: YKY Yanyınları, 2007); Firro, *Metamorphosis of the Nation (al-Umma)*.

28. This article was also published in the 3rd issue of *Hetawî Kurd*.

29. Babanzade Ismail Hakkı, 'Kürdler ve Kürdistan' [Kurds and Kurdistan], *KTTG*, No. 1, December 5, 1908.

30. Nonetheless, as we will see later, the ideology of Ottomanism diminished in the discourse of *Rojî Kurd*, where Kurdishness consisted of Kurdish national identity and Islam, with the Ottoman component left out. Babanzade himself, one of the authors of *Rojî Kurd*, dismissed Ottomanism as a major element of Kurdish identity. Kurdishness gradually came to be the dominant element of Kurdish national identity discourse superseding Ottoman, or even Islamic identity.

31. Hobsbawm, Eric John. *Nations and Nationalism since 1780: Programme, Myth, Reality* (2nd ed.). (Cambridge: Cambridge University Press, 1992), 10.

32. Hastings, *The Construction of Nationhood Ethnicity*, 31–32; Lapidus, *Between Universalism and Particularism*, 47.

33. Babanzade Ismail Hakkı, 'Kürdler ve Kürdistan' [Kurds and Kurdistan], *KTTG*, No. 1, December 5, 1908.

34. Cf. Wodak et al., *The Discursive Construction of National Identity*, 100.

35. "Then and now" is a powerful rhetorical device in the strategy of discontinuation/dissimilation to emphasize the differences between the previous and current period.

36. Halil Hayali, 'Weten û Îttîfaqa Kurmanca' [The Homeland and the Unity of the Kurds], *KTTG*, No. 8, January 23, 1908.

37. Anonymous, 'Kürdçe Lisanımız' [Our Kurdish Language], *KTTG*, No. 4, December 26, 1908.

38. British Indian intellectuals, including Muslim Indians, found themselves in a similar situation. Particularly after the Indian uprising of 1857 was defeated, Muslim Indian intellectuals, such as Syed Ahmad Khan, found it wise to prove their loyalty to the triumphant British rule *See,* Deringil, *They Live in a State of Nomadism,* 337.

39. A number of articles presented Ottomanism through the same radical approach, for example, see the article by Bediuzzaman, in *KTTG*, No. 6, January 9, 1909.

40. Fairclough, *Media Discourse,* 45; Billig, Michael. "Discursive, Rhetorical and Ideological Message," in *Discourse Theory and Practice: A Reader,* edited by Margaret Wetherell, Stephanie Taylor, and Simeon J. Yates. (London: Sage Publications, 2002), 211–221, 220.

41. This is the case throughout the *KTTG* corpus every time the word "Kurd" is employed to refer to the people of this region.

42. Hanioğlu, *Bir Siyasal Düşünür,* 212–213; Hanioğlu, *Turkism and the Young Turks,* 3–19; Akşin, *Turkey from Empire to Revolutionary Republic,* 84–87.

43. Klein, *Claiming the Nation,* 96.

44. An exception to this was Halil Hayali's article where he invited the Kurds to the realm of modern education through the divine voice of a hadith from the Prophet. *See,* Halil Hayali, 'Weten û Îttîfaqa Kurmanca' [The Homeland and the Unity of the Kurds], *KTTG*, No. 8, p. 8, January 23, 1908.

45. Bedri, 'Makale-i Mahsuse: Kürdler ve Şecaat-i Akvam' [Special Article: Kurds and Heroism of Nations], *KTTG*, No. 6, January 9, 1909.

46. This article was also translated into Ottoman Turkish and published in the 2nd issue of *KTTG*.

47. Molla Saîd-î Kurdî, 'Kürdçe Lisanimiz: Bediüzzaman Molla Saîd-î Kurdî'nin Nasayihi' [Our Kurdish Language: Advice by Bediüzzaman Molla Saîd-î Kurdî], *KTTG*, No. 1, December 5, 1908.

48. Saîd-î Kurdî, 'Kürdler Neye Muhtac?' [What do the Kurds Need?], *KTTG*, No. 2, December 12, 1908.

49. Starting from the Tanzimat period and running until the early republican years, the military remained the most favorable institution whose members enjoyed the priority of having privileged access to modern science and technology before all other state institutions.

50. *KTTG* authors, including Saîd-î Kurdî, Sayyid Abdulkadir, and Süleymaniyeli Fethi, promoted the Hamidian Cavalries, despite the fact that these forces were involved in many crimes against civilians, including Armenians and Kurds. They opposed the Young Turks' plans to dissolve the Hamidian Regiments, arguing that the regiments consolidated ties between Kurds and the state.

51. Cf. Gellner, *Nations and Nationalism*, 24–29; Breuilly, *Reflections on Nationalism*, 142.

52. Fairclough, *Language and Power*, 27.

53. van Leeuwen, Theo (2005). "Multimodality, genre and design," in *Discourse in Action: Introducing Mediated Discourse Analysis*, edited by Sigrid Norris and Rodney H. Jones. (London: Routledge, 2005), 73–94; Kress, Gunther and van Leeuwen, Theo. *Multimodal Discourse: The Modes and Media of Contemporary Communication*. (London: Edward Arnold, 2001).

54. Halliday, *An Introduction to Functional Grammar*, 202–227.

55. van Leeuwen, *Multimodality Genre and Design*, 77; Sheyholislami, *Kurdish Identity, Discourse, and New Media*, 135–136.

56. *KTTG*, No. 3, December 19, 1908.

57. *KTTG*, No. 6, January 9, 1909.

58. *KTTG*, No. 4, December 26, 1908.

59. *KTTG*, No. 8, January 23, 1909.

60. *KTTG*, No. 5, January 2, 1909.

61. *KTTG*, No. 9, January 30, 1909. The journal also published images with sceneries of Istanbul, the capital city of the Ottoman state, including images of Kizkulesi (Maiden's Tower), also known as Leander's Tower; the Golden Horn; and Mektebi Sultani (Galatasaray Imperial Hight School).

62. van Leeuwen, *Multimodality, Genre and Design*, 81–82.

63. Soleimani, *Islam and Competing Nationalisms*.

64. Hanioğlu, *Bir Siyasal Düşünür Abdullah Cevdet*, 209.

65. For an interesting discussion on how the use of multiple Kurdish dialects and alphabets on the Kurdish Internet has contributed to the further fragmentation of the Kurds along linguistic line, *see*, Sheyholislami, *Kurdish Identity, Discourse, and New Media*.

66. Cf. Sadoğlu, Hüseyin. *Türkiye'de Ulusçuluk ve Dil Politikaları [Nationalism and Language Policies in Turkey]*. (İstanbul: Istanbul Bilgi Üniversitesi Yayınları, 2003), 89–90.

67. Babanzade Ismail Hakkı, 'Kürdler ve Kürdistan' [Kurds and Kurdistan], *KTTG*, No. 1, December 5, 1908.

68. For an excellent discussion on Sheikh Ubeydullah of Nehri's nationalist revolt in the context of the nexus between religion and nationalism, *see*, Soleimani, *Islam and Competing Nationalisms*.

69. Bozarslan, *Kürd Milliyetçiliği ve Kürd Hareketi*; Kreyenbroek, *Religion and Religions in Kurdistan*.

70. Babanzade Ismail Hakkı, 'Kürdçeye Dair' [On Kurdish Language], *KTTG*, No. 3, December 13, 1908.

71. Cf. Deringil, *They Live in a State of Nomadism*.

72. *See*, Erzincanli Hamdi Süleyman, 'Kurdistan'da Maarifin Tarz-i Tensik ve Ihyasi' [Regulation and Revitalization of Education in Kurdistan], *KTTG*, January 23, 1908, No. 8.

73. Cf. Wodak et al., *The Discursive Construction of National Identity*, 39.

74. *KTTG* became the first journal to publish texts in the two major Kurdish dialects, namely Sorani and Kurmanji.

75. Zeine, *The Emergence of Arab Nationalism*, 98–99; Firro, *Metamorphosis of the Nation (al-Umma)*, 37; Makdisi, *Ottoman Orientalism*, 784.

76. Open Correspondence, *KTTG*, No. 6, January 9, 1909.

77. Since Kurds lacked an educational institution at their disposal, Kurdish intellectuals set up the Kürd Neşr-i Maarif Cemiyeti (Kurdish Society for the Diffusion of Education), a subsidiary organization under *KTTC*, which established the Meşrutiyet Okulu [Constitutional School] for Kurdish children in Çemberlitaş district of Istanbul. It is not clear whether the language of instruction was Kurdish in this school. The Society saw to the establishment of branches in Kurdistan as well. According to Sureyya Bedir Khan, the Young Turks were wary of this society's activities and particularly disturbed by the word "Kurd" in the header. Although the Young Turks did not dare to order the shutdown of the society directly, they resorted to intimidation and harassment, which eventually led to the breakup of the society, see, Silopî, *Doza Kurdistan*, 15; Malmisanij, *Kürd Teavün ve Terakkî Cemiyeti ve Gazetesi*, 37; Jwaideh, *The Kurdish National Movement*, 298; Sureyya Bedir Khan, *Vahdet-i Osmaniyeyi Kimler Parçaliyor?* [Who Is Disrupting the Unity of the Ottomans?], *Kürdistan*, No. 8, December 14, 1917, cited in Malmîsanij, *Kürd Teavün ve Terakkî Cemiyeti ve Gazetesi*, 15.

78. Hüseyin Paşazade Süleyman, 'Kürdler ve Ermeniler' [Kurds and Armenians], *KTTG*, No. 9, January 30, 1909.

79. Molla Saîd-î Kurdî, 'Bediuzzaman Saîd-î Kurdî'nin Milletvekillerine Seslenişi,' [Bediuzzaman Saîd-î Kurdî's Call on the Members of the Parliament], *KTTG*, No. 4, December 26, 1908.

80. Halil Hayali, 'Weten û Îttîfaqa Kurmanca' [The Homeland and the Unity of the Kurds], *KTTG*, No. 8, January 23, 1908.

142 Chapter 3

81. Babanzade Ismail Hakkı, 'Kürdler ve Kurdistan' [Kurds and Kurdistan], *KTTG*, No. 1, December 5, 1908.

82. Tevfik, 'Untitled,' *KTTG*, No. 1, December 5, 1908.

83. Erzincanli Hamdi Süleyman, 'Kurdistan'da Maarifin Tarz-i Tensik ve Ihyasi' [Regulation and Revitalization of Education in Kurdistan], *KTTG*, No. 8, January 23, 1908.

84. Announcement, *KTTG*, No. 4, December 26, 1908.

85. Babanzade Ismail Hakkı, 'Kürdçeye Dair' [On Kurdish Language], *KTTG*, No. 3, December 13, 1908.

86. Bedri, 'Kürdler ve Şecaat-i Akvam' [Kurds and Heroism of Nations], *KTTG*, No. 2, December 12, 1908.

87. Süleymaniyeli A. Hilmi, 'Kürd Vatandaşlarıma Hitaben Birkaç Söz' [Addressing my Fellow Kurdish Compatriots in a Few Words], *KTTG*, No. 9, January 30, 1909.

88. Ahmed Cemil, 'Milletin Id-i Ekber-i Hurriyeti' [People's Grand Festival of Freedom], *KTTG*, No. 3, December 19, 1908.

89. For the historicization of the relations between Ottomans and Kurds, *see*: Ahmed Cemil, *KTTG*, No. 3; Babanzade Ismail Hakkı, *KTTG*, No: 4; Erzincanlı Hamdi Süleyman, *KTTG*, No: 8.

90. Wodak et al., *The Discourse-Historical Approach*, 4.

91. Malatyalı Bedri, 'Makale-i Mahsuse: Kürdler ve Şecaat-i Akvam' [Special Article: Kurds and Heroism of Nations, *KTTG*, No. 6, January 9, 1909.

92. Chatterjee, *The Nation and Its Fragments*, 120.

93. Ibid.

94. Bediüzzaman-i Kurdî, 'Molla Saîd-î Kurdî'nin Tımarhane Hatırâtı', [Molla Saîd-î Kurdî's Memoires of the Mental Hospital], *KTTG*, No. 5, January 2, 1909.

95. On one occasion, Saîd-î Kurdî refused to give up his traditional Kurdish outfits while in the capital city of Istanbul, because he saw his outfits as an expression of his Kurdish identity, even though he was aware that others found his outfits "unfashionable" or "inappropriate."

96. Makdisi, *Ottoman Orientalism*, 771.

97. Bediüzzaman-i Molla Said El-Kurdî, 'Devr-i Istibdadda Timarhaneden Sonra Tevkifhanede iken Zaptiye Nâziri Şefik Paşa ile Muhaveremdir' [My Quarrel with the Minister of Security Şefik Paşa, during the Tyrannical Period when I was sent to Prison from the Mental Hospital], *KTTG*, No. 5, January 2, 1909.

98. Khani, Ahmad. *Mem û Zîn*, edited by Mehmet Emin Bozarslan. (Uppsala: Weşanxana Deng, 2005), 192.

99. Bedri, 'Kürdler ve Şecaat-ı Akvam' [Kurds and Heroism of Nations], *KTTG*, No. 2, December 12, 1908.

100. Sayyid Abdulkadir Ubeydullah Efendi, Cem'iyetimizin Reis-i Fezail'enîsî Sayyid Abdülkadir Ubeydullah Efendi'nin Nümûne-i Fikr-ü Irfani [An Example from the Thoughts and Wisdom of Sayyid Abdulkadir Ubeydullah Efendi, the Honorable President of Our Association], *KTTG*, No. 1, December 5, 1908.

101. Anonymous, 'Kürdçe Lisanımız' [Our Kurdish Language], *KTTG*, No. 4, December 26, 1908.

102. Allison, Christine. "Yezidis," in *Encyclopaedia Iranica*, online edition, (New York, 1996). (Accessed June 28, 2010: http://www.iranicaonline.org/articles/yazidis-i-general-1).

103. Noteworthily, Yezidis are actually considered Kurds in Sharaf al-Din [Sharaf Khan] Bitlisi's *Sharafname* (1596).

104 Babanzade Ismail Hakkı, 'Kürdlerin Mevki-i Coğrafi ve Siyasîsi', [The Geopolitical Posizion of the Kurds], KTTG, No. 4, December 26, 1908.

105. For a detailed discussion on the types of local coherence relations between clauses, clause complexes or sentences, *see*, Fairclough, *Media Discourse*, 121.

106. As a matter of fact, Armenian ambitions, backed by European powers, were among the major reasons behind Sheikh Ubeydullah's Revolt, *see*, Jwaideh, *The Kurdish National Movement*, 75–101.

107. Hüseyin Paşazade Süleyman, 'Kürdler ve Ermeniler' [Kurds and Armenians], *KTTG*, No. 9, January 30, 1909.

108. Halil Hayali, 'Weten û Îttîfaqa Kurmanca' [The Homeland and the Unity of the Kurds], *KTTG*, No. 8, p. 8, January 23, 1908.

109. The mountainous terrain of Kurdistan was also utilized in the construction of the common Kurdish homeland. As we saw earlier, Saîd-î Kurdî used mountains as a symbol of the Kurdish national landscape. Similarly, Ahmed Cemil, commemorating Ishak Sukûtî, evokes the mountains of Kurdistan and associates them with the notion of freedom. *See*, *KTTG*, No. 5, January 2, 1909.

110. Billig, *Banal Nationalism*, 75.

111. Seyyah Ehmed Şewqî, 'Geli Welatiya!' [O Fellow Countrymen!], *KTTG*, No. 2, December 12, 1908.

112. *See*, Seyyah Ahmed Şewqî, 'Ey Gelî Kurdan!' [O Kurdish People], *KTTG*, No. 1, December 5, 1908; and Diyarbekir'den telgrafci Mehmed Tahir Cezeri, 'Kurdce Lisanımız' [Our Kurdish Language], *KTTG*, No. 6, January 9, 1909.

113. M. Tevfik, 'Geli Welatiya!' [O Countrymen!], *KTTG*, No. 3, December 19, 1908.

114. Anonymous, 'Makale-i Hikemiye' [An Article on Philosophy], *KTTG*, No. 4, December 26, 1908.

115. Erzincanli Hamdi Suleyman, 'Kurdistan'da Maarifin Tarz-i Tensik ve Ihyasi' [Regulation and Revitalization of Education in Kurdistan], *KTTG*, No. 8, January 23, 1908.

116. Huseyin Paşazade Suleyman, 'Makale-i Mahsuse' [Special Article], *KTTG*, No. 6, January 9, 1908.

117. For similar rhetoric on the territorial integrity of the Ottoman Empire and the construction of the Ottoman territory as the common homeland for all Ottoman communities, *see*, articles by E. A. 'Siyasîyât' [Politics], *KTTG*, No. 1, December 5, 1908; Süleymaniyeli A. Hilmi, 'Kürd Vatandaşlarıma Hitaben Birkaç Söz' [A few Words to My Kurdish Compatriots], *KTTG*, No. 9, January 30, 1909; and Seyyah Ahmed Şewqî, 'Geli Welatiya' [O Countrymen!], *KTTG*, No. 3, December 19, 1908.

118. The "Dahili" section in the 2nd issue is particularly illustrative in this matter; *See*, *KTTG*, Dahili, No. 2, December 12, 1908.

119. Cf. Fairclough, *Media Discourse*, 128.

120. Tevfik, 'Untitled,' *KTTG*, No. 1, December 5, 1908.

121. Interestingly, the same allegory was used by Sharaf al-Din [Sharaf Khan] Bitlisi (1543–1598/99) in his Sharafname (1596), where Sharaf Khan praised the Ottoman Sultan Mehmet Han III by comparing him to Alexander the Great.

122. Seyyah Ahmed Şewqî, 'Geli Welatiya' [O Countrymen!], *KTTG*, No. 3, December 19, 1908.

123. A similar theme of humiliations is dominant in Indian nationalist discourse, which shames Indians, "the descendants of of Aryans," for being subordinated to others, *see*, Chatterjee, *The Nation and Its Fragments*, 97.

124. Halil Hayali, 'Weten û Îttîfaqa Kurmanca' [The Homeland and the Unity of the Kurds], *KTTG*, No. 8, January 23, 1908.

125. 'Telgrafat-i Hususiye' [Special Telegram], *KTTG*, No. 6, January 9, 1909.

126. Bozarslan, *Kürd Milliyetçiliği ve Kürd Hareketi*.

127. 1904 according to the Gregorian calendar.

128. 'Telgraf'[Telegram], *KTTG*, No. 2, December 12, 1908.

129. 'Telgraf' [Telegram], *KTTG*, No. 9, January 30, 1909.

130. 'Telgraf, Musul Kürd Teavün ve Terakkî Cem'iyeti Şu'besi'[Telegram from KTTG Mosul Branch], *KTTG*, No. 7, January 16, 1909.

131. 'Musul Hâdise-i Fecîasi' [Terrible Incident in Mosul], *KTTG*, No. 7, January 16, 1909.

132. Hodge and Kress, *Social Semiotics*, 5–6.

133. Cf. Wodak at al., *The Discursive Construction of National Identity*, 40.

134. This same point has been repeated in a Kurdish article penned by Ercişli Seyyah Ehmed Şewqî, where he states "the government is investigating the real reason behind the Sheikh's death." Ercişli Seyyah Ehmed Şewqî, 'Gelî Kurda!' [O Kurds!], *KTTG*, No. 7, January 16, 1909.

135. Anonymous, 'Şüûnat: Teessüf-i azim' [Happenings: Great Sorrow], *KTTG*, No. 6, January 9, 1909.

136. Klein, Janet. *Power in the periphery: the Hamidiye Light Cavalry and the struggle over Ottoman Kurdistan, 1890–1914*. (New Jersey: Princeton University, 2002), 210–212.

137. Klein, *Kurdish Nationalists and Non-nationalist Kurds*, 145.

138. Ibid., 142–144.

139. Klein, *Claiming the Nation*, 119.

140. Ang, *Desperately Seeking the Audience*, 28–29.

141. Ey Kürdler; O Kurmancino; Gelî Kurmancan; O Kurdino!; Gelî Kurda (Kurmanc and Kurd were used interchangeably); Gelî Welatiya; Gelî Biran; Gelî Birakên Ezîz; Gelî Hevalan; Gelî Bira; Ya ma'serel Ekrad; Kürd Vatandaşlarıma.

Chapter 4

The Journal *Rojî Kurd*
Kurdish Identity Redefined

THE SHATTERED OTTOMAN IDEALS
AND THE CUP'S REIGN OF TERROR

The CUP came to power after the Young Turks Revolution of July 1908, which marked the start of the Second Constitutional Period in Ottoman history. The new regime generated great enthusiasm among the Ottoman communities of various ethnic and confessional backgrounds since it promoted liberty and equality, promised reforms, and envisaged the decentralization of the state. However, the euphoria of the 1908 Young Turk revolution did not last long, as it soon became evident that the CUP, now in total control of the state, was not willing to live up to its promises. In the face of the duplicity and false promises of the CUP government, which started to resemble a one-party system,[1] non-Muslim communities such as Greeks, Macedonians, Bulgarians, and Armenians gradually moved away from the new government. They began to ponder how they could turn the new political landscape to their own advantage to accomplish their own projects for national unity and independence at the expense of the Ottoman establishment. On the other hand, non-Turkish Muslims of the empire, such as Arabs, Kurds, and Albanians, recognized that secession would be extremely difficult due to the circumstances. Nonetheless, they also took measures to defend their own national identity and gain political autonomy.

The first Muslim revolt against the Young Turks and the CUP regime started when Albania and Yemen rose in rebellion.[2] Consequently, the Young Turks and the CUP came to realize that Turks comprised the only group that favored the new state's centralization strategies, which provided further impetus to fall back on Turkish nationalist policies. In any case, the Young Turks were already in the grip of Turkish nationalism long before the 1908

145

coup d'état. Their interpretation of Ottomanism had always been based on the Turkification of other Ottoman communities, which immensely damaged Ottomanism's credibility in the eyes of both the non-Turkish and non-Muslim communities. On September 6, 1910, Sir G. Lowther, the British Ambassador in Constantinople, wrote to Sir Edward Grey, the British foreign secretary:

> That the Committee has given up any idea of Ottomanizing all the non-Turkish elements by sympathetic and constitutional ways has long been manifest. To them, "Ottoman" evidently means "Turk," and their present policy of "Ottomanization" is one of pounding the non-Turkish elements in a Turkish mortar.[3]

After the military coup known as the *Raid on the Sublime Porte* (Babi Ali Baskını) on January 23, 1913, the CUP tightened its grip on the Ottoman state apparatus by purging anti-CUP elements from the government, particularly non-Muslims and non-Turks. Now unopposed, the CUP had little regard for any political opposition as it started to govern with an iron fist and a reign of terror. Particularly after the myth of Ottomanism was shattered in the aftermath of the First Balkan Wars, the Committee made the Turkish nationalist ideal and Turkish racial superiority the basis for the state by openly embracing the idea of Turkism formulated by Yusuf Akçura nine years earlier. In 1908, nationalist Turkish intellectuals and students organized around Pan-Turkist or Turanian cultural associations such as *Turk Derneği* (Turkish Society) (1909), *Turk Yurdu Cemiyeti* (Turkish Homeland Society) (1911), and *Turk Ocakları* (Turkish Hearths (1912), all of which were closely linked to the CUP.[4] Akçura himself was among the founding members of the Turkish Society. These Pan-Turkist associations published such journals as *Türk Dili Dergisi* (Turkish Language Journal) and *Turk Derneği Dergisi* (Turkish Association Journal). The Young Turks and the CUP were also influenced by the ideas put forward by Mehmet Ziya (Gökalp), for whom "society" meant "nation," which in turn meant *Pan-Turkism*. Gökalp's version of *Pan-Turkish* required not only the cultural and political reorganization and unification of the Turkish race from Central Asia to Anatolia, but also the transformation of non-Turkish communities into subjects. It is worth noting that the emblem of *Türk Ocakları* was a gray wolf head.[5] Although the CUP, the Pan-Turkist organization and their publications continued to advocate Ottomanism in order to prevent the growth of non-Turkish ethnic nationalist sentiments and movements, CUP policies further stimulated nationalist feelings, particularly among the Muslim areas of the empire in Anatolia and Arabia.[6] For instance, it was during this historical period that the Turkish language was imposed in all educational institutions and all geographical place names were changed to Turkish.[7] Also, it has been suggested that Balkan nationalism and, in particular, the First Balkan Wars, catalyzed a more radical and chauvinist form of Turkish nationalism, which in turn nurtured Kurdish and Arab nationalisms. It was under these sociocultural and political circumstances that Kurdish intellectuals and students founded the *Kurd Talebe-Hêvî Cemiyeti* or the *Kurdish Students-Hope Society*, which published the journal *Rojî Kurd/Hetawî Kurd*. (Figure 4.1)[8]

The Proprietors of *Rojî Kurd*: Patterns of Ownership and the Control of Media

The *Hêvî Society*, the owner of the journal *Rojî Kurd*, was founded as the first legal Kurdish student organization on August 9, 1912, in Istanbul by a group of students at Halkalı Agricultural College. The *Hêvî Society* and *Rojî Kurd* were dominated by the new generation of Kurdish youth that came from nonaristocratic backgrounds, which in turn made possible broader discursive participation in the dissemination of a new form of Kurdish nationalism. Founding members of the organization included Kadri Cemilpaşa (Zinar Silopî), Omer Cemilpaşa, Fuad Temo, and Diyarbekirli Cerrahzade Zeki, while notable members included Kerküklü Necmeddin, Ekrem Cemilpaşa, Memduh Selim, Ihsan Nuri, Kemal Fevzi, Nuri Dersimi, Asaf Bedir Khan, Müküslü Hamza, Şefik Arvasi, Mehmet Mihri [Hilav], and Abdurrahim Rahmi.[9] Moreover, Halil Hayali, Şükrü Mehmet Sekban, and Abdullah Cevdet, among others, provided the *Hêvî Society* with material as well as ideological and intellectual support. The first secretary general of the society was Omer Cemilpaşa, who was later succeeded by Memduh Selim. The *Hêvî Society* attracted Kurdish students from various colleges and its membership reached 200 soon after its foundation.[10] The headquarters of the society was located in the Erzurum Office Blocks in Sirkeci district of Istanbul. Kadri Cemilpaşa, along with his cousin Ekrem Cemilpaşa, established the European branch of the *Hêvî Society* in 1913 in Lausanne/Switzerland, where the Cemilpaşas, as well as Babanzade Recai Nuzhet and Dersimli Selim Sabit were studying.[11]

The Cemilpaşa Family

As their last name suggests, the family is descended from Ahmed Cemil Paşa (1837–1902), a son of Hafiz Mustafa Efendi, an influential and affluent religious authority from Diyarbakır, where he also served as governor. The family belonged to the urban landed notable class, which produced some of the most active members of the Kurdish nationalist movement.[12] Among the Cemilpaşas, Kadri Cemilpaşa (aka Zinar Silopî), born in Diyarbakir in 1891, was the son of Fuat Bey and the grandson of Ahmed Cemil Paşa. He first enrolled in Halkalı Agricultural College in Istanbul and two years later went

Figure 4.1 The First Issue of *Rojî Kurd*.

to Lausanne for his studies. He was among the founding members of *Hêvî Society* branches in both Istanbul and Lausanne. He was also an active member of *KTC*[13] and *TIC*.[14] He left Turkey in 1929 for Syria, where he joined the Kurdish nationalists organized around *Xoybûn*[15] in opposition to the new Turkish regime. He died in Damascus in 1973. It is worth noting that Kadri

Cemilpaşa was not actually an Ottoman *paşa* by profession; the word *paşa* was just part of his family name.

Ekrem Cemilpaşa (1891–1974), another grandson of Ahmed Cemil Paşa, was schooled in Istanbul and Europe. He studied engineering in Lausanne, where he joined Kadri Cemilpaşa in establishing the Lausanne branch of the *Hêvî Society*. He was a founder of *TIC* and a member of *Xoybûn*.[16]

Abdullah Cevdet (1869–1932)

Cevdet was born in Arapgir in 1869, where he received his primary educa-tion from his uncle, an imam, and his father, who was an assistant clerk for the Ottoman army's First Battalion. After attending Mameratülaziz provin-cial military school, he went to Istanbul and enrolled in the Military Medical School, where he participated in the growing liberal and reformist Ottoman movement. In 1889, along with three other non-Turkish colleagues, he formed a secret political society, which, after a succession of name changes, would become the CUP. To join the Young Turks' political activities against the despotic Hamidian regime, he fled to Europe, where he published two periodicals, *Osmanlı* and *Ictihad*. Two important collections of his essays are *Science and Philosophy* (1906) and *An Examination of the World of Islam from a Historical and Philosophical Viewpoint* (1922). He also trans-lated Shakespeare's plays into Turkish. Cevdet returned to Istanbul after the 1908 coup d'état, or July Revolution, and resumed his journalistic activi-ties, this time in opposition to the CUP, which had abandoned its original liberal policies in favor of a centralist, authoritarian, and Turkish nationalist line. Cevdet became a member of the *Kurdish Society for the Diffusion of Education* and contributed to the publication of *Rojî Kurd*, *Hetawî Kurd*, and *Jîn*. He broke from the Kurdish movement after the establishment of the Turkish Republic.[17]

Beni Erdelanî Ehmed Muhsin (Mehmed Mîhrî Hîlav) (1889–1957)

Originally from Sinneh (Sanandaj) in Iranian Kurdistan, he studied in Kurdish medreses before he went to Istanbul and participated in *Hêvî Society* activities. Like many other *Hêvî Society* members, he joined the KTC and became the editor-in-chief of the journal *Kurdistan*, one of the KTC's organs. Later, he published a book on Kurdish grammar.[18]

Mehmed Salih Bedir Khan (1874–1915)

He was born in Latakia in 1874. He started middle school in Istanbul but finished in Damascus. After dropping out of Damascus Military High School in Cairo in 1900, he published the journal *Umid* (Hope) against the Hamidian regime. He was exiled and imprisoned several times by the Hamidian regime due to his political activities. He returned to Istanbul after the 1908 coup d'état and wrote for the second *Kurdistan*, published by Sureyya Bedir Khan. He was one of the most prolific writers in *Rojî Kurd*, where he sometimes wrote under the pen name M. S. Azîzî. He was court-martialled and imprisoned by the CUP for an article he published in *Rojî Kurd*. He died in Kayseri in 1915.[19]

Süleymaniyeli Abdulkerim (1880–1929)

Abdulkerim was the publisher of *Rojî Kurd*, for which he wrote seven articles in the Sorani variety of Kurdish. He received his preliminary education in a medrese in Suleimania. After graduating from Suleimania Military High School, he went to Istanbul in 1908 to study law. He worked at the Collection Agency in Suleimania, in 1914, and served as a judge in Kirkuk and Suleimania between 1922 and 1927.[20] In some of his articles, he used the pen names Silêmanî Ebdulkerîm or Kurdî.

Fuad Temo

Fuad Temo, the son of the deputy for Van Tevfik Bey, was a founding member of the *Hêvî Society*. He is the author of the first modern Kurdish short story, entitled *Çîrok*, which was published in the first and second issues of *Rojî Kurd*.

Xelîl Xeyalî (1864–1946)

See the previous chapter for his short biography.

Babanzade Ismail Hakkı (1876–1913)

See the previous chapter for his short biography.

Lutfi Fikri (?–1934)

Fikri was born in Istanbul. Upon his graduation from the School of Political Science in 1890, he went to Paris to study law. Soon after his return to Istanbul in 1894, he was sent into exile on account of his connections with anti-Sultan activities. He returned to Istanbul after the 1908 coup d'état and became the deputy for Dersim in the Ottoman parliament. Although he wrote extensively for many Kurdish journals of the era, he was never actively involved in the Kurdish nationalist movement. He became the head of the Istanbul Bar Association after the establishment of the Turkish Republic. Fikri died in 1934 in Paris while receiving medical treatment.

Due to space limitations, as well as the scarcity of information, it is not possible to provide detailed biographies of all the members of the *Hêvî*

Table 4.1   The Social Background of "Hêvî Society" Members

Bedir Khan family	1
Bâbânzâde family	2
Cemilpaşazade family	6
Sheikly or other religious background	4
Bureaucrats	1
Civil servants	1
Working class	1
Petty urban notables	4

Society. Nonetheless, table 4.1 reflects the familial and social background of twenty-one members of the society:[21]

Obviously, most members of the society came from a new generation of nonaristocratic Kurdish youth. A number of them studied in Europe, spoke European languages, and were exposed to European movements of thought. Although they were born into the Ottoman state system and were educated in Ottoman schools as the children of the Kurdish urban elite, the majority of *Hêvî Society* members and *Rojî Kurd* writers were not incorporated into the Ottoman state bureaucracy, nor were they involved in the Ottoman state's power structure, the way the proprietors of *Kurdistan* and *KTTG* had been a generation earlier. These new circumstances, coupled with the CUP's policies of Turkish racial superiority, led to a waning emotional attachment to the idea of Ottomanism and the rise of Kurdish ethnic nationalism among this new generation of Kurdish youth. In an increasingly Turkist political setting, they were concerned more about the future of the Kurds than they were for the future of the Ottomans. This transformation becomes evident in discursive discontinuities around the idea of Ottomanism, which came to be replaced with Kurdish nationalism. However, *Rojî Kurd* writers had to adopt a very subtle discursive strategy to promote Kurdish nationalism because the state put pressure on them through both legal and illegal channels in the form of imprisonment, intimidation, and assassination.[22] *Rojî Kurd* was nonetheless shut down by the CUP after its 4th issue.

Each issue of *Rojî Kurd* was thirty-two pages long. Issue numbers and publication dates are as follows:

Table 4.2   *Rojî Kurd*'s Publication Dates and Places

Issue Number	Publication Date	Printing House	Place
1st	June 19, 1913	Hukûk Printing House	Istanbul
2nd	July 19, 1913	Hukûk Printing House	Istanbul
3rd	August 14, 1913	Hukûk Printing House	Istanbul
4th	September 12, 1913	Hukûk Printing House	Istanbul

Rojî Kurd's management and the *Hêvî Society* shared the same office.[23] Although it received some financial support from Kurds in Istanbul, *Rojî Kurd* was published on a limited budget and therefore relied heavily on subscription fees. The *Hêvî Society* ceased its activities with the outbreak of World War I, as most of its members were conscripted into the Ottoman army and fought on various fronts during the war. Although the society resumed its activities in 1919, the state shut it down in 1922.[24]

DISCOURSE PRACTICES AND TEXTUAL ANALYSIS OF THE JOURNAL *ROJÎ KURD*

Kurdish Identity Redefined: The Waning Power of Ottomanism and the Rise of Islamic Modernism

As we saw earlier, the discourse of *Kurdistan* fluctuated between the Hamidian notions of Pan-Islamism or Islamic Ottomanism and Kurdish secessionist nationalism, while the *KTTG* discourse revolved around the hegemonic ideology of secular Ottomanism to carve out a space for Kurdish politics within the new Ottoman political landscape. In both journals, the Kurdish intelligentsia explored the future of the Kurds within an Ottoman political framework. However, parallel to the shifting political landscape at home and abroad, the construction of a Kurds' common political present and future kept evolving in the discourse of *Rojî Kurd*. One such development was the gradual demise of the Ottoman state and the idea of Ottomanism, which led to the rise of nationalist movements, including Turkish nationalism, which further alienated non-Turkish elements of the empire. Accordingly, one of the primary discursive shifts that occurred in *Rojî Kurd* was the replacement of Ottomanism with Islamic modernism and a more refined form of Kurdish nationalism. These changes eventually led to debates over political decentralization in favor of the Kurds. In what follows, I will chart these discursive shifts in *Rojî Kurd* to reflect on the momentous alterations to explain how Kurds articulated their present political crises and dangers, and how they imagined a common future for themselves.

The major thematic elements in *Rojî Kurd* concerned such issues as the collective liberation of the Kurdish community through political reforms and decentralization; the education of the Kurdish masses; reforming the alphabet; the modernization, industrialization, and agricultural progress of Kurdistan; ending the disunity among Kurdish leaders, and so on. Not only did *Rojî Kurd* differentiate itself by bringing in new themes, but also by adopting a new approach to older concerns. Some of the goals of the *Hêvî Society*, the owner of *Rojî Kurd* and *Hetawi Kurd*, were outlined in its founding declaration published in *Hetawi Kurd*:

In any case, our righteous religion commands that Muslims learn sciences and arts and work hard for progress and happiness . . . If we want to obey the will of glorious God, we should understand clearly that hard work is the only way to acquire sciences, the arts, and progress.

[. . .]

Today every Kurd, young or old, wealthy or poor, should realize his debt to his religion and nation and carry out his duty. Working individually is not rewarding. The best and the most beneficial way to do this is through collective work. All other newly awakening nations [millet] first started by establishing associations, and as a result, they advanced their nations and attained their desire. . . . We, the Kurdish youth who have gathered at medreses and schools in Istanbul to acquire sciences and skills, have legally established the Kurdish Students-Hope Society to pay our dues to our nation and religion. The purpose of our society is as follows:

1. To introduce Kurdish students to one another so that they can work collectively
2. To cultivate the Kurdish language and literature
3. To open medreses and schools and build mosques in Kurdistan
4. To educate poor Kurdish children in medreses, to help them acquire arts and skills [and] provide them with financial support
5. In short, to work toward the welfare and happiness of the Kurds

The ultimate purpose of our society is to aid the Kurds, who are an essential pillar of Muslimness [Müslümanlık], and in this way to serve the religion and the state.

Today, the Kurdish ulama and nobles have no greater duty than their national and religious duty. The destiny of a great component of Islam is in your hands.

And then, once we comprehend the saying that "the sheep is not for the shepherd, but the shepherd is for the sheep's service,"[25] we will have, for the most part, paved the way for the prosperity of Muslimness [Müslümanlık] and Kurdishness [Kürdlük].[26]

As evident in the Society's founding declaration, education and progress remained two key themes and were clustered tightly around a dense religious allusion. For instance, utilizing religion for nationalist purposes, the founding declaration stated that education in sciences and the arts first and foremost was God's command and a religious duty in order to convince conservative Kurdish commoners. Similar to the previous journals, this was not because the members of the society or the writers of their journals were devout Muslims who propagated religion. Rather because of the deep-seated Islamic faith among the Kurdish masses, Kurdish intellectuals sought to reconcile traditional (Islamic) values and secularism in the service of Kurdish interests. Even Abdullah Cevdet, an ardent positivist and secularist Kurdish intellectual who, due to his materialist views, was "accused" of being an atheist, utilized a similar discursive act.[27]

The extract also highlighted the importance of collective work, which allegedly would lead to the collective progress and happiness of the Kurds as *a newly awakening nation*, whose youth had already set an example by establishing associations to advance their nation. The word "duty" (vazîfe) was probably meant to convey, in a nationalist context, the common rights, and duties of the members of the Kurdish community. The declaration also highlighted the social composition of the society, which was made up of Kurdish youth who were proudly portrayed as the torchbearers for this new phase of Kurdish nationalism. This view was reinforced by the lexemes youth, university, science, skills, hope, hard work, progress, and so on.

It is important to note that, in stark contrast to the heavily Ottomanist rhetoric of the *KTTC/KTTG*, the *Hêvî Society* and its press organs, for the most part, dropped Ottomanism. As a result, the declaration of the *Hêvî Society* never endorsed Ottomanism at any point. On the contrary, the text, from an Islamic modernist perspective, designated the Kurds as an essential pillar of Islam , and not Ottomanism. The last two paragraphs of the declaration encouraged hard work for the prosperity of Kurds and Muslims, but significantly neither paragraph mentioned Ottomanism, although the word "state" is mentioned vaguely in passing. Also, notice that in line 21, where the duties of Kurdish society were specified, the word "nation" (*millet*), that is, the *Kurdish nation*, preceded the word religion, giving priority and urgency to Kurdish national identity, not religion.[28] A similar discursive act, in which Kurdish identity was foreground vis-à-vis Islamic identity, can be observed in one of Halil Hayali's articles, where he wrote: "O brothers! I expect you not to neglect your duty to either Kurdishness or Muslimness."

As far as *Rojî Kurd's* general treatment of Ottomanism is concerned, on only a few occasions did it pay lip service to the notion of Ottomanism. With the publication of *Rojî Kurd*, Ottomanism ceased to exist in Kurdish journalistic discourse as a discernible part of Kurdish identity. It was replaced with a refined form of Kurdish nationalism, and with a broader notion of Islamic modernism that essentially served Kurdish modernism. In fact, the journal's general narrative promoted Kurds' relations with and service to Islam, and not Ottomanism. In the first issue of *Rojî Kurd*, Kerküklü Necmeddin stated: "In short, in the columns of *Rojî Kurd*, we are going to write of Kurds' loyalty and service to Islam, which is proven by historical evidence, during the time of the four Caliphs, such as Othman and Ali, as well as during the reigns of the Umayyads, Abbasids, and Ottomans."[29] While previous Kurdish journals painstakingly promoted Kurdish service to the Ottoman state and Kurds' loyalty to Ottomanism, here there is no reference to Kurdo-Ottoman relations. Instead, the author emphasized Kurdish contributions to the Islamic states and empires throughout history, which *inevitably* includes the era when the Ottomans held the title of Caliph. Hence, the Ottoman era is presented as a mere chapter in a much longer Kurdo-Islamic history.

One figure who persistently championed the idea of Ottomanism in the *KTTG* corpus was Babanzade Ismail Hakkı. In Babanzade's arrangements of the various layers of Kurdish identity, Islam and Ottomanism were the two primary and indispensable components that preceded Kurdish ethnic identity.[30] What is more, Babanzade and other *KTTG* authors encouraged education and modernization for the sake of one specific outcome: to train Kurds as better Ottomans so that they could better serve Ottoman ideals and the Ottoman state. However, in an article suggestively entitled "Muslimness and Kurdishness," Babanzade wrote:

> As evident from history as well as the present situation, one of the most robust and the most important pillars of the vast Islamic family is the Kurdish nation [Kürd kavmi]. The place of such a deeply rooted and noble nation, who has brought up many renowned rulers, emirs, scholars, and poets for Islam during the 1300 year-long Islamic civilization, is no less important than other Islamic nations [akvâm-ı İslâmiyye] . . .
>
> For the defence of Islam, which is the sacred property and inheritance of the entire Islamic community, there is a need for a new weapon. This weapon is the introduction of schools everywhere, even in the remotest villages of the Islamic nations, to give a bright life to the nations, that is, to elevate the scientific level of the nations [akvâm] . . .
>
> The only way to salvation and safety for the Islamic nations is first Muslimness, then Arab[ness], Turkish[ness], Kurdish[ness,], and Persian[ness] . . .
>
> Hence, Kurds, like other Islamic nations, should set their agenda as follows: First Islam, then Kurdish[ness].[31]

While Babanzade, an Islamic modernist, in his articles for *KTTG* presented the Kurds as the most important pillar of Ottomanism and as a nation in the service of the Ottomanist ideals, here he bypassed this Ottomanist rhetoric altogether and instead presented the Kurds as "the most robust and important member of the Islamic family for the past 1300 years of great service" with no mention of Ottomanism whatsoever.[32] Then, in the second paragraph, he promoted education and progress in the sciences as the only way to advance the Islamic nations, whose members would ultimately come to the defense of Islam. Nations—here the author's primary, if not the only concern, was the Kurdish nation—could better serve "Islam"—not Ottomanism—if they

improved themselves first. This discursive *strategy of dissimilation* and dis-
identification with the Ottomans marked that Kurdish identity was no longer
subordinated to Ottoman identity.

Still, as far as identity is concerned, the author's punchline falls in the
last paragraph, where he dismissed the idea of Ottomanism by rearranging
the layers of Kurdish identity he had previously proposed in *KTTG*. While
Ottomanism, along with Islam, used to constitute the two primary components of Kurdish identity, now Kurdish identity is composed of just Kurdish
national identity and Islam. In this formulation, Islam or Islamic modernism
is expected to facilitate the modernization of the Kurdish community.

Similarly, in the 3rd issue of *Rojî Kurd*, Babanzade wrote: "If Kurds, like
some of other nations [akvam], manage to start a campaign for education and
establish a committee whose only work would be the promotion of primary
education without getting involved in politics or politicians, then they would be
doing a great service *not only* to Kurdishness [Kürdlüğe] *but also* to Muslimness
and Ottomanness [Osmanlılık]."[33] Here, using a correlative conjunction *not
only . . . but also* [yalnız . . . değil . . . de], Babanzade foregrounded Kurdish
service to Kurdishness and backgrounded not only Ottomanism but also Islam.
His suggestion about not getting involved in politics will be discussed below,
along with an analysis of an article by M. Salih Bedir Khan.

A comparison between Babanzade's views in *Rojî Kurd* and those
expressed in *KTTG* demonstrates the extent of the discursive shift from
Ottomanism to Kurdish ethnic nationalism. This shift can be observed in the
attitudes of other Kurdish intellectuals, among them Halil Hayali. A seemingly ardent supporter of Ottomanism in the *KTTG*'s discourse, all seven of
his articles published in *Rojî Kurd* dropped the notion of Ottomanism altogether and replaced it with a clearly defined Kurdish national identity and the
notion of Islamic modernity.[34]

Furthermore, despite their use of a dense religious intertextuality, *Rojî
Kurd* writers did not shy away from questioning the "one-sided" Kurdish
service to the Islamic *ummah* through the discourse of victimhood. M. Salih
Bedir Khan, for example, wrote:

From the advent of Islam up to the present day, Kurdish mîrs have always been
active in wars and shone on the front lines; they have always been unselfish for
the sake of religion and the state by sacrificing their lives. But unfortunately, and
with great regret, they have never benefited from those sacrifices. Those that are
not from us [ji xeyrî me] have always benefited from our sacrifices.

[. . .] Therefore, we have always been and remain servants [xulam] in the
service of those people that are not from us [wan mirovînî ne ji me].

We Kurds [me Kurda] have always been like that . . .

If we Kurds do not comply with that command of God [regarding education], we will never make progress. We will always remain behind. We will be slaves to others [kes û nakes].[35]

The author questioned the entire sweep of Kurdo-Islamic history and regretted the Kurds' "unreciprocated" service to the Islamic *ummah*. By deconstructing the Islamic *ummah* into its ethno-national components, the author claimed that *those that are not from us*, which means "those that do not have the same ethno-national identity as *us Kurds*"—perhaps particularly the Turks, Arabs, and Persians—have been the beneficiaries of the sacrifices that "we Kurds" have made. His argument, coupled with his use of powerful discursive devices such as deictic pronoun, for example (*us/we [Kurds], them [all Muslims]*, etc.), reinforces the presentation of Kurdish identity at a unique and exclusive ontological level beyond religious affiliation. The author's use of the term "servant" is meant to underline ostensibly unrecognized Kurdish contributions to Islamic civilization. Perceiving this history as such indicates the extent of the author's national feelings and the degree of his frustration, disappointment, and perhaps regret about non-Kurdish Muslims' "exploitation" of Kurds.

Despite these criticisms, Kurdish intellectuals did not see nor present Islam as an impediment to the development of Kurdish national identity and national goals. On the contrary, they argued for the compatibility of Islam and nationalism by presenting nationalism as a force that could empower Islam and modernize the Islamic world. In this act of nationalizing religion, Kurdish intellectuals created what could be called a *micro ummah* within the Kurdish community, whereby all Kurds were bound to each other with the feeling of a religious fraternity who ought to strive, as a nation, for the well-being of Islam and not necessarily for non-Kurdish Muslims. As a matter of fact, the term *al-ummah al-Kurdiyyah* (Kurdish *ummah*) appeared much earlier in a reader's letter published in the 8th issue of *Kurdistan*.[36] For that reason, it can be argued that Islam or Islamic modernity in the form of religious intertextuality or interdiscursivity was instrumental in reinforcing national sentiments among the Kurds.[37] Another important point about M. Salih Bedir Khan's article is that it was published in both Turkish and Kurdish in the same issue of the journal, with noteworthy differences between the two versions. For instance, the last paragraph of the above extract is significantly different from its Turkish version: "Unfortunately, in spite of this, [Kurds] have never been able to escape the misfortune of being forgotten and abandoned."[38] While the Kurdish version was much more radical in its nationalist tone, in terms of both its content and its realization, the Turkish version remained moderate in tone and content. Moreover, a patriotic poem by Khani is missing from the Turkish version. It seems that the use of less radical language and the exclusion of Khani's patriotic poem in the Turkish version both stemmed from the fear of Young Turk retaliation. In a similar way, a section of the text where the author claimed Kurdistan for the Kurds against "unjust" Armenian claims and refuted claims of Kurdish antagonism toward the Armenians does not appear in the Turkish version, perhaps to avoid Armenian reaction.

Similarly, in his article entitled "The Misfortune and Deprivation of the Kurds," Modanli Halil (Halil Hayali) lamented the unrecognized and unappreciated Kurdish service to Islam with the following words: "All these services [of the Kurds] . . . have been lost [on Muslims] . . . Their names [Kurdish leaders in Islamic history] have been ignored. The ones that are recognized are claimed by Arabs and Persians."[39] This unrecognized Kurdish contribution to Islamic civilization and the Islamic community was one of the dominant themes of *Roji Kurd* that we can observe throughout the journal.

One should bear in mind that state retribution directed at dissidents was not a baseless concern but a reality during this period, which had a significant impact on the nationalist narrative of the journal. As we saw, the CUP was extremely intolerant of any non-Turkish nationalist inclinations or any other form of opposition, even from their fellow Turks. The extract below from an article by M. S. Azîzî sheds light on these circumstances:

> Today there is no nation [qewm] without at least fifteen or sixteen newspapers. In these newspapers, they make their situation known, present their troubles and make demands. . . . A nation without a paper is like a mute person who can neither express his/her troubles nor be aware of his/her situation. Here, the youths of the Kurds have gathered and established a Kurdish association [Hêvî]. . . . And now they have begun publishing a newspaper. This newspaper talks [only] about science and skills. It cannot talk about anything else because a clause in the state's law stipulates that "those who wish to publish a political newspaper should deposit 500 gold pieces." It is we Kurds who cannot obtain that money. Therefore, for now, they [Hêvî] have contented themselves with this newspaper.[40]

Expressing the crucial role of newspapers for a nation, the author stated that a paper is not a mere *cultural artefact*, but a pragmatic tool that addresses a nation's collective social and political problems and proposes solutions. He next pointed to the state law that requires journals to deposit 500 gold pieces in the state treasury to be able to discuss political issues. However, he said, since this was beyond *Roji Kurd*'s financial resources, the journal had to refrain from overt discussions of important political issues pertaining to the

Kurds. Obviously "political issues" meant Kurdish political demands. Thus, it is hardly surprising to see that *Rojî Kurd*, for the most part, avoided overt political discussions.[41] In any case, the state persecuted all those who opposed the CUP regime. Still, M. S. Azîzî himself was tried in a martial court and imprisoned owing to his articles in *Rojî Kurd*.[42]

This further confirms the fact that due to the legal and illegal measures taken by the CUP, the Kurdish intelligentsia and Kurdish leaders were unable to overtly engage in politics in the pages of Kurdish journals. However, missing this crucial fact, some of the relevant scholarship has maintained the misconception that *Rojî Kurd*, like its predecessors, never went beyond being the publication of a "cultural club" since it did not make any overt or funda-mental political demands on behalf of the Kurds. Thus, it would be unfair to describe the Kurdish intellectuals of the period as "Ottoman nationalists with Kurdish colours" or label them as "Young Kurds," an allusion to the name "Young Turks."[43] Despite the ban and policies of intimidation, the Kurdish intelligentsia daringly problematized the social and political situation of the Kurds in the pages of *Rojî Kurd* and thus challenged the status quo. M. S. Bedir Khan wrote in the same article:

> Our Kurdish brothers need to be awakened. If from now on, we do not open our eyes and do not wake up from this heavy sleep, they will leave nothing of our Kurdishness [Kurdanî] and they will annihilate us . . . Friends are weeping and the enemy is cheerful. I said "friends," but do not think we [truly] have friends other than ourselves . . . From now on . . . be it our learned or our ignorant, we should all open our eyes and hold one another's hands and work hard for the salvation [silamet] of Kurds and the liberation of the homeland [welat] . . . Today there are six million Kurds; no one is as courageous as Kurds . . . But it is a great pity that Kurdishness [Kurdanî] is not known among the [community of] nations [li nav qewma].[44]

First, using the concept of *national reawakening*, one of the central doctrines of nationalism, Bedir Khan called on his Kurdish *brethren* to wake up from their state of dormancy and to defend their national identity.[45] Then, utiliz-ing the strategy of *unificatory warning* against the loss of Kurdish national identity, he alerted the Kurds to the threat of extinction of Kurdish identity.[46] The third person plural pronoun "they" enabled the author to avoid specifying the source of the *threat* in lines 2 and 3, where he claimed that an unspecified agent, that is, *they*, will annihilate the Kurds. Still, the Kurdish language has afforded the author with an even better linguistic device that enabled him to avoid the use of a subject or agent of the action altogether via the pro-drop feature of Kurdish.[47] In this *strategy of avoidance*, the author left it to the reader to fill in the blanks and see the primary source of this threat, which probably was none other than the Young Turks and the CUP. The powerful rhetoric of "we have no friends" suggested that Kurds were now on their own and should no longer expect support from other Muslims, perhaps particularly the Ottoman Turks who were in control of the state. This also marked the end of the "we are all in the same boat" narrative of Kurdish Ottomanism, which was especially dominant in *KTTG*. Perhaps that is why *Rojî Kurd* did not criticize the Ottoman state the way *Kurdistan* and *KTTG* did: because it did not expect the state to concern itself with or address Kurdish demands. In any case, the author called on Kurds from all walks of life to unite in a *"horizontal comradeship"* and take the matter into their own hands.[48] Lastly, the author estimated the number of Kurds to be around *6 million*, a statement that was probably meant to highlight another factor that certified the Kurds as a true national community.[49]

This over-careful attitude that refrained from explicit expressions of political needs and desires became too obvious, and even strange, in some articles. Consider the following extract from Silêmanî Ebdilkerîm:

> Humans, from time immemorial [rozî ezelewe], have been in need of one another's help. Nothing could happen without collaboration. Even states are always in need of their people's collaboration. If people do not provide soldiers and money through their taxes, there cannot be a basis for a state. [. . .] Today, France has made such great progress that it boggles the mind. It is proven based on statistical evidence that every year 20,000 people die in France and 20,000 people are born in Germany. If today Germany declares another war against France, who could guarantee that the Germans would prevail; if having a greater population guarantees victory, then why was Russia defeated by Japan?
>
> Thus, if there is collaboration, anything can be accomplished. Today, if the Kurds collaborate, they will canonize Kurdish literature, reform our language, and hence gain a name and fame like other peoples.[50]

First, Ebdilkerîm evoked the basic terms and concepts of the social contract, for example, the origin of societies and cooperation between the society and the state. Then, he further elucidated this essential cooperation in political terms: France and Japan, two strong states that defeated their enemies thanks to collaboration, hard work, and the sacrifices of their people, rallied around their respective legitimate national causes.[51] After foregrounding his discussion around state-society cooperation in the lead paragraph, he related it to Kurdish society in the final paragraph. A typical reader would expect the author to, in a logical sequence, relate the topic in the lead paragraph to the Kurds within the same theme of state-society cooperation. However, the author left out the political substance in the lead paragraph. Instead, he limited the scope of the social contract or state-society cooperation to the intellectual activities around Kurdish literature and language reform. Analyzing this argument in connection with what M. S. Bedir Khan had said earlier about the Kurds' inability to discuss politics, it suffices to understand the unwillingness of Ebdilkerîm to relate the political topic in his lead paragraph to the Kurds explicitly, because it would mean encouraging Kurds to rally around a prospective Kurdish state or a state-like political body. Perhaps the author expected readers to connect the dots on their own.

Similarly, Lutfî Fîkrî, a positivist Kurdish intellectual, penned an article entitled "Kurdish Nation" [Kürd Milliyeti] that was also carefully worded to avoid the wrath of the CUP regime:

> In this world, it is not possible to resist natural or social laws . . . The evolution and rejuvenation of societies are subject to the same fixed and unchanging laws of nature . . .
>
> Today nobody questions what being an Arab, an Albanian, or a Kurd means . . . because in an era where nationalist [milliyet] thoughts prevail, no idea that is based on the denial of nations can last long. The necessity to accept, sooner or later, the existence of those nations is a requirement of the social laws.[52]

The importance of this article is twofold: first, from a Comptian point of view, the author stated that a society, like the physical world, operates according to general laws; second, he explained social evolution from a sociocultural evolutionism perspective, which holds that if organisms can develop and change over time, so too can societies following the discernible laws of nature. Based on these two arguments, the author justified the rise of the Kurdish nation and nationalism by presenting them as "natural" phenomena or the inevitable result of social evolution that should not be opposed but accepted. Finally, he asserted that attempts to prevent this evolution would be futile. However, the author did not seem willing to take the next step by putting forward a well-defined political program for the future development of Kurdish nationalism.

As we saw in both *Kurdistan* and *KTTG*, education was deemed a prerequisite for the modernization and progress of Kurdish society into a *real* nation. Although *Rojî Kurd* also concerned itself with these themes, the discourse of *Rojî Kurd* differentiated itself by not promoting education per se, but by sponsoring ethno-nationalism as a condition for the modernity, progress, and ultimately national unity of the Kurds, a view that parallels Gellner's understanding of nationalism as a necessary step toward industrialization and a modern economy.[53] This discursive shift found its most apparent manifestation in an article by Harputlu H. B. His point of departure resembled Anderson's argument about the way sacred imagined communities reacted to the rise of nationalism.[54] After praising the Enlightenment and the ideas put forward by Voltaire that laid the foundations of modern Western civilization, he added:

> This breeze, this spirit, caused new ideas and feelings in Christian minds. The most important of these was the nationalist current. These supreme and innate feelings spread very quickly. Undoubtedly, what served the current development and progress of France and Germany was the idea of Frenchness [Fransızlık] and Germanness [Almanlık].
>
> This power that exalted Christianity pervaded Eastern Christians, too. Even though they lived under Islamic dominion, the lives and the social rules of the Eastern Christians still improved; they made progress and became prosperous.
>
> Undeniably, the power of this novelty that is spreading from the West to the East will bring about significant changes in the Islamic world, too.
>
> I sincerely hope that the current situation [the spread of nationalism] causes a great awakening in the Islamic world and especially among Kurds, Islam's most backward element.[55]

First, holding the West in high regard was a common theme in *Rojî Kurd* because its writers were convinced that Westernization and modernization were one and the same thing.[56] In the first paragraph, the author asserted that the most consequential outcome of the modern era was the rise of nationalism, which became the driving force behind the social, scientific, industrial, and commercial progress of the European nations, for example, France and Germany, as well as the nations of Eastern Europe. Attributing all these progressive qualities to nationalism was the most crucial part of the author's overall argument, in the sense that for him nationalism, and not education, was the primary agent of sociopolitical change toward progress, prosperity, and the well-being of nations. In other words, for him, nationalism, as in the cases of German and French nationalisms, was a precondition for the progress of the Kurds. This was a common perception among Kurdish intellectuals writing for *Rojî Kurd*, since they believed that the French Revolution had established nationalism as a political force capable of reforming societies. Author Harputlu H. B. not only explicitly endorsed the outcome of nationalist movements, that is, their power to form nation-states, but he implicitly wished the same for the Kurds. The author's claim that nationalism would exalt Islam was—from a religious-nationalist point of view—perhaps a reassuring argument to assuage worries that nationalism—or Kurdish nationalism—was a threat to Islam and the Islamic *ummah*.

Another Kurdish intellectual who spoke his mind about Kurdish political aspirations was Abdullah Cevdet. In one article, first, he mentioned a conversation he had with one of his Turkish friends who, on seeing an issue of *Rojî Kurd* on Abdullah Cevdet's desk, claimed that *Rojî Kurd* was a separatist publication because it contained articles in Kurdish language. Clearly,

Cevdet's friend found the use of the Kurdish language to be a challenge to the supremacy of the Turkish element of the empire. Abdullah Cevdet added:

> I think this is a noteworthy incident. It is a deplorable common misperception.
> [. . .]
> Turkey remains a vast empire that consists of various elements [unsur] even after the loss of its territories in Ottoman Europe. We have not yet missed the chance to unite these elements or at least bring them closer to one another . . . The most effective way of unification is by separation. Undoubtedly, you will find this contradictory. . . . Let me explain. God has separated humans to [eventually] unite them. In His Qur'an, God says: "We made you into peoples and tribes so that you may come to know one another." It is obvious that to establish a close friendship between the elements, every element should experience its own natural and racial evolution in a free environment. In empires consisting of various elements, it is a false conviction that these elements can be united through one language, one set of laws and politics [. . .]
> Switzerland consists of twenty-two cantons. The administration and the judiciary of each canton are completely independent [of the central government] . . . Switzerland . . . which is the size of one of our provinces, is made up of smaller republics. . . . It consists of three nations [kavim] based on three different races [ırk].
> [. . .]
> Our century is the century of nations [milliyet], and even the most durable and the strongest governments and states have not been and will not be able to avert this movement.
> [. . .]
> If we want the unity of the elements, then we should accept their separation, too . . .
> Kurds want to use their language and write their own history. They want to know their national personages and they want to elevate them to the level they deserve. I am sure that our enlightened government will be in favour of these wishes.[57]

First of all, it is noteworthy that Cevdet's Turkish friend considered the publication of a non-Turkish journal—regardless of content—to be a nationalist act that posed a threat to the cultural, linguistic, and political supremacy of the Turks. Second, this small confrontation between Cevdet and his Turkish friend reveals the degree to which the Ottoman Turks were intolerant and suspicious of the use of national languages other than Turkish, an attitude that Cevdet found deplorable (*te'essüf iderim*).[58] After welcoming the inevitable arrival of nationalism to the Ottoman territories, Cevdet made some "daring" remarks about the "false conviction" that the whole empire should be united around one nation, one language, and one state governed by a single set of laws. These remarks were followed by the author's most fundamental suggestion: that the empire should adopt an administrative model based on decentralization, similar to Switzerland. But, before he got to the Swiss example, he first felt the need to wrap this Christian/Western style of governance in dense religious intertextuality by invoking a Qur'anic verse, which would make it more "acceptable" to his predominantly Muslim audience. As we saw, promoting Western concepts and ideas often required religious sanction to relate them to the Islamic heritage. Cevdet's use of religious intertextuality is particularly relevant here. The use of religious allusions by a prominent positivist figure like Cevdet, who was often "accused" of being an atheist, strengthens my argument that religion, similar to Ottomanism, was a mere rhetorical resource and a way of framing political claims in the hands of nationalist Kurdish intelligentsia. In other words, religious intertextuality, as a practical tool, help them justify the demands of Kurdish nationalism, which were secular, Western, and modern in nature. Cevdet's use of religious references made his subsequent argument for the adoption of the Swiss model more compatible with Islam and, therefore, palatable to a conservative Muslim society. To further justify his proposal, Cevdet presented decentralization as the only viable option to keep the empire intact. His position—that no state could prevent the inevitable consequences of the nationalist current—added further justification to his argument that his primary concern was the unity and safety of the empire, rather than Kurdish nationalist demands. But at the same time, he hinted at the Ottoman state's oppressive measures to prevent the growth of non-Turkish nationalist movements.

Cevdet's use of such terms as "independent" (*müstakil*), "republic" (*cumhûriyyet*), and "race" (ırk) were parts of a newly forming Kurdish public discourse on nationalism. The word choices, as well as the content of that paragraph, implied that each Ottoman element needed a separate *republic* based on their *racial* and linguistic difference, with their own national language, set of laws, and a certain degree of *independence* from the Ottoman Turks. The term "element" implied a particular component of the empire: the Kurds. This implication became more evident as the author immediately related his argument on decentralization to the Kurds. The last sentence where the author referred to the CUP as the "enlightened government" was perhaps meant to smooth the Young Turks' ruffled feathers. Despite his subtle tone, Abdullah Cevdet always found himself in trouble with the Young Turks and the CUP. Due to his criticism of the government, the CUP shut down his newspapers *İçtihat*, *İşhad*, and *Cehd* one after another.[59]

In the previous two chapters, we saw the importance of deictic pronouns, for example, *us*, *we*, *they*, *them*, with their context-bound meanings in the formation of taken-for-granted assumptions. Due to its dense Ottomanist rhetoric, it was sometimes difficult to tell the denotational meaning of deictic pronouns in the discourse of the *KTTG*, as it was not immediately clear whether a deictic pronoun referred to the Kurds or the Ottomans. Such ambiguity hardly exists in the *Rojî Kurd* because Ottomanism ceased to exist as a core element of Kurdish national identity. Consider the following extract taken from an article by Silêmanî Ebdilkerîm:

> Even though we [ême] have been doing business for the past three years, why doesn't our capital [sermayekeman] exceed one hundred thousand liras? Why does a businessman in Baghdad make one hundred thousand liras in three years? For God's sake, it is not my intention to insult [you], I [just] want [you] to be as intelligent as they [ewan] are.[60]

In this extract—and the whole article for that matter—Ebdilkerîm did not use the word *Kurd* once, yet the reader knew with the starkest clarity that every single deictic or enclitic pronoun, such as "ême," and "-man" referred to "us/we Kurds," while "ewan" and "-yan" univocally referred to "them" who are "not of us." In the corpus of *Rojî Kurd*, the constant use of these deictic pronouns, whose referents were either "us/we Kurds" or "the non-Kurdish others," rendered a deliberately *habitual assumption* about intranational sameness around Kurdish national identity.

Another point that deserves attention concerns the journal's use of certain terms. In both *Kurdistan* and *KTTG*, there was ambiguity around such terms as *qewm/kavm and milet/millet* (nation) as to whether they referred to "our *Kurdish* nation" or "our *Ottoman* nation." Nonetheless, these terms acquired a more refined meaning in the discourse of *Rojî Kurd* and came to denote only the Kurdish nation since Ottomanism was no longer a central trait of Kurdish identity, as evident from the following excerpts:

> There are many reasons for the trouble and disease that have fallen upon us. The first reason is that . . . we are a nation [qewmêkî] without unity . . .[61]
> I want to tell my nation [qewm] that there is no nation [qewm û milet] on earth that has achieved its objectives only with their swords and shields . . .[62]
> But we know and believe that a nation [millet] cannot survive if it just relies on its essential talents and its innate abilities . . . Isn't it a necessity for Kurds too . . .to show a sign of life?[63]

Moreover, unlike *Kurdistan* and the *KTTG*, the authors of *Rojî Kurd* added new terms, perhaps neologisms, to their nationalist discourse, which included *Kurdanî, Kurmancinî, Kurdîtî, and Kürdlük,*[64] which could be rendered to as *Kurdishness*. These terms were instrumental in the journal's *strategy of unification and cohesivation*, which emphasized intranational sameness and unity among Kurds. Another new term was *Kurdayetî* or *Kurdeyetî*, which might be rendered as *Kurdish nationalism* or the *Kurdish nationalist movement or ideology*.[65] For example, H. Hayali, in one article, wrote: "Let those Kurds who have decency, honour, and zeal for Kurdish nationalism [kurdiyetî] . . .

help them [Hêvî and *Rojî Kurd*]."[66] Given the political substance of the term, the use of *kurdayetî/kurdiyetî* intended to unite Kurds around *Hêvî* and *Rojî Kurd* for a common *national cause, ideology,* or *movement.* In brief, all these terms, *kurdayetî* in particular, suggested a strong ideological commitment to Kurdish nationalist ideology without leaving much room for Ottomanism or parochial Kurdish identities.

Multimodality and Consolidation of Kurdish National Identity through Photographic Images

Multisemiotic analysis is an indispensable aspect of text analysis in the case of the printed press due to the use of photographic images and the overall visual organization of pages. Like *KTTG*, the corpus of *Rojî Kurd* might be considered a multimodal text because of the visual images featured on the cover pages for each issue. To analyze these images as a semiotic modality in interaction with the text in the meaning-making process is therefore necessary. While all photographic images in *KTTG* were related to the hegemonic

Figure 4.2   O You the Wonderful Creation of this Universe, Do Not Think That the Mother of Time Will Bring the Likes of You into this World Again. One of the exceptional Kurds: Sultan Saladin Ayyubid.

discourse of Ottomanism and hence contributed to that journal's ostensibly Ottomanist narrative, those in *Rojî Kurd* were related to great Kurdish figures and in this way contributed to the journal's overall Kurdish ethno-nationalist line. As far as the multimodality of the text is concerned, the photographic images in *Rojî Kurd* can be considered examples of the *extensive mode* as opposed to the *elaborative mode* because none of the images were directly related to the articles in their immediate proximity.[67]

The first image championed by the journal was a portrait of Saladin (1137–1193), along with a caption, on the cover of *Rojî Kurd*'s first issue (Figure 4.2):[68]

While the first sentence of the caption depicted Saladin as an irreplaceable historical figure, the second sentence proudly specified his Kurdish identity in an attempt to generate a sense of national pride among the readership. Although Saladin's portrait was unrelated to any articles found in that issue, the image was still closely connected to the overall content of *Rojî Kurd* as it supplemented the paper's general Kurdish ethno-nationalist line.

An image that appeared on the cover of the 2nd issue (Figure 4.3) was a portrait of Karim Khan Zand (ca. 1705–1779),[69] the founder of the Kurdish Zand

Figure 4.3   One of the Great Kurdish Figures: Shah Abd al Karim Khan Zand.

dynasty and the ruler of Persia for thirty years during the third quarter of the eighteenth century.[70]

Similar to the Saladin example, this portrait was not connected to any specific article either. Nevertheless, as an *extensive* type of multimodality, it fits into the Kurdish nationalist discourse of *Rojî Kurd*. The caption reinforced this discursive act as it proudly announces the Kurdish identity of this historical figure. As I argue later on in detail, certain discursive acts and strategies in *Rojî Kurd* aimed at the dis-identification of Kurds from Ottomans by

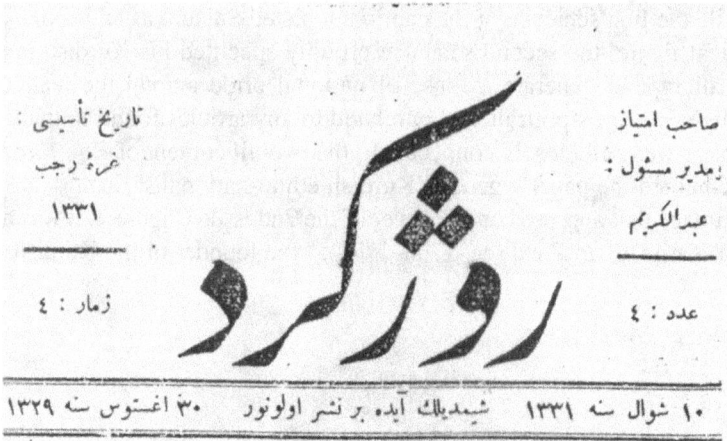

Figure 4.4   Erzurum Province, One of the Fortified Towns of Kurdistan.

evoking pre-Ottoman Kurdish culture, history, and territory. Parallel to this practice, both of the Kurdish personages above were selected from outside Kurdo-Ottoman history.

Another image that appeared in the 4th issue was a panoramic landscape of the city of Erzurum (Figure 4.4).[71] The caption specified the Kurdish identity of the city by evocatively locating it in Kurdistan rather than portraying it as an Ottoman city. This is an outstanding discursive strategy, especially when read in relation to *KTTG*'s discourse in which most visual images were related to the Ottoman capital of Istanbul and thereby closely connected with the journal's Ottomanism.

A picture that stood out in comparison to the other images from the pre-Ottoman or pre-Islamic Kurdish history is the portrait of Hüseyin Kenan Paşa (Figure 4.5) from the renowned Bedir Khan family. The image was published alongside an obituary following the Paşa's death.[72]

Figure 4.5   The Late Bedir Khani Huseyin Kenan Pasha.

Publishing the portrait and obituary of an Ottoman Kurdish figure like Kenan Paşa might seem an ordinary act at first. However, what makes it extraordinary is that Kenan Paşa, along with his brothers Kamil Paşa and Osman Paşa, had recently instigated and led a Kurdish revolt against the Ottoman state in the Botan district of Kurdistan. Promoting a figure like Kenan Paşa implied an endorsement of his political activities, even though the journal made no mention of the revolt in his obituary owing to the unfavorable political circumstances of the period.[73]

Cultivation of Kurdish Language and Literature in *Rojî Kurd*

As we saw, although *Kurdistan* preferred Kurdish as its primary medium of communication, it never explicitly politicized Kurdish by making demands for the official recognition of this language or its use in public schools. *KTTG*, on the other hand, did politicize Kurdish as the most vital component of Kurdish national identity by demanding its use in public schools as a language of instruction. Despite this demand, *KTTG* published predominantly in Ottoman Turkish due to the politico-symbolic as well as the pragmatic communicative function of Turkish. The Kurdish language maintained its position as the most fundamental marker of Kurdish national identity in the discourse of *Rojî Kurd*, nevertheless with a new approach that distinguished this journal from both *Kurdistan* and *KTTG*. *Rojî Kurd*, like *Kurdistan*, preferred to use Kurdish as its dominant language of communication. Like *KTTG*, it problematized Kurdish in political terms as the most crucial element of Kurdish national identity. Nevertheless, there are three noteworthy differences between *KTTG* and *Rojî Kurd*'s stance on language policy. First, when Kurdish became the predominant language of communication in *Rojî Kurd*, Turkish ceded its politico-symbolic value to Kurdish, which resumed its function of being an exclusive Kurdish national symbol and a boundary marker between Kurds and non-Kurds. Nevertheless, Turkish remained an important medium of communication, perhaps due to both its communicative function as the *lingua franca* of the empire and to circumvent Turkish nationalist claims that those who did not use Turkish were receptive to foreign influences).[74]

Second, while *KTTG* demanded Kurdish be used as a medium of instruction in Ottoman public schools, *Rojî Kurd* never made such a demand, nor did it ask for the support of the state to foster Kurdish. Instead, as we will see, it encouraged the Kurds to take matters into their own hands by establishing schools and producing books on Kurdish literature, grammar, and the lexicon, another point that suggests the gradual demise of Ottomanism among Kurdish intelligentsia. Third, while in *KTTG*, the language issue was usually subsumed under the general narrative of Kurdish nationalism, many *Rojî Kurd* articles were specifically dedicated to the promotion and cultivation of Kurdish literature and language. Finally, while *KTTG* was a Turkish acronym, *Rojî Kurd* was in Kurdish.

Orality versus Literacy

With the advent of modernity, the printing press and printed materials undermined the importance of oral communities.[75] Orality was deemed inferior to literacy because the proponents of literacy were convinced of literacy's key role in developing intellectual competence. They felt that this development would transform oral or traditional societies dominated by the spoken word into Western literate societies of the printed word.[76] Moreover, in the comparative analysis of modes of thinking and communication, *great divide* theories frequently refer to a binary divide between orality, on the one hand, and literacy or scripturality on the other, promoting the supremacy of the latter. A process that started in the discourse of the previous journals but intensified in *Rojî Kurd* also addressed the orality and literacy dichotomy and the increasing value of printed materials. Kurdish intellectuals, influenced by the West, saw the dominance of orality over literacy as an impediment to the social and intellectual progress of Kurdish society.[77] The theory of a *great divide*, coupled with the lasting prestige bestowed on literacy, standardized languages, and printed materials by the ideology of nationalism, generated an even greater impetus for Kurdish intellectuals to transform Kurdish society into a literate society of the printed word and thereby a *"true"* nation.[78]

Certain sections of its declaration on the Kurdish language illustrate the *Hêvî Society*'s position on the binary divide between orality and literacy:

> Then, every nation has a language, and just as it speaks in that language, it also writes and publishes books in it. While in the past, Kurds possessed an excellent language for reading, writing, and speaking and had many books written in that language, later on, this language was gradually forgotten and came to be spoken only outside of towns and cities. Hence Kurdish lost its former prominence. However, a nation cannot exist without an adequate

Table 4.3   Distribution of Kurdish and Ottoman Turkish Articles in the Early Kurdish Journals

	Kurdistan	KTTG	Rojî Kurd
Kurdish	107 texts	14 texts	37
Ottoman Turkish	43 texts	168 texts	32

language . . . Therefore, the first and foremost purpose of this society is to make Kurdish a language of reading and writing, and publishing and disseminating books in that language.[79]

The declaration first established the national language as an indispensable element of the nation, in which it speaks and writes. Second, although Kurdish literature mainly remained based in oral tradition, the text invented a prestigious Kurdish past based on its literary productions.[80] This prestige was later lost, according to the text, when the Kurdish language disappeared from urban areas, the centers of literacy and printing activities. It was confined merely to being a language spoken in the impoverished countryside. Consequently, the Society's declaration set freeing Kurdish from the status of an "inadequate" rural language under the dominance of orality and elevating it to the status of an urban print-language by way of intensive publication activities as the Society's first and foremost objective. Kurdish intellectuals such as Halil Hayali believed that an ethnicity transforms naturally into a nation when its vernacular moves from being an oral language to a written one to the extent that it is regularly employed in the production of literature. Therefore, it can be argued that in the discourse of *Rojî Kurd*, language cultivation was not only a cultural or an intellectual endeavor, but also a *political activity* and an instrument to transform Kurds from an ethnic group into a full-fledged nation.

Turkish nationalists, who claimed that Kurdish was merely a primitive spoken language ill-suited for literature or science, created another impetus for Kurdish nationalists to cultivate the Kurdish language and prove it was capable of a written tradition in science, literature, and education. Perhaps in response to these claims, Babanzade presented language cultivation as a *sacred duty* for the Kurds: "While there are doubts even about the possibility of education and book writing in Kurdish [Kurdce] . . . it is the duty of those who see the social and moral improvement of Kurdishness [Kurdluk] as a sacred [mukaddes] goal to prove that such concerns are baseless and that Kurdish is suitable for science and education."[81]

One figure who in particular took up the issue of language was Halil Hayali. In all of his seven articles written in Kurdish, Hayali attended to such matters as language standardization, literature, alphabet, and so forth. In an article entitled, *Ziman* [Language], Hayali offered a ten-point proposal for "what Kurds need today." The most relevant points for the issue of language and literature were:

1. Reading and writing swiftly
2. A new alphabet based on a new style

3. A dictionary for the entire [temamê] Kurdish language
8. A Kurdish grammar book
10. Cultivation of Kurdish literature and poetry

> To realize these, you must send us all available books in Kurdish. [Also] write down Kurdish religious songs as well as stories and folktales that you can gather from bards and send them to us.[82]

The first two points in Hayali's list suggested the adoption of a new alphabet that would suit the needs of Kurdish orthography, an issue taken up by several other *Rojî Kurd* writers, including Silêmanî Ebdulkerîm, M. S. Bedir Khan, Bulgaristanli Dogan, Abdullah Cevdet, and Babanzade. Likewise, later on, in one of his articles published in the 2nd issue of *Hetawi Kurd*, Mevlanazade Rıfat would propose the adoption of the old Urartian script, claiming that the Urartian alphabet had been the ancient Kurdish and Armenian alphabet.[83] Hayali's 3rd point expressed the need for a Kurdish lexicon that would cover the *entire* Kurdish language. By the word "entire" [temamê], he probably meant all Kurdish dialects, a step toward the standardization of Kurdish as a single unified language. In his 8th point, he suggested the preparation of a "Kurdish grammar book," whereby he created the assumption that Kurdish is a single unified standard language.[84] None of the *Rojî Kurd* authors made any explicit reference to the multidialectal reality of the Kurdish language. Instead, they always used the term *Kurdish* or *Kurdish language* as a singular noun, which downplayed the fragmented nature of this language into dialects. This convention is hardly surprising given the importance of the one-to-one correspondence between the nation and its language summarized in the nationalist motto, "one nation one language." The 10th point, in line with the theory of "Great Divide," promoted the cultivation and canonization of oral literature into printed literature. The canonization of Kurdish oral literature was also highlighted in the paragraph that followed the author's ten points, this time in his call to the common people to collect, record, and send any piece of oral literature, for example, folktales and folksongs, they could gather from the Kurdish bards.

Hayali's call underlines the importance attached to the Herderian notion of plebeian authenticity, in which the commoners' use of language was referred to as *native speech* and a source of authenticity, the functional equivalent of sanctity, vis-à-vis the diluted language of the cosmopolitan city dwellers influenced by *foreign* languages.[85] Simply put, in line with the Herderian view of nationalism, in an attempt to distinguish Kurds from their others, Hayali sought the pure and primordial roots of Kurdish national identity in the rural people's folktales and folksongs. In this sense, the cultivation, codification, and canonization of Kurdish folklore would free Kurdish from the private domain and give solidity to Kurdish literature. It would also underline Kurdish national particularities.[86] This bottom-up approach "was particularly attractive to those whose communities had long been incorporated in, and subjected to, large and often oppressive empires, and who lacked powerful institutions which could carry and impose the new vision and its political aims."[87]

Examples of Kurdish literature, such as classical poems by Ahmad Khani, Haji Qadir Koyi, and Sheikh Riza, embellished the pages of *Rojî Kurd*. Canonizing these works proved the capacity of Kurdish to be a language of *high culture*. They also generated a sense of national pride among the readers. What is more, *Rojî Kurd* authors had an opportunity to subtly express and propagate Kurdish nationalism through the patriotic contents of these poems.

Several *Rojî Kurd* authors, especially Hayali, Babanzade, and Benî Erdalanî Ahmed Muhsîn, expressed their regrets and criticized Kurdish religious dignitaries and other literate Kurds for not using Kurdish in their writings. Hayali, in a sarcastic way, questioned Kurdish religious figures who saw Kurdish as unsuitable for writing. He wrote, "No matter how much I try, I do not comprehend why our mullahs and our literates talk and lecture in Kurdish in medreses, [but] use Arabic, Persian or Turkish, and not Kurdish, when they need to write a paper or a document. There must absolutely be a pearl of wisdom or a mystery in this that we cannot comprehend [mutleq di vê da hikmetek, sirrek heye ku em pê nizanin]."[88]

In another article, Hayali criticized Kurdish men of letters who had previously written their literary works in Turkish, Arabic, or Persian and were therefore claimed by Turks, Arabs, and Persians: "Their names are no more; the ones that have remained have become the property of the Arabs, Persians ['Ecem] and Turks [Romî]. They [Kurdish men of letters] have done no good for the Kurds."[89] This is a point highlighted by Kreyenbroek and Allison, who assert that "those Kurds who had the talent and inspiration to create *high culture* therefore tended to be absorbed into the dominant traditions of Arabic, Persian, and Ottoman Turkish. The fact that a celebrated scholar or artist was a Kurd is now usually known only to Kurds, while others think of such figures as Arabs, Persians, or Turks."[90] However, influenced by the feelings of nostalgia for the glorious past of Kurdish literature, Hayali did not fail to honor the Kurdish men of literature who did write in Kurdish, as he proudly mentioned the works of Elî Herîrî, Melayê Cizîrî, Ehmedê Bateyî (aka Melayê Bateyî), Ehmedê Kor ê Sablaxî, Ahmad Khani, and Hajî Qadir Koyi.[91]

Benî Erdalanî Ahmed Muhsîn (Mehmed Mîhrî Hîlav) launched a similar discussion about language, writing:

Although the Kurdish language is so beautiful and courtly, it has neither [a fixed grammatical] basis nor books. That's why the Kurd is compelled [mecbûr ebê] to devote his time to learning Persian, Turkish, and other languages [zimanî dî] and remains deprived of his own language [zimanî xoy]. If he tries to lay a foundation for Kurdish, he will not be compelled to learn another language; and [in this way] Kurdish will escape the danger of vanishing . . . Now I am asking, is it possible that a Kurd would be willing to see his language disappear [laçûn] and his moral values vanish [gumkirdin]?[92]

First, using the personification metaphor, "the Kurd" in its third-person singular form, the author humanized the Kurdish community as a unified single entity or organism. Next, by asserting that "the Kurd" was "deprived" of his own language and was "compelled" to use the languages of the others, he created a strong nexus between language and national identity at the expense of Turkish and Persian, not to mention Arabic, the secret language of God. This connection was more obvious in his rhetorical question, which echoed the German romantic view that designates language as the unique source of national character and moral values, that is, the *Volk*.

Still, the most fundamental, comprehensive, and sophisticated account of the significance of language came from Babanzade:

particularly during the last century, this nation [kavim] has been completely abandoned, forgotten, and neglected by its own sons as well as by the surrounding nations. This nation that has brought up so many celebrated poets and scholars, [who have written their works] in Arabic, Turkish and Persian, has given little importance to its own language . . .

In the past, the Islamic world had a distinguished intellectual stratum that was not in a defensive position but rather in a superior position vis-à-vis the intellectually inferior Western nations [akvâm-ı garbiyye]. Writing in Arabic used to meet the needs of this very small stratum. Thereby the virtuous pioneers of all [Muslim] nations, seeing their own native languages as secondary, utilized Arabic, the language of our religion, in their scientific endeavours. Latin was serving the same purpose in Europe and thus various nations that composed Christianity paid little attention to writing in their own languages. However, their civilization developed immeasurably. Their experience taught them that a foreign language [yabancı lisân] could no longer meet their needs . . .

It seems that a long-term development similar to the one in Europe, albeit to a lesser degree, is starting to appear on the horizons of the East. This is an exigency and inevitability.

> The Kurd will not be abandoning his religion if he starts reading and writing in Kurdish . . . Did the Turks abandon Islam after they started to standardize and use their language? Did the language of the Persians turn them into the enemies of Islam? . . .
>
> Rendering a written form for a language never means supporting the idea of nationhood [kavmiyyet fikri] or what Europeans call nasyonalite. This has been banned by the Sharia, in any case . . . Islam will advance if it is protected, defended, and disseminated in different languages.[93]

In the first paragraph, the author echoed Ahmed Muhsin and Hayali's arguments about the negligence of the Kurdish language by Kurdish men of literature, significantly referred to as *the nation's sons*, a powerful metaphor of anthropomorphism. Next, Babanzade blamed the surrounding Islamic nations for abandoning the Kurds. The second paragraph is particularly important, as Babanzade attributed the inferiority of the Muslim East and the superiority of the Christian West to the issue of language. First, he recalled the glorious past, when the Islamic world was superior to the Christian West thanks to the intellectual endeavors of Islamic scholars. Then, he asserted that the Islamic world had to take a "defensive position" vis-à-vis the Christian West because the "virtuous pioneers" of the Islamic world continued to use "sacred" Arabic "in their scientific endeavors," although Arabic could no longer meet the needs of the Islamic intellectual stratum. Meanwhile, Christian Europeans did not hesitate to abandon Latin and replace it with their various vernaculars, which resulted in "immeasurable" scientific progress. Clearly, Babanzade perceived the enduring hegemonic power of Arabic over the vernaculars as an impediment to progress in the Muslim world, while he felt that the use of vernaculars had facilitated scientific progress in Europe. Moreover, by emphasizing the adverse effects of *foreign languages* on progress, the author implicitly presented Arabic as a "foreign language" that should be abandoned—by non-Arab Muslims—in favor of national languages.

Another fascinating point is articulated in the third paragraph, when Babanzade "broke" the news of the dawn of nationalism in the "East," that is, the Ottoman Middle East. Outstandingly, decades before McLuhan and Anderson, Babanzade could analyze the decline of religion, the dynastic realm, and sacred languages in the face of the ideology of nationalism in the West and predicted that the same process would "inevitably" take place in the East. In the fourth paragraph, he tried to convince the Young Turks and the CUP that fostering Kurdish would not alienate Kurds from religion, or more precisely, from the Pan-Islamic policy of the Young Turks. Through his rhetorical question, he daringly emphasized the Young Turks' double standard, which allowed the Turks to promote their language while it tried to prevent or limit the use of Kurdish in the public sphere. Perhaps this paragraph was also meant for Kurdish ears, particularly Kurdish religious scholars, to encourage them to write in Kurdish, like the Turks and Persians, two prominent Islamic communities who abandoned "holy" Arabic to write in their national languages. Babanzade painstakingly refrained from conceptualizing these changes in a nationalist framework. Instead, he labeled this process as a "civilizational development," which had spread from Europe to the other parts of the globe, including the Ottoman East. This excessively cautious attitude is most obvious in the last paragraph, where he tried to assure the Young Turks that the promotion of one's language *"never"* meant supporting the idea of nationalism, or "nasyonalite." Babanzade reinforced this point by stating that in any case, nationalism was "banned by the Sharia law," perhaps a word of caution also intended for Turkish nationalists urging them not to commit a sin by imposing Turkish culture onto non-Turkish Ottoman subjects. Religious intertextuality lingers into the following sentence, where he justified the use of Kurdish by claiming that it would contribute to the modernization and improvement of the Islamic *ummah*, which supposedly was in line with the Ottoman Turks' modernity project.

In one article, Halil Hayali made a similar point -by trying to ease the Young Turks' anxiety: "[T]oday there are three hundred million Muslims. They all read and write in their own languages. [But] they have never intended to harm the religion [by using their own languages]."[94] He next reproduced a section of a poem from Haji Qadir Koyi's Diwan, which includes the following powerful verses:

We are believers [Muslim] not Russians [Christian]
Why is it blasphemy for us to write in our language [zibanman binûsîn]

Noticeably, several *Rojî Kurd* writers also highlighted the waning power of Arabic as the sacred language, in favor of Kurdish.

Rapprochement between Kurmanji and Sorani

Rojî Kurd, like its predecessors, devoted generous space to the issue of language and literature, including poems by Ahmad Khani, Haji Qadir Koyi, and Sheikh Riza. This was meant to prove the capacity of the Kurdish language to be a vehicle for *high culture* and generate a sense of national pride among the readership. Among the contributors to *Rojî Kurd*, Hayali

devoted articles to the promotion of Kurdish language by reproducing stanzas from classical Kurdish literature. One figure that Hayali most promoted
was Haji Qadir Koyi, whose Sorani Kurdish poetry provided Hayali with
the opportunity to create the assumption that Sorani and Kurmanji were
two mutually intelligible varieties of the same language. For instance, after
quoting one of Koyi's poems, he stated: "A Kurd who has perseverance
and Kurdish bravery needs to know the meaning of Haji Abdul Qadir's
poems."[95] In this discursive act, Hayali ignored the fact that not all Kurds
speak the Sorani variety and hence cannot *know the meaning of Haji
Qadir's poems*[96]

What makes this strategy of rapprochement between the two varieties
more obvious is Hayali's constant and deliberate use of Sorani words in all
his Kurmanji articles. For instance, he deliberately used the Sorani preposi-
tion "le" instead of the Kurmanji "li," the Sorani "çak" instead of "baş,"
"meramim" instead of "merama min," "nûsîn" instead of "nivîsîn," and so
forth. This practice seems to be another instance of language cultivation
that can be related to Kloss's tripartite concept, that is, *Abstand, Ausbau*,
and *Dachsprache*. In this deliberate language cultivation activity, Hayali
attempted to close the distance between the two varieties, toward the formation of a "roof language" (Dachsprache).[97]

What is more, *Rojî Kurd* used the Kurdish language as a Kurdish cultural particularity that differentiated the Kurds from all other *Oriental* or
Ottoman communities. In one article, Kurdî, aka Silêmanî Ebdilkerîm,[98]
claimed that Kurds, like Germans, belong to the Aryan people: "Germans
and the German language resemble Kurds and Kurdish. Today, if a Kurd
goes to Germany, he could learn German [zebanî elman] in two months.
However, if a Turk or Arab try to learn the German language, it would take
them more than a year."[99] From a comparative linguistics point of view
and based on their linguistic and racial differences, the author did not only
emphasize Kurds' Aryan roots, but he also dis-identified the Kurds from the
Turks and Arabs, two hegemonic identities that posed a threat to Kurdish
identity. Furthermore, given their "racial roots," the author sought to align
Kurds with the West.

Reclaiming Kurdish Common Past

History is one of the most effective preexisting cultural tools at the disposal
of nationalists to cultivate a glorious heritage. Like its predecessors, *Rojî
Kurd* produced a historical narrative based on a selective national history to
reinvigorate a collective Kurdish past with an uninterrupted social, political,
and cultural continuity. To that end, the authors of *Rojî Kurd* played the role

of *nationalist historians* and incorporated such recurrent themes as historical personages, splendid social and political moments in history, genealogical research, and so forth into their narrative of Kurdish national history. One of the themes that was most discussed in *Rojî Kurd* was Kurdish historiography, or rather, its lack. Thirteen out of sixty-one *Rojî Kurd* articles were about Kurdish history as well as the importance of history writing. For instance, Abdullah Cevdet wrote:

> We are in an epoch whereby nations [milliyetler] are rising and acquiring a character . . .
>
> Memory to individuals is what history is to a nation . . . A human that has been infected by "amnésie complète," which refers to the disease of complete loss of memory, is no different from a tree . . . whose green leaves sway every which way depending on the direction of the wind . . .
>
> If a nation does not possess a perfectly written history, it is as if that nation has never lived. Do the Kurds have a history? Just with a *Sharafname*, a nation cannot lay claim to the glory of its past . . .
>
> A nation that does not lay claim to its past/ancient history . . . cannot be master in its own house. A nation that is not master in its own house is doomed to be a slave to others.[100]

First, Cevdet warned the Kurds by establishing the fact that they live in the era of nations, when peoples grow, develop, and acquire particular national characters. Then, through the metaphor of anthropomorphism, he personified the Kurdish society as a unified body or organism with a collective disease, that is, *amnésie complète* or total amnesia, to emphasize the importance of written history as a society's collective memory. Next, he presented the lack of national autonomy and collective memory as an ontological matter: history-less nations do not really exist or matter. He criticized the fact that *Sharafname* was the only Kurdish book written on the history of the Kurds and did not suffice to present Kurdish history. Cevdet's article could also be read as an unintended introduction to "Kurdish national history" by implying that Kurds do, in fact, have a national history, and that it is contained in the *Sharafname*. Cevdet's reference represents one of the first instances in which the *Sharafname* is presented as a book of Kurdish national history.

Similarly, M. S. Bedir Khan wrote:

> The Kurd has produced many great and magnificent scholars, geniuses, poets, and writers; however, they have remained unknown or forgotten . . . by Kurds, owing to the lack of a written history . . .

. . . we have even lost the right to claim Saladin Ayyubi for ourselves . . . . There is no bigger disgrace and crime against history than neglecting and forgetting this magnificent Kurd as a source of pride, who had the honour of being the saviour of Islam . . . we are on the verge of being doomed to extinction, to be forgotten, and to disappear as a nation.[101]

M. S. Bedir Khan and other *Rojî Kurd* writers acted as historians to *remind* the Kurds of their splendid national heritage, which was unknown due to the lack of a modern Kurdish historiography. For that reason, the author lamented the fact that Kurds are unable to claim Saladin's Kurdish identity. Although the passage presents Saladin as "the savior of the Islam," what the author was really trying to accomplish was the nationalization of a Kurdish Sultan and his legacy.[102] In this context, Bedir Khan, much like Abdullah Cevdet, perceived historiography and historical consciousness as an ontological matter.

Rojî Kurd, like *Kurdistan*, produced a pantheon of Kurdish historic personages as the protagonists of the *Kurdish national history*, in which the most prominent figure was Saladin, promoted by Halil Hayali in a lengthy article in the 2nd and 3rd issues of *Rojî Kurd*. As we saw, *Rojî Kurd* also disseminated an image of Saladin on the cover of its very first issue. Besides, the journal devoted space to figures such as Karim Khan Zand, Ahmad Khani, Haji Qadir Koyi, Molla Gurani, Idris-i Bitlisi, Sheyholislam Ebu's Suud, Elî Herîrî, Khanî, Nalî, Fuzûlî, Sheikh Riza Talabanî, Khoyî, the Princes of Ardalan, and so on. In one article, Halil Hayali nostalgically mentioned the names of previous Kurdish rulers and then harshly criticized the current traditional Kurdish leadership for not uniting and leading the Kurds: "It seems that you have no intention to protect miserable Kurds . . . Where are Alî Eyûb and Marwan the Kurd? Where is Alî Wexnaz, the governor of Sanandaj? Where is the prince of Rawanduz? Where are the princes of Jazeera and Botan [and] the ruler of Soran and Baban? Raise your heads and see the [miserable] situation of the Kurds."[103] In this nostalgic account, the author expressed his longing for the long-vanished romantic past when Kurds were allegedly united under Kurdish rulers such as Alî Eyûb and Marwan the Kurd. Was there, in fact, such a period in Kurdish history, in which a Kurdish ruler showed the capacity to unify all Kurds under a broad political roof, like a state? Did the Kurdish leaders cited by the author really concern themselves with the idea of Kurdishness or Kurdish nationalism in the modern sense? The fact that manufactured nostalgia or golden ages always invokes a past that was unified and comprehensible, unlike the incoherent, divided present, makes these questions irrelevant. "Such golden ages embody the 'essence' of the community, their 'true' character. They epitomize all that is great and noble in 'our community,' now so sadly missing but soon to be restored."[104] Consequently, the misrepresentation of the object of desire, that is, the unity of the Kurds, in this nostalgia, is a reasonable response, within the framework of nationalism, to the needs and demands of nationalists. This conceived heritage works as a political resource to encourage and invite the Kurdish masses to be involved in the nation-building process.

Construction of Pre-Islamic Kurdish History

Nationalists frequently utilize ancient history as a means to foster uncritical identification with the ancient past and to present their nation as possessing historical antiquity, which in turn justifies the nation's political, social, and territorial claims. As we saw in the previous sections of this chapter, *Rojî Kurd* authors attempted to disidentify the Kurds from the Ottomans and occasionally from the Islamic *ummah*. Similar practices can be observed in the journal's reproduction of the ancient Kurdish past, particularly the pre-Islamic period. Kurdî (Silêmanî Ebdilkerîm), in one article significantly entitled "The Origin and Lineage of the Kurds," wrote:

> Kurds existed before the time of the prophets. Kurds, as a part of the Aryan nations [eqwamî aryen], accepted Islam like the Afghans and Iranians ['Ecem] . . . The others, such as the Greeks, Armenians, and Germans, remained on the path of ignorance [by not accepting Islam]. Be it the Greeks, Armenians, Germans, or Portuguese, they all belong to the Kurdish race [le irqî kurd] . . . Notice how our cuisine, clothes, and traditions resemble those of the Iranians [Ecem], while they differ from the traditions of those in Baghdad . . . Germans and the German language resemble Kurds and the Kurdish language . . . If the claim that Germans belong to the Kurdish race [ɪrq] explains why Kurds are intelligent and brave, then why have they [Germans] made such progress while we [Kurds] have remained ignorant? The reason for this is obvious, because, first and foremost, Germans refused internal conflict and instead collaborated with each other.[105]

To place emphasis on the pre-Islamic roots of the Kurds, the author traced Kurdish history back to the "Aryan nations," which also included the Iranians [Ecem] and Afghans. Next, he added Greeks, Armenians, Germans, and Portuguese to the same group, this time calling it the "Kurdish race." To prove his point, he mentioned similarities between Kurds and other Aryans in terms of their cuisine, clothing, and traditions, which were different from those of Baghdad, a metonym for the Arabs and their culture. In this racial politics, the author exploited the issue of race as a natural, rigid, and involuntary concept of identity that differentiates the Kurds from Arabs and perhaps the Ottoman Turks, bringing the Kurds closer to the West. Another outstanding aspect of the author's primordial racial politics pertains to his use of what is known as *race science*, which claims that there is a link between race and intelligence. The author argued that since they belong to the same Aryan race, Kurds are as smart as the Germans, which indirectly establishes Kurds as superior to the non-Aryans. Finally, Kurds lag behind only due to their internal conflicts, while Germans have made progress thanks to their national unity.

A similar historical narrative about the origins of the Kurds comes from Xezal, who wrote:

> O, Brothers! First and foremost, we need to know the times of our ancestors. So far, whoever has forgotten their ancestors has vanished . . . The history of us Kurds [Kurmanc] and Christians [Armenians][106] goes back to the Assyrians. Assyrians constituted a great power back then . . . In the past, we had everything, including our own language as well as our own writing and reading system. After we became subordinate to the Arabs, we lost everything but our language . . . When the Arabs lost power, we fell into the hands of the Roms [Turks].[107]

After emphasizing the importance of history for nations as an existential matter, Xezal traced the history of the Kurds and the Christian Armenians back to the time of the Assyrians, a pre-Islamic, pre-Arab, and pre-Ottoman period. Moreover, the author presented the Kurds as an identifiable "national" entity during three distinctive historical periods, namely: the time of the ancient Assyrians (2500 BCE); the advent of Islam and the Arabs (seventh century CE); and the arrival of the Ottoman Turks (sixteenth century CE). After nostalgically recalling the glorious days of Kurdish language and literature, the author depicted the reign of the Arabs and Turks as periods of collective suffering—perhaps owing to forced cultural and linguistic assimilation—when the Kurds lost everything but their language. As far as the significance of the ancient Kurdish history is concerned, *Rojî Kurd*'s debates on genealogy were in pursuit of authenticity found in the ancient past. These debates were instrumental in dissociating and distancing Kurdish identity from hegemonic Islamic, Arab, and Turkish identities.

The Invention of Kurdish Common Culture and National Self-Admiration

Parallel to its predecessors, in its identity politics, *Rojî Kurd* continued to reproduce and reinterpret Kurdish cultural particularities such as values, memories, behaviors, customs, traditions, symbols, and so forth, which amounted to "the Kurdish national character." Nevertheless, while *Kurdistan* and especially the *KTTG* tried to create a particular Kurdish national culture within the broader Ottoman framework, *Rojî Kurd* introduced another fundamental discursive shift by dropping the Ottomanist rhetoric in favor of a new image of Kurdish culture based in folkloric and exclusive racial features. Believing that the nation-forming power of language and literature were essential parts of national culture, *Rojî Kurd* expanded its repertoire of Kurdish collective culture to include various prosaic and poetic genres ranging from articles, short stories, and historical anecdotes to classical and contemporary poetry. In this generic abundance, the journal presented a richer form of Kurdish literature in both Sorani and Kurmanji varieties. As we saw, the contents of the stanzas taken from Khani's and Koyi's poetry were no less important than their original Kurdish form. Much like the editors of *Kurdistan*, Halil Hayali often reproduced such stanzas to lend weight and substance to his nationalist argument. Moreover, through the poems of Khani and Koyi, he could express Kurdish resentment against Turkish, Arab, and Persian rulers.

Rojî Kurd also published the first example of a modern Kurdish short story, entitled *Çîrok* [Story], by Fû'ad Temo in a serialized fashion.[108] *Çîrok* depicts the poverty-stricken life of a Kurdish agrarian community in a village setting. It follows the life of a shepherd and his son, Şewêş, who every night waits for his father to return from the grazing fields. When one day, the father falls sick and is unable to get out of bed, the villagers start to take care of Şewêş. The story is meant to reflect the typical life of poor Kurdish villagers, their communal solidarity, manners, and customs. At this juncture, it should be noted that in *Rojî Kurd*, Kurdish intellectuals' treatment of agrarian Kurdish communities evolved. As we saw in their critiques of Kurdish commoners and the peasantry, all three journals, particularly *Kurdistan* and *KTTG*, developed a contempt for peasants and adopted a harsh paternalist and authoritarian discourse of discipline in which they reproached and humiliated the peasant commoners for their ignorance and backwardness. However, *Rojî Kurd* distinguished itself with a more populist approach that glorified the lower classes and peasantry as the repository of authentic Kurdish national identity, language, and culture. This populist attitude was most visible in Hayali's writings. In an article proudly siding with the Kurdish peasantry, Hayali called upon city dwellers to resist assimilation and return to their original Kurdish roots:

O people of the city: You and we were brothers in the same tribe and village . . . We shared our joy and sorrow . . . Time set you apart from us; you went to the cities . . . You got rich . . . we remained poor and deprived . . . You gave up your Kurdish identity [Kurdîtî] and peasant roots when you learned the language of the city people[109] and considered yourselves members of another nation [cins].[110] We might be peasants, ignorant, and deprived, but at least we have not given up our nationality. Why are you ashamed of us? You blame us for our ignorance, but you are responsible for this situation . . . We could be civilized like you had you helped us. Our essence [cewher] and yours were the same.[111]

Analogous to the Herderian notion of *cultural populism*, which had long endorsed the nurturing peasant culture from which the nation's native genius ostensibly sprang, Hayali gave a voice to Kurdish peasants. He argued that the peasantry and the lower classes faithfully preserved the authenticity, the folklore, and the glory of the Kurdish ethno-cultural heritage and distinctiveness thanks to limited influence from the outside world. Accordingly, country-dwellers were not simply primitive peasants, the way the urbanites saw them, but were the repository and the guardians of Kurdish folk culture and identity against foreign influences. Next, Hayali lamented how urbanization and corrupt alien influences brought about the loosening of ties between an authentic Kurdish culture and cosmopolitan Kurds.[112] In fact, the Kurds who lived in cities were more easily exposed to the Turkish language and culture than their peers who stayed in villages. Even though linguistic assimilation might not always lead to a change in ethnic identity, Hayali asserted that linguistic assimilation resulted in ethnic assimilation and the loss of true national culture and identity among estranged urban Kurds. Like Herder, who exhorted his fellow Germans to return to their indigenous roots and native culture, Hayali encouraged urban Kurds to go back to their authentic culture and essence (*cewher*).[113] It is important to remember that the Ottoman state had already begun imposing Turkish on non-Turkish Ottomans in the mid-nineteenth century. Finally, the author lamented the attitude of arrogant urbanized Kurds for being ashamed of the "primitive" Kurdish culture and invited them to take pride in it, which constitutes an approach similar to Herder's, who once said: "Let us follow our own path . . . let all men speak well or ill of our nation, our literature, our language: they are ours, they are ourselves and let that be enough."[114] A similar glorification of authentic peasant culture is observed in Ergani Medenli Y. C.'s article, where the author claimed that Kurdish women in rural areas were more liberal compared to conservative Kurdish women in cities who lost their original Kurdish character.

Several articles emphasized the Kurds' ostensibly distinctive and "superior" cultural particularities to highlight racial identity and differences from other Muslim nations. Fahri argued: "As we said, Kurds, throughout their history, have had a great tendency for progress and the ability to raise their level of civilization . . . the proof of this is their national [kavmiyye] and racial [ırkiyye] particularities . . . in addition to their spiritual and characteristic virtues and moral values such as generosity, bravery, hospitality, and trustworthiness."[115] We saw in the previous section that a significant distinction between Kurds, on the one hand, and Arabs and Turks on the other, was made through racial politics in which the authors traced the origins of the Kurds to the Aryan and Assyrian civilizations. In this excerpt, the same racial politics is utilized to claim the cultural idiosyncrasies of the Kurds, described with the lexemes of bravery, generosity, and so on. It followed that these distinctive racial or phenotypical characteristics differentiated the Kurds from Ottoman Turks and Arabs.

This perennialist or essentialist approach to racial and national character is reiterated in another article by Salih Bedir Khan. He claimed: "The inherent bravery of Kurdishness and its noble character that stems from its race [ırkiyye] have shown the merit of being on the front lines of armies since the beginning of Islam. Kurds have worked wonders on the battlefield. But unfortunately, despite this, [Kurds] have not been able to recover from the state of being forgotten and abandoned."[116] Employing discourses of racial dissimilarities, the author attempted to produce an image of the nation in order to underline the distinctive, inherent, and superior qualities of the stereotypical Kurdish mind and character, which in turn would create a sense of national self-admiration. Then, utilizing *the strategy of the shift of blame*, the author holds, albeit implicitly, the Ottomans and other Islamic communities responsible for the backward situation of the Kurds.

Rojî Kurd problematized gender relations, too, as another distinguishing quality of Kurdish society vis-à-vis other Muslim communities. As we saw, *Kurdistan*, from a male-gendered perspective, presented women as the chaste mothers of the nation who had to be protected against "infidel" aggressors.[117] *KTTG* adopted a more refined treatment of women, depicting them as bravely assisting their husbands in difficult times, including wars, by fighting side by side with them on the battlefield. In both journals, these peculiarities of Kurdish women were meant to emphasize the uniqueness of Kurdish culture within the broader Ottoman/Muslim culture. *Rojî Kurd*, on the other hand, addressed the women issue from a more sophisticated perspective rooted in gender equality. Its authors not only put stress on the uniqueness of Kurdish culture, but also worked to dissociate it from Ottoman culture's conservatism. The most elaborate such argument came from Ergani Madenli Y. C. in an article entitled, *The Issue of Women in Kurdish Society*. After explaining the advanced role of women in Western societies and the spread of these ideas to the Ottoman East, he stated:

I think it goes without saying that the moral and material situation of women in almost the entire Ottoman world is heart-rending . . . This disease has also infected the [vast] Kurdish family . . .

Kurds have an advantage when it comes to reforming women's issues. Let me explain: In Kurdistan -except for the urban centres which have lost their original [Kurdish] character- the place of women in village life is satisfactory; despite some primitive elements, the Kurds show great respect for women.

. . . the use of the hijab in Kurdish villages and towns is also at a moderate level . . . Kurdish women are never trapped in thick and exhausting sacks.[118] Instead, they walk around freely . . . Women constitute half the workforce in Kurdistan . . . this means in a Kurdish family, women are close to the level of men in the public sphere . . . the only thing women lack is a modern education and science.

The reformation of the urbanized women, who have lost their original character and the sense of being Kurdish, will require a greater effort and work.

The progress of a nation is measured by the [role of] its women.[119]

At the outset, the author Y. C. expressed the "heart-rending" place of gender relations in the broader "Ottoman world." Then he proudly depicted the more prestigious place of women in the "Kurdish family" as a distinguishing feature of the Kurdish culture vis-à-vis the socially and religiously conservative culture of other Muslim communities of the empire. It is remarkable that the author mockingly referred to the Ottoman women's outfit as a "sack" in which women are trapped, while he emphasized how Kurdish women move freely in the public sphere and participate in the workforce side by side with men. The author presented the scarcity of the hijab among Kurdish women as a sign of their modernity and gender equality. He did not attribute this aspect of modernity to Western civilization, but instead presented it as an inherent characteristic of authentic Kurdish culture. While peasant women were isolated from the influences of outside forces and thus managed to retain this liberal character, urbanized Kurdish women lost it due to the impact of the broader conservative Arabo-Islamic and Ottoman-Islamic cultures. The author also called for help to bring these assimilated urbanite women back to the modern Kurdish culture and identity through education. Finally, remarkably, the author asserted that gender relations should be the yardstick by which the progress of a society should be measured. A number of other *Roji Kurd* contributors concerned themselves with the issue of Kurdish women, among them Halil Hayali, who, in one article, promoted gender equality in the context of schooling through religious intertextuality by stating, "education is a religious obligation for Muslim women and men alike."[120]

Kurdish National Homeland: From Ottoman Kurdistan to Greater Kurdistan

Kurdish nationalism transformed the Kurdish inhabited territories from a mere geographical space into a new ontological space as a national territory and as the primary factor in defining Kurdish national identity. To consolidate this new perception of the land, *Rojî Kurd* authors made extensive use of assumptions or presuppositions that established Kurdistan as the Kurdish national homeland. Consider the following extract: "When you return to your national territory [muhît-i milliye], first you should lay the foundations for primary education based on solid and rational methods and disseminate it as much as possible."[121] The author Bulgaristanli Togan called on the Kurdish leadership and youth in Istanbul to return to their "muhît-i milliye" [national territory], where "muhît-i milliye" established Istanbul as a foreign territory or a *general elsewhere*. Notably, he did not explicitly mention the name *Kurdistan* because the reader is expected to know the "national territory" of the Kurds.

Likewise, in the obituary for Hüseyin Kenan (Paşa), Bedir Khan stated: "Compelled to live off the holdings he had inherited from his family, Hüseyin Kenan Paşa felt the necessity to return to his 'original homeland' [vatan-ı aslîye] . . . therefore he has returned back to Kurdistan with his brother Osman Paşa."[122] Here, the adjective "original" [aslî] and "homeland" [vatan] together formed a strong homeland-making phrase, conveying that Istanbul, or any other Ottoman territory for that matter, was outside the "original" or "native" homeland of the Paşa, that is, Kurdistan.

Although we still do not come across any visual cartographic maps of Kurdistan, we observe that the editorial board of *Rojî Kurd* also constructed discursive maps of the Kurdish homeland. For instance, Kerküklü Necmeddin wrote: "I want to explicate, as much as possible, the service provided to the office of the Caliphate by the Kurds, who occupy all of Mosul, Van, Diyarbakir, Elazig, and Erzurum provinces as well as parts of Aleppo, Damascus, Baghdad and Sivas—which accounts for the Kurds living under Ottoman dominion alone."[123] In this excerpt, the author draws a map of Ottoman Kurdistan by naming cities and presenting them as essentially homogeneous geo-ethnic Kurdish territories whose borders were demarcated by territories inhabited by non-Kurdish *others*. The spatial reference in the last clause, that is, "which accounts for the Kurds living under Ottoman dominion alone," implies that a part of the *Greater* Kurdish territory extends beyond the limits of Ottoman sovereignty, an indirect reference to the Kurdish territories under the Qajar Dynasty.[124] This point deserves special attention because this is the third time that the early Kurdish journals under consideration are making references to *Greater Kurdistan* partitioned between the Safavid—later the Qajar—and Ottoman Empires.[125]

As we have seen so far, whenever Kurdish journals attempted to endorse a concept that was new to Kurdish society, especially an idea that originated in the West or might be perceived to contradict religion, religious allusion proved an indispensable strategy. Such an approach was evident in *Rojî Kurd*'s construction of a common homeland in nationalist terms, as reflected in an article by Kurdî (Silêmanî Ebdilkerîm) in which he stated: "All these indicate that we should act in accordance with the sayings of the Prophet; because he has commanded: love of one's homeland is part of faith."[126] The author provoked patriotic sentiments by invoking the Prophet's command, which asserts that love of the national homeland is a part of Islamic faith and thus a religious duty. Miqdad Midhat Bedir Khan in *Kurdistan* and Halil Hayali in *KTTG* used the same hadith to promote Kurdistan as the Kurdish national homeland.

Kurdish-Armenians relations did not constitute a major topic in *Rojî Kurd* in the same way that they did in *Kurdistan* and *KTTG*. Nevertheless, a few *Rojî Kurd* authors did take up this issue. For example, while Abdullah Cevdet presented the Armenians as a role model for Kurdish modernity, others such as Kurdî (Silêmanî Ebdilkerîm) and Xezal claimed that Armenians and Kurds were descended from the same race. Essentially, both views encouraged friendly relations between the two communities despite the territorial disputes inherent in their respective nationalist discourses. After the Treaty of Berlin (1878), the Armenians were the only Christian community not to attain some sort of autonomy or independence from the Ottomans. Furthermore, both the Treaty of Berlin and the Treaty of San Stefano stipulated reforms under the provision of the Great Powers in six provinces of Anatolia (Van, Bitlis, Elazig, Diyarbakir, Erzurum, and Sivas [referred to as historical Armenia]), all of which were claimed by both the Kurds and the Armenians. M. S. Bedir Khan took up the territorial disputes between the two peoples. Much like Diyarbekiri Fikri Necdet, he perceived Armenian nationalist ambitions as a threat: "Although the Armenians [file] and we, as two nations [milet], have the same homeland, Armenians are far fewer than us; we are stronger and manlier than them; however, today, the whole world assumes that they are the owners of this dear-homeland [welat]."[127]

The author acknowledged the fact that the national homeland claimed by both the Armenians and Kurds overlaps. Nevertheless, he tried to strengthen the Kurdish claim by asserting the territory was predominantly Kurdish despite the common assumption that it belonged to the Armenians. As was typical of the Kurdish press, the passage above was excluded from the Turkish translation of the article published in the same issue, perhaps to avoid offending the Armenian audience.

The use of the term *welat* (homeland) in Kurdish journalistic discourse served as a barometer to measure the gradual semantic progress and evolution of the concept of the homeland in Kurdish nationalist narratives. The term *welat* acquired a more established meaning as it came to signify the "national homeland," as opposed to the "native region or province." Still, it somewhat remained vague or elusive in the nationalist discourses of the *Kurdistan* and *KTTG*, as both journals occasionally stretched the meaning of *welat* to include the whole Ottoman territory. However, in *Rojî Kurd*, the term *welat*, for the most part, completed its semantic evolution and denotational meaning and came to signify the Kurdish national homeland unmistakably. In an article, M. S. Bedir Khan stated: "From now on all of us . . . our learned as well as our ignorant, should open our eyes and hold one another's hand and work hard for the salvation of Kurds [silameta Kurdanî] and liberate the homeland [welat]."[128] Particularly due to the concordance of the words "Kurd" and "welat" in this article and elsewhere in the corpus of *Rojî Kurd*, the latter indisputably came to refer to the Kurdish national homeland.[129]

The Formation of a New Elite-Commoners' Relation

As we saw, in its semantic complexity, language produces three categories of meanings concurrently, namely *ideational, textual,* and *interpersonal metafunctions.* The latter metafunction mainly concerns the linguistic choices made in a text that entail not only particular types of relations between the participants of a communicative event, but also enact social identities.[130] This metafunction differentiates *Rojî Kurd* from *Kurdistan* and *KTTG*. The class composition of the *Hêvî Society* and *Rojî Kurd* was dominated by the new generation of Kurdish youth who came from various predominantly non-dynastic and nonaristocratic backgrounds. This new organizational character made possible the broader discursive participation of Kurds from different walks of life. Some of the journal's nonaristocratic figures included Diyarberkirli Fikrî Necdet, Kerküklü Necmeddin [Hüseyin], Abdullah Cevdet, Suleymaniyeli Abdulkerim, and Halil Hayali. Inevitably, this new situation changed the nature of relations between the Kurdish elite and the commoners. Their role in the Kurdish political landscape allowed the Kurdish national identity narrative to go beyond the monopoly of an aristocratic or religious elite and move toward a more populist discourse. Therefore, *Rojî Kurd* became the site of an elusive confrontation between this new social and political force and the previous Kurdish leadership, as manifested in the *Hêvî Society*'s declaration:

O Kurdish ulama, sheikhs, leaders, nobles!
. . . You comprehend better than us the situation of Kurdishness [Kürdlüğün]; and are capable of determining its needs and priorities. Therefore, we never dare to offer you guidance or give you advice. Nevertheless, with your permission, we would like to point out that one thing the Kurdish nobility has not comprehended is the damage caused by their internal-discord . . . today, the Kurdish ulama and nobility have no greater duty than their national and religious duty. The destiny of this great component of Islam is in your hands.[131]

In this text, the deictic "we" and "us" powerfully refer to the new generation of Kurds and Kurdish youth, establishing it as a force in the new Kurdish political landscape vis-à-vis the traditional aristocratic elite. The text smooth-talks the traditional aristocratic elite in carefully worded expressions, such as "you comprehend better than us," "we never dare to offer you guidance or give you advice," "with your permission," and so on. This approach is meant to avoid any pontifical or boastful statements that might offend the older generation of Kurdish leaders. Immediately after these phrases, the text articulates a severe criticism of the traditional leadership, accusing it of internal discord and rivalries, and hence holding it responsible for the current calamitous social and political situation. Next, in the rhetoric of humility, it does actually "dare" to give advice by calling on this stratum to fulfill its national and religious duty. Also, by giving priority to the word "national" vis-à-vis "religious," the religious aspect of this duty is subordinated to the national unity of the Kurds or, perhaps, religious duties were mentioned just to mitigate the Kurdish nationalist tone of the text.

If this new generation of Kurdish leadership did not seem too eager to claim the leadership position for themselves, it was perhaps because they thought that the traditional Kurdish community was not ready to be led by the youth. However, this novelty in the nature of Kurdish leadership added a new dimension to the *interpersonal metafunction* in Kurdish journalistic discourse in that the Kurdish youth attempted to rally the traditional Kurdish leadership and the Kurdish masses around the same national cause while they set them-selves up as the watchdogs of this new mode of relations.[132] This view was expressed in an announcement by the journal's management:

> For anyone with a bit of understanding and wisdom, it is beyond all doubt that Kurdishness [Kürdlük], in the midst of the vibrant masses of the 20th century, is paralyzed and ailing, if not a dead organ altogether. With this paralysis and illness coupled with destitution and the lack of leadership, the Kurd day by day gets closer to extinction. Although we refrain from saying much in this regard, we appeal to the Kurds, particularly to the Kurdish nobles, who have seen themselves as the rightful traditional and historical leaders of the Kurds, to think deeply with logic and reason on this issue.
>
> The collaboration of a few youths will not provide much benefit, because the national mass [kütle-i milliyye] that matters will still fall behind. It is the influential, prominent figures, rather than the youth, that are capable of mobiliz-ing this mass.
>
> At best, the youth can utilize such instruments as *Rojî Kurd* and the *Hêvî Society*. The continuation and the success of these instruments depend on assis-tance from the Kurdish community, but particularly from the Kurdish upper stratum.[133]

The text identifies the problems using the metaphors of body politic, where the Kurdish nation is presented as a corporeal entity like a human body that is stricken with "illnesses" and hence "paralyzed," a topos of threat that was popular in all Kurdish journals. Accordingly, a chief reason for this situation was the Kurdish upper class' lack of "deep logical thinking" and "reason." Nevertheless, the author of the announcement, a representative of the Kurdish youth, made sure that every criticism directed at the traditional Kurdish leadership was delivered in a humble and flattering voice via the strategy of euphemism to mitigate the harsh tone.

Many other *Rojî Kurd* texts assigned the role of supreme leadership in the mobilization of the Kurdish masses to this upper stratum. Consider the following extract from Hayali entitled, *To the Kurdish Nobles*: "O Kurdish nobles, you know too well that your ancestors took great pride in Kurdishness, and when the situation arose, they sacrificed their wealth and their lives for the cause of Kurdishness and Muslimness for which history is the witness. What happened [to you] that you have ceased to lead the Kurds? Is it because you no longer carry the blood of your ancestors in your veins?"[134] By creating a sense of political continuity through the metaphor of blood and kinship and ancestral narrative, Hayali was trying to inspire the Kurdish nobles and invite them to fulfill their leadership role as their ancestors had done throughout history. Kurdish identity is foregrounded and religious identity, or Muslimness, is backgrounded, while Ottoman identity is dismissed altogether.[135]

Silêmanî Ebdilkerîm also concerned himself with the issue of disunity and the failure of the traditional Kurdish leadership. In an article entitled, *Always Me and No One Else*, he asserted:

> There are many reasons for the trouble and disease that have befallen us. The first reason is that . . . we are in fact a nation [qewmêkî] without unity. The reason for our disunity [bê ittifaqîşman] . . . [is that] our noblemen (gewrekanman) . . . have invented a profession for themselves . . . However, this has resulted in their own and the Kurdish nation's destruction. This profession consists of a few words: "always me and no one else (her min bim û kesî tirî nî)."[136]

He openly blamed the traditional Kurdish leadership for disunity on account of their rivalries, which failed to unite and lead the Kurdish masses. Although the author refrained from citing any specific names, he was perhaps referring to the competing Baban and Bedir Khan families.

Rojî Kurd did not only play the role of intermediary between the Kurdish aristocratic elite and the commoners, but also sided with the Kurdish masses by calling on the Kurdish aristocracy and elite through the voice of the Kurdish commoners: "Our sheikhs, mullahs, mîrs, leaders, and notables! You know too well that we are in the midst of a fire . . . nobody comes to our aid

. . . Let them (the nobles) collaborate and protect us miserable, us placeless, us deprived, [and] rescue us from this fire."[137] Using inclusive deixis such as "we," "our," and "us," the author of the article claimed co-membership with the commoners both as an individual and as a member of *Rojî Kurd* and *Hêvî Society*, a populist and anti-elitist stand, that can be observed throughout the corpus of *Rojî Kurd*. Gradually, this approach spread among traditional Kurdish leaders who abandoned, for the most part, their previous paternalistic position and language in favor of a more populist attitude.

The genres of journalism acquired their present association with the lower classes or socially and ethnically inferior human groups by validating and celebrating them. Similarly, *Rojî Kurd* elevated the Kurdish commoners from a dispersed and inferior peasant status into the position of subject matter. Seeing the Kurdish commoners as the driving force behind the realization of national ideals, *Rojî Kurd*, unlike *Kurdistan* and the *KTTG*, adopted an egalitarian and populist voice. This strategy revealed itself in the journal's forms of addressivity, such as:

O, Brothers!
O, Friends!
O, Our Kurdish Brothers!
O, Kurds!
O, Friend![138]

In the examples above, the predominant use of such forms of addressivity as "brothers" and "friends" were perhaps inspired by the French Revolution's motto of "liberté, égalité, fraternité." Moreover, despite frequent calls on the traditional Kurdish leadership to fulfill its role, some *Rojî Kurd* contributors found the Kurdish youth the most dynamic segment and thus the worthiest of leadership. M. Salih Bedir Khan expressed this view in the following words:

> Only you, O shining youths of my beloved Kurdishness [Kürdlüğümün]! In this glorious clash, the heaviest duty is on your shoulders. . .
> . . . O earnest youth! You are the saviour Noah who will deliver this ill and orphaned Kurdishness [Kürdlüğün] from the flood of ignorance by your determination and benevolence.[139]

The author, who had a way with words, eloquently suggested the Kurdish youth for national leadership through the powerful flood narrative, in which he likened the activities of the Kurdish youth to Noah and his ark. He presented the Kurdish youth as the messiah-savior and liberator of the Kurdish people. Interestingly, the author of these lines was a member of the dynastic Bedir Khan family. A similar point was expressed in an article by Bulgaristanlı Doğan, in which he offered the following advice to the Kurdish youth:

> Neither the laws nor the officials of the country nor the traditional elite class [sınıf-ı mumtaz] of your nation's notables nor anyone else for that matter could carry out this duty as successfully as you . . . You should not settle in centres of civilization far from your national region [muhît-i millî]; on the contrary, you are obliged to return with enlightened ideas to your birthplaces that are pure and sacred to you.
>
> If you do not do this and remain outside of your national region and look down upon people like the Ottoman Turkish youth does [Osmanlı Türk gençleri gibi], you will expose yourself to grave accusations. Everyone will assume that you are pretending to be the privileged intellectual class of your society, with the dream of establishing a class of intellectual aristocrats. As if the other two aristocratic classes are not enough, people will rightfully call you the "third" trouble.[140]

Disregarding the traditional Kurdish nobility, the author first designated the Kurdish youth as the new leaders of Kurdish society. Secondly, he warned the Kurdish intellectuals in Istanbul about a matter hardly mentioned in previous Kurdish journals: the trap of developing an aristocratic, elitist attitude toward Kurdish commoners in Kurdistan, similar to the degrading Ottoman Orientalist attitude of the Turks toward commoners on the Ottoman periphery.[141] In a sense, Dogan's voice urged the intellectual Kurdish youth to return from the imperial center, that is, Istanbul, to its ancestral homeland and embrace the Kurdish masses, unlike the arrogant, Turkish intellectuals who had already alienated themselves from the people by looking down on the provinces of the empire. It is hard to determine what exactly the author intended to convey by the term "the third trouble." Perhaps he meant the rival Baban and Bedir Khan families as the first two "troubles."[142]

NOTES

1. Bozarslan, *Kürd Milliyetçiliği ve Kürd Hareketi*.

2. Zürcher, *The Young Turk Legacy*, 84, 85, 127; Akçam, *From Empire to the Republic*, 129.

3. Gooch and Temperley, vol. IX, Part I (No. 38) Confidential, enclosure in F.O. 371/1014, pp. 208–209, cited in Zeine, *The Emergence of Arab Nationalism*, 86–87.

4. Kevorkian, Raymond. *The Armenian Genocide: A Complete History*. (New York: I.B. Tauris, 2011), 131; Akşin, *Turkey from Empire to Revolutionary Republic*,

84–87; Üstel, Füsun. *İmparatorluktan ulus-devlete Türk milliyetçiliği: Türk Ocakları 1912–1931 (Turkish Nationalism from the Empire to the Nation-State: the Turkish Hearths 1912–1931).* (İstanbul: İletişim, 1997), 15, 70–75; Zürcher, *The Young Turk Legacy,* 120, 216.

5. According to Turkic grey wolf mythology, the Turks consider themselves the descendants of a she-wolf called Asena, *see,* Türk Ocakları Tüzüğü (Turkish Hearths Bylaw) available at: http://www.turkocagi.org.tr/kitaplar/Tuzuk.pdf.

6. Zeine, *The Emergence of Arab Nationalism,* 93.

7. Silopî, *Doza Kurdistan,* 15; Firro, *Metamorphosis of the Nation (al-Umma),* 64.

8. The *Hêvî Society* published a total of three journals: *Rojî Kurd* (Kurdish Day/Sun), *Hetawî Kurd* (Kurdish Sun) and *Yekbûn* (Unity), see, Malmîsanij, Mehemed and Lewendî, Mahmud. *Li Kurdistana Bakur û Tirkiyê Rojnamegeriya Kurdî (1908– 1992) [Kurdish Journalism in Northern Kurdistan and Turkey (1908–1992)]* (2nd ed.). (Ankara: Özge, 1992).

9. For a complete list of members, *see,* Silopî, *Doza Kurdistan,* 27–30, 35, 164.

10. Malmîsanij, Mehemed. *Kürt Talebe-Hêvî Cemiyeti [The Kurdish Student Hope Society].* (İstanbul: Avesta Yayınları, 2002), 86–87; Silopî, *Doza Kurdistan,* 27, 37; Cemilpaşa, Ekrem. *Muhtasar Hayatim [A Brief Account of My Life].* (Brussels: Kurdish Institute, 1989), 20.

11. Özoğlu, *Kurdish Notables and the Ottoman State,* 106; Malmîsanij, *Kürt Talebe-Hêvî Cemiyeti,* 134.

12. Cf. Malmîsanij, Mehemed. *Diyarbekirli Cemilpaşazadeler ve Kürt Milliyetçiliği [Cemilpaşazades of Diyarbekir and Kurdish Nationalism].* (İstanbul: Avestam, 2004), 11–27.

13. Kurdistan Teali Cemiyeti (KTC) or the Society for the Rise of Kurdistan (1918).

14. Teşkilat-i Içtimaiye Cemiyeti (The Society of Social Organization) (1920).

15. For Khoybun, *see,* Jwaideh, *The Kurdish National Movement,* 145.

16. Cf. Malmîsanij, *Diyarbekirli Cemilpaşazadeler ve Kürt Milliyetçiliği,* 237– 245; Özoğlu, *Kurdish Notables and the Ottoman State,* 104–106.

17. Hanioğlu, *Bir Siyasi Örgüt Ittihat ve Terakki*; Malmîsanij, *Yüzyılımızın Başlarında Kürt Milliyetçiliği.*

18. Koma Xebatên Kurdolojiyê [Kurdology Study Group]. *Di Sedsaliya Wê De Rojî Kurd 1913 [Rojî Kurd (Kurdish Sun) on Its 100th Anniversary 1913].* (İstanbul: Istanbul Kurdish Institute Publication, 2013), 70.

19. Ibid., 75.

20. Ibid., 71.

21. Malmîsanij, *Kürt Talebe-Hêvî Cemiyeti,* 73–74.

22. In an article published in *Jîn,* Memduh Selim, the secretary general of the Hêvî Society, mentioned the intimidation and harassment of many *Hêvî Society* members by the police, *see,* Memduh Selim, 'Iki Eser-i Mebrur: Kürd Kadinlari Teali Cemiyeti, Kürd Talebe Hêvî Cemiyeti' [Two Auspicious Works: The Society for the Advancement of Kurdish Women and Kurdish Students-Hope Society], *Jîn,* No. 20, June 4, 1919. For a list of journalists and other opponents assassinated by the

CUP, *see*, Akşin, *Turkey from Empire to Revolutionary Republic*, 69; Silopî, *Doza Kurdistan*, 43; Hanioğlu, *Bir Siyasal Düşünür Abdullah Cevdet*, 292.

23. In the first issue of the paper, it is indicated that the paper's office was the same as Hukûk Publishing House on Ebu Suud Street. However, starting from the second issue, the paper shared an office with Hêvî Society's headquarters, first on Bab-i Ali Slope across from Meserret Hotel, and then on Bab-i Ali Street, *see*, *Rojî Kurd*, No.1, June 9, 1913; *Rojî Kurd*, No. 2, July 1913; *Rojî Kurd*, No. 3, August 14, 1913.

24. Malmîsanij, *Kürt Talebe-Hêvî Cemiyeti*, 161, 185; van Bruinessen, *Agha, Shaikh and State*, 276.

25. This is a quote from Islamic scholar Sheikh Sadi Shirazî (1193–1292). *See*, http://www.tasavvufdunyasi.net/tasavvuf-buyukleri/seyh-sdi-srz-kimdir/.

26. The Founding Declaration of Kurdish Students-Hope Society [Kürt Telebe-Hêvî Cemiyeti'nin Beyannamesidir], *Hetawî Kurd*, No. 4–5, pp. 1–4, May 10, 1914, in Malmîsanij, *Kürt Talebe-Hêvî Cemiyeti*, 257–261.

27. Hanioğlu, *Bir Siyasal Düşünür Abdullah Cevdet*, 21.

28. Halil Hayali, 'Ziman' [Language], *Rojî Kurd*, No. 3, August 14, 1913.

29. Kerküklü Necmeddin, 'Kurd Talebe Cemiyyeti ve Kürdlerin Makam-i Hîlafete Hidmetleri' [Kurdish Hope Society and the Kurdish Service to the Office of Caliphate], *Rojî Kurd*, No. 1, June 19, 1913.

30. Babanzade Ismail Hakkı, Kürdler ve Kurdistan [Kurds and Kurdistan], *KTTG*, No. 1, December 5, 1908.

31. Babanzade Ismail Hakkı, 'Müslümanlık ve Kürdlük' [Muslimness and Kurdishness], *Rojî Kurd*, No. 2, July 19, 1913.

32. Historicization of the Kurdo-Islamic ties and Kurdish service to Islam is one of the dominant themes in the entire corpus of *Rojî Kurd*; *see*, for instance, Kerküklü Necmeddin, 'Kurd Talebe Cemiyyeti ve Kürdlerin Makam-i Hîlafete Hidmetleri' [Kurdish Hope Society and the Kurdish Service to the Office of Caliphate], *Rojî Kurd*, No. 1, June 19, 1913; Salih Bedir Khan, 'Kılıçtan Evvel Kalem' [Pen before the Sword], *Rojî Kurd*, No. 3, August 14, 1913; H. . . 'Dertlerimiz/Nîfakımız' [Our Troubles/Our Disunity], *Rojî Kurd*, No. 3, August 14, 1913; M.X., 'Bextreşî û Mehrûmiya Kurdan' [The Misfortune and Deprivation of the Kurds], *Rojî Kurd*, No. 3, August 14, 1913.

33. Babanzade Ismail Hakkı, 'Kürdelerin Te'âlîsi' [The Rise of the Kurds], *Rojî Kurd*, No. 3, August 14, 1913.

34. For instance, see two articles by Halil Hayali: M.X., 'Tefsîrê Şerîf' [Interpretation of the Holy Text], *Rojî Kurd*, No. 3, August 14, 1913 and Halil Hayali, 'Ziman' [Language], *Rojî Kurd*, No. 3, August 14, 1913.

35. M. Salih Bedir Khan, 'Berî Şîrê Qelem' [Pen before the Sword], *Rojî Kurd*, No. 3, August 14, 1913.

36. Eli Kurê Huseynê Amedî, *Kurdistan*, No. 8, December 1, 1898.

37. Cf. van der Veer, *Religious Nationalism*.

38. Salih Bedir Khan, 'Kılıçtan Evvel Kalem' [Pen before the Sword], *Rojî Kurd*, No. 3, August 14, 1913.

39. M. X., 'Bextreşî û Mehrûmiya Kurdan' [The Misfortune and Deprivation of the Kurds], *Rojî Kurd*, No. 3, August 14, 1913.

40. M. S. Azîzî, 'Hişyar Bin!' [Wake up!], *Rojî Kurd*, No. 2, July 19, 1913. (M. S. Azîzî was one of a few pen names used by M. Salih Bedir Khan in *Rojî Kurd*. Azîzî is one of the names used for the Bedir Khans).

41. As we saw earlier, Babanzade was among those most concerned about the Kurdish youth's involvement in politics, perhaps due to the same reasons, that is, state retaliation.

42. *Tercüman-i Hakikat*, No. 11687, p. 3, October 9, 1913, in Koma Xebatên Kurdolojiyê, *Di Sedsaliya Wê De Rojî Kurd*, 67.

43. *See*, Bajalan, *Kurds for the Empire*; Bajalan, *Kurdish Response to Imperial Decline*.

44. M. S. Azîzî, 'Hişyar Bin!' [Wake up!], *Rojî Kurd*, No. 2, July 19, 1913.

45. The same central doctrine of nationalism was also taken up by several *Rojî Kurd* writers including H., Süleymaniyeli Ebdulkerim, and Halil Hayali.

46. Cf. Wodak et al., *The Discursive Construction of National Identity*, 38.

47. Kurdish has a *pronoun-dropping* phenomenon whereby a sentence requires no expressed subject because the subject is pragmatically inferable as the conjugated verb forms have an implied subject.

48. The alienation of the Kurds from the Ottoman state revived the radical view that Kurds should side with Armenians, a non-Muslim, "Christian" entity, against the Sultan Caliph. In an article published in the journal *Hetawî Kurd*, Mevlanazade Rıfat claimed that Armenians and Kurds belonged to the same race and hence should collaborate, *see*, Mevlanazade Rıfat, 'Muhterem Hetawi Kurd Gazetesi Muessislerine' [To the Honorable Founders of *Hetawi Kurd* Journal], *Hetawi Kurd*, No. 2, December 3, 1913, in Malmîsanij, *Kürt Talebe-Hêvî Cemiyeti.*

49. Halil Hayali gives the same figure in a similar socio-political context, *see*, Halil Hayali, 'Ziman' [Language], *Rojî Kurd*, No. 3, August 14, 1913.

50. Silêmanî Ebdilkerîm, 'Be Firya Keyn-Mu'awenet' [Competition and Cooperation], *Rojî Kurd*, No. 3, August 14, 1913.

51. Here the author refers to the Franco-Prussian War and the Russo-Japanese War (February 8, 1904–September 5, 1905).

52. Lütfî Fikrî, 'Kürd Milliyeti' [Kurdish Nation], *Rojî Kurd*, No. 4, September 12, 1913.

53. Gellner, Ernest. *Nationalism*. (London: Weidenfeld & Nicolson, 1997); Gellner, *Nations and Nationalism*.

54. Anderson, *Imagined Communities*, 42.

55. Harputlu H. B., 'Garbla Şark, Milliyet Cereyanlari' [West and East, National Currents], *Rojî Kurd*, No. 1, June 19, 1913.

56. ; *See*, for instance, Silêmanî Ebdilkerîm, 'Her Min Bim û Kesî Tirî Nî' [Always Me and No One Else], *Rojî Kurd*, No. 2, July 19, 1913.

57. Abdullah Cevdet, 'Ittihad Yolu' [The Path to Unity], *Rojî Kurd*, No. 2, July 19, 1913.

58. For an excellent discussion on linguistic nationalism as a significant element of Turko-Ottoman nationalism, *see*, Soleimani, *Islam and Competing Nationalisms*.

59. Hanioğlu, *Bir Siyasal Düşünür Abdullah Cevdet*, 292.

60. Silêmanî Ebdilkerîm, 'Tal û Şîrîn' [Bitter and Sweet], *Rojî Kurd*, No 1, June 19, 1913.

61. Silêmanî Ebdilkerîm, 'Her Min Bim û Kesî Tirî Nî' [Always Me and No One Else], *Rojî Kurd*, No. 2, July 19, 1913.

62. M. Salih Bedir Khan, 'Berî Şîrê Qelem' [Pen before the Sword], *Rojî Kurd*, No. 3, August 14, 1913.

63. Anonymous, 'Gaye ve Meslek' [The Purpose and the Method], *Rojî Kurd*, No. 1, June 19, 1913.

64. *KTTG* used the term *Kurdayetî* seven times compared to thirty-three times in *Rojî Kurd*.

65. Hassanpour, *Nationalism and Language in Kurdistan*, 46; Hassanpour, *The Making of Kurdish Identity*, 106; Sheyholislami, *Kurdish Identity, Discourse, and New Media*, 202

66. Halil Hayali, 'Ziman' [Language], *Rojî Kurd*, No. 3, August 14, 1913.

67. van Leeuwen, *Multimodality genre and design*, 77; Sheyholislami, *Kurdish Identity, Discourse, and New Media*, 135–136.

68. *Rojî Kurd*, No. 1, June 19, 1913.

69. le gewrekani Kurdekan]: Shah Abd al Karim Khan Zand. *Rojî Kurd*, No. 2, July 19, 1913.

70. Jwaideh, *The Kurdish National Movement*.

71. *Rojî Kurd*, No. 4, September 12, 1913.

72. *Rojî Kurd*, No. 3, August 14, 1913.

73. For more details, *see*, Malmîsanij, *Cizira Botanlı Bedirhaniler*, 147–149; Malmîsanij, *Kürt Talebe-Hêvî Cemiyeti*, 30–31; Zeki, *Dîroka Kurd*, 144.

74. Soleimani, *Islam and Competing Nationalisms*; Hanioğlu, *Bir Siyasal Düşünür Abdullah Cevdet*.

75. Meyrowitz, *Shifting Worlds of Strangers*, 63.

76. McLuhan, Marshall. *Understanding Media: The Extensions of Man*. New York: Mentor Books, 1964.

77. Allison, Christine. "From Benedict Anderson to Mustafa Kemal: Reading, Writing and Imagining the Kurdish Nation," in *Joyce Blau: l'eternelle chez les Kurdes*. (Paris: Karthala, 2013), 101–134, 120.

78. Cf. Hastings, *The Construction of Nationhood Ethnicity*, 13.

79. The Founding Declaration of Kurdish Students-Hope Society [Kürt Telebe-Hêvî Cemiyeti'nin Beyannamesidir], *Hetawî Kurd*, No. 4–5, pp. 1–4, May 10, 1914, in Malmîsanij, *Kürt Talebe-Hêvî Cemiyeti*, 257–261.

80. Kreyenbroek, Philip and Allison, Christine. "Introduction," in *Kurdish Culture and Identity*, edited by Philip Kreyenbroek and Christine Allison. (London: Zed Book Ltd., 1996), 1–6, 2.

71. Babanzade Ismail Hakkı, 'Kürdlerin Te'âlîsi [The Rise of the Kurds], *Rojî Kurd*, No. 3, August 14, 1913.

82. Halil Hayali, 'Ziman' [Language], *Rojî Kurd*, No. 3, August 14, 1913.

83. Mevlanazade Rıfat, 'Muhterem *Hetawi Kurd* Gazetesi Muessislerine' [To the Honorable Founders of *Hetawi Kurd* Journal], *Hetawi Kurd*, No. 2, pp. 2–3, December 3, 1913, in Malmîsanij, *Kürt Talebe-Hêvî Cemiyeti*.

84. The Hêvî Society, the owner of *Rojî Kurd*, published the "Kurdish Language Tutorial" [Hînkerê Zimanê Kurdî] in 1921. It was a booklet composed of basic phrases, vocabulary and short texts in Ottoman Turkish, Kurmanji and Babanî (Sorani). The booklet was transcribed into the Latin alphabet and republished in 2008 in Istanbul by Bgst Publication.

85. Brennan, *The National Longing for Form*, 53; Fishman, Joshua. *Language and Nationalism*. (Massachusetts: Newbury House Publishers, Inc., 1972), 80.

86. Halil Hayali intensified his work on the cultivation of plebeian authenticity in the journal *Jîn*.

87. Smith, *Nationalism: Theory, Ideology, History*, 115.

88. Modanî X., 'Ziman û Nezaniya Kurdan' [The Language and Ignorance of the Kurds], *Rojî Kurd*, No. 2, July 19, 1913.
Halil Hayali also used the pen name Modanî X. (Modanî Xalîl).

89. M. X., 'Bextreşî û Mehrûmiya Kurdan' [The Misfortune and Deprivation of the Kurds], *Rojî Kurd*, No. 3, August 14, 1913.

90. Kreyenbroek and Allison, *Introduction*, 2.

91. Salih Bedir Khan also offered a list of Kurdish notables to emphasize their Kurdishness. The list includes Sheyhulislam Ebu's-suud, the historian Ibn-al Esir, Ebu Zadra, Molla Guran, Fuzuli, Nefi, Nali, and so forth. *See*, 'Kiliçtan Evvel Kalem' [Pen before the Sword], *Rojî Kurd*, No. 3, August 14, 1913.

92. Benî Erdelanî Ehmed Muhsin, 'Le Tarîkî bo Ronakî' [From Darkness to Enlightenment], *Rojî Kurd*, No. 4, September 12, 1913.

93. Babanzade Ismail Hakkı, '*Müslümanlık ve Kürdlük*' [Muslimness and Kurdishness], *Rojî Kurd*, No. 2, July 19, 1913.

94. Halil Hayali, 'Ziman' [Language], *Rojî Kurd*, No. 3, August 14, 1913.

95. M. X., 'Bextreşî û Mehrûmiya Kurdan' [The Misfortune and Deprivation of the Kurds], *Rojî Kurd*, No. 3, August 14, 1913.

96. Similarly, M. S. Bedir Khan, referring to the poetry of Khani and Koyi, stated that, "Every Kurd should know those poems by heart," *see*, M. Salih Bedir Khan, 'Berî Şîrê Qelem' [Pen before the Sword], *Rojî Kurd*, No. 3. August 14, 1913.

97. A similar discursive strategy can also be observed in one of Xezal's articles, *see*, Xezal, '*Dema Kalê Me—Çaxa Me—Dema Tê*' [The Time of Our Ancestors—Our Time—The Future], *Rojî Kurd*, No. 1, June 19, 1913.

98. According to Abdullah Zengene, 'Kurdî' was a pen name used by Silêmanî Ebdulkerîm, cited in Koma Xebatên Kurdolojiyê, *Di Sedsaliya Wê De Rojî Kurd*, 74.

99. Kurdî (Silêmanî Ebdilkerîm), 'Esl û Neslî Kurd' [The Origins and Ancestors of the Kurds], *Rojî Kurd*, No. 4, September 12, 1913.

100. Abdullah Cevdet, 'Bir Hitab' [And Address], *Rojî Kurd*, No. 1, June 19, 1913.

101. Salih Bedir Khan, 'Kiliçtan Evvel Kalem' [Pen before the Sword], *Rojî Kurd*, No. 3, August 14, 1913.

102. We observed the same practice in the discourse of *Kurdistan*.

103. M. X., 'Ji Mezinên Kurdan Ra' [To the Kurdish Nobles], *Rojî Kurd*, No. 4 September 12, 1913.

104. Smith, *Nationalism: Theory, Ideology, History*, 140.

105. Kurdî (Silêmanî Ebdilkerîm), 'Esl û Neslî Kurd' [The Origins and Ancestors of the Kurds], *Rojî Kurd*, No. 4, September 12, 1913.

106. The original term used in the text is 'file' (Christian), which refers to the Armenians.

107. Xezal, 'Dema Kalê Me—Çaxa Me—Dema Tê' [The Time of Our Ancestors—Our Time—The Future], *Rojî Kurd*, No. 1, June 19, 1913.

108. This incomplete story was published in the 1st and 2nd issue of the paper. Although a note in the second part of the story reads "to be continued," the rest of the story was never published.

109. The author means the Turkish language.

110. Here the Arabic term "cins" signifies nationality.

111. X., 'Gilî û Gazin' [Complaint and Reproach], *Rojî Kurd,* No. 4, September 12, 1913.

112. Cf. Fishman, *Language and Nationalism*, 8.

113. Herder (1877–1913), cited in Smith, *Nationalism: Theory, Ideology, History*, 27.

114. Ibid.

115. Fahrî, 'Kürdlerde Kabiliyyet-i Temeddün' [Kurds' Civilizational Abilities], *Rojî Kurd*, No. 1, June 19, 1913.

116. Salih Bedir Khan, 'Kiliçtan Evvel Kalem' [Pen before the Sword], *Rojî Kurd*, No. 3, August 14, 1913.

117. Cf. Mojab, *Women and Nationalism*, 76.

118. The author refers to the "çarşaf," a garment worn by women that covers them from head to toe so as to hide their body from the view of men.

119. Ergani Madenli Y. C., 'Kürdlerde Kadin Meselesi' [The Issue of Woman Among Kurds], *Rojî Kurd*, No. 4, September 12, 1913.

120. Modanî X., *'Ziman û Nezaniya Kurdan'* [The Language and Ignorance of the Kurds], *Rojî Kurd*, No. 2, July 19, 1913.

121. Bulgaristanli Togan, 'Milletinize Karşu Vazifeniz' [Your Duty Towards Your Nation], *Rojî Kurd*, No. 2, July 19, 1913.

122. Anonymous, 'Hayat-i Meşahir: Bedirhanî Hüseyin Paşa' [The Lives of Notables], *Rojî Kurd*, August 14, 1913, No. 3.

123. Kerküklü Necmeddin, 'Kurd Talebe Cemiyyeti ve Kürdlerin Makam-i Hîlafete Hidmetleri' [Kurdish Hope Society and the Kurdish Service to the Office of Caliphate], *Rojî Kurd*, No. 1, June 19, 1913.

124. Halil Hayali drew a similar discursive map in the 2nd issue of *Rojî Kurd*.

125. As discussed in the previous chapter, Babanzade Ismail Hakkı was the first to make reference to the Greater Kurdistan in *KTTG, see*: 'Kürdlerin Mevki-i Coğrafi ve Siyasîsi', [The Geopolitical Posizion of the Kurds], *KTTG*, No. 4, December 26, 1908.

126. Kurdî (Silêmanî Ebdilkerîm), 'Esl û Neslî Kurd' [The Origins and Ancestors of the Kurds], *Rojî Kurd*, No. 4, September 12, 1913.

127. Salih Bedir Khan, 'Berî Şîrê Qelem' [Pen before the Sword], *Rojî Kurd*, No. 3, August 14, 1913.

128. M. S. Azîzî, 'Hişyar Bin!' [Be Awake!], *Rojî Kurd*, No. 2, July 19, 1913.

129. Cf. Baker, *Using Corpora in Discourse Analysis*, 71.

130. Halliday, *An Introduction to Functional Grammar*; Halliday, Michael Alexander Kirkwood, *Spoken and Written Language*. (Oxford: Oxford University Press, 1985); Fairclough, *Critical Discourse Analysis*; Wodak, *The Discourse-Historical*; Kress, *From Saussure to Critical Sociolinguistics*.

131. The Founding Declaration of Kurdish Students-Hope Society [Kürt Telebe-Hêvî Cemiyeti'nin Beyannamesidir], *Hetawî Kurd*, No: 4–5, pp. 1–4, May 10, 1914, in Malmîsanij, *Kürt Talebe-Hêvî Cemiyeti*, 257–261.

132. During the *Hêvî Society*'s first congress in 1913, Memduh Selim, the secretary general of the society, complained about the traditional Kurdish leadership's lack of interest in the Kurdish cause, *see*, Silopî, *Doza Kurdistan*, 43.

133. Journal Management, 'Yükselmek İçün Himmet Lazımdır' [Progress Requires Hard Work], *Rojî Kurd*, No. 4, September 12, 1913.

134. M. X., 'Ji Mezinên Kurdan Ra' [To the Kurdish Nobles], *Rojî Kurd*, No. 4 September 12, 1913.

135. For a similar argument *see*, Halil Hayali, 'Ziman' [Language], *Rojî Kurd*, No. 3, August 14, 1913.

136. Silêmanî Ebdilkerîm, 'Her Min Bim û Kesî Tirî Nî' [Always Me and No One Else], *Rojî Kurd*, No. 2, July 19, 1913.

137. M.X., 'Bextreşî û Mehrûmiya Kurdan' [The Misfortune and Deprivation of the Kurds], *Rojî Kurd*, No. 3, August 14, 1913.

138. Gelî bira[yan]!; Gelî hevala[n]!; Gelî birayê me Kurdino!; Gelî Kurdino!; Hevalo!

139. Salih Bedir Khan, 'Kiliçtan Evvel Kalem' [Pen before the Sword], *Rojî Kurd*, No. 3, August 14, 1913.

140. Bulgaristanlı Doğan, 'Milletinize Karşu Vazifeniz' [Your Duty Towards Your Nation], *Rojî Kurd*, No. 2, July 19, 1913.

141. Cf. Makdisi, *Ottoman Orientalism*.

142. van Bruinessen asserts that the Kurdish aristocracy "shared the Ottomanist ideals of the Young Turk movement, but not its liberal ideas. Their attitude towards the common Kurdish people was extremely paternalistic. They had no serious contacts with Kurdistan." *See*, van Bruinessen, *Agha, Shaikh and State*, 275–276. However, the extent to which their Turkish counterparts, that is, the Young Turks, succeeded in internalizing liberal ideas and incorporating the Turkish masses into their nationalist ideas is also questionable. It was the state, and not an independent bourgeoisie class or devout liberalists or a grassroots movement that spearheaded the social changes in the empire. One should also keep in mind the arrogant Ottoman orientalist attitude of the Turks toward commoners. From this perspective, the CUP's brand of liberalism does not appear to be a genuine one. The spirit or deeper meaning of liberalism was adapted only in form and thus never prevailed, *see*, Göçek, *Rise of Bourgeoisie*; Makdisi, *Ottoman Orientalism*.

Discussion and Conclusion

The late Ottoman period marked a formative stage in the development of nationalist ideologies and movements among various Ottoman ethnic communities. One momentous innovation that coincided with and contributed to the growth and dissemination of nationalism was the introduction of the printing press in the eighteenth century and print media in the mid-nineteenth century. During this period, not only the Ottoman Turks but also political intellectuals from diverse ethnic groups throughout the empire published newspapers to articulate and disseminate their respective national identity narratives. Similarly, the formation of Kurdish nationalism as an ideology and a political project emerged around the same time as the inception of the first nationally oriented Kurdish journals and organizations, which opened a communicative space for articulating the Kurdish nationalist discourse. However, some academics have argued that the Kurdish leadership and their journals are not nationalist because (1) Kurdish journalistic discourse of the period stopped short of making political demands; and (2) it was, if anything, Pan-Islamist and Ottoman nationalist. Therefore, this book has called into question the claims that dominate academic accounts on early Kurdish journals by revealing the sources of common methodological, theoretical, and linguistic misconceptions that have led to such inaccurate assumptions. In contrast to these claims, this book has argued that Kurdish journals promoted a clearly defined Kurdish ethnic nationalism. Pan-Islamism or Ottoman nationalism were merely discursive tools in the hands of Kurdish nationalists to subtly foster Kurdish national interests within the limits of the Ottoman political setting.

The historical context or what Foucault calls the "historicization of discourses"[1] is crucially important in understanding the circumstances whereby discourses emerge because discursive elements are time-specific and are

meaningful only within their specific historical, cultural, and political contexts. This approach is vital to understanding Kurdish nationalism because
the unstable sociocultural environment of the chaotic late Ottoman period
led to heterogeneous and shifting discourse practices. Therefore, this book
revealed that the specific sociocultural and political setting that prevailed in
each period in which Kurdish journals were published had a decisive effect on
how each journal constructed its unique form of nationalism. In other words,
as a result of a close textual analysis of numerous extracts from the corpora of
early Kurdish journals, this study unveiled how each journal adopted different sets of discursive strategies, practices, and language devices following the
various requirements of their own social, political, and cultural conditions of
existence. For instance, the journal *Kurdistan* was published under the reign
of Sultan Abdulhamid II and his policy of Ottoman-Turkish Pan-Islamism,
while *KTTG* came out in the immediate aftermath of the 1908 Young Turk
Revolution and the ensuing liberal environment in which a more secular form
of Ottomanism prevailed as the dominant ideology. *Rojî Kurd*, on the other
hand, started publication during a historical period whereby European colonialism and rising nationalist tendencies in the empire had further weakened
Ottomanism and precipitated the radicalization of Turkish nationalism into
a chauvinist state ideology. It can be argued that Kurdish identity discourse
developed different shades of nationalism over a period of sixteen years during the final decades of the Ottoman Empire in response to three complex
historical periods, each dominated by different ideological currents, that is,
Ottomanism, Ottoman-Turkish Pan-Islamism, and chauvinist Turkish nationalism. Hence, these discursive shifts served as a sensitive barometer of the
discursive evolution in Kurdish journals' nationalist narratives.

Although *Osmanlılık*, or Ottoman official nationalism, dominated much
of the late Ottoman period, the reign of Sultan Abdulhamid II distinguished
itself by elevating Ottoman-Turkish *Pan-Islamism*, *Islamic Ottomanism*,
or Turkish-style *Ummahism* into a hegemonic ideology. This policy was a
response to both "Christian" Europe's colonialist ambitions and rising ethno-
national inclinations among non-Turkish Muslim communities. To that end,
more than any previous Ottoman ruler, Sultan Abdulhamid II, made extensive
use of his title as the Caliph of Islam to foster Islamic solidarity and rally
Muslims around his rule.

Kurdistan, which appeared during the reign of Sultan Abdulhamid II, was
an irregularly published Kurdish journal, edited by the Bedir Khan Brothers
and published in exile. It provided a discursive space to articulate, negotiate, and disseminate a distinctive Kurdish national identity narrative and a
Kurdish nationalism among Kurdish elements of the empire. The analysis of
Kurdistan revealed that the hegemonic discourses of the CUP's Ottomanism,
but particularly Sultan Abdulhamid II's Ottoman-Turkish Pan-Islamism,

had a determining effect on the type of nationalist discourse expressed in *Kurdistan*. Since the Sultan and his statesmen did not tolerate ethno-nationalist inclinations among non-Turkish Muslims, the Bedir Khan Brothers felt compelled to profess and sponsor both religion (Islam) and Ottomanism in their journalistic discourse. In this way, they disguised their nationalist intentions and aimed at finding a niche in the Ottoman political landscape. What is more, in a Sunni Muslim Kurdish community that was predominantly socially and religiously conservative, both religious piety, as well as some sort of religious lineage, were vital to finding an audience and achieving a leadership position. This reality gave the Bedir Khan Brothers another incentive to trace their ancestry to Arabia and adopt a religiously tinted language and discourse in their Kurdish nationalist narrative. To that end, the Bedir Khan Brothers adopted, in an essentially pragmatic manner, a dense religious intertextuality, that is, Ottoman Pan-Islamism, to justify their ethnonationalist project. In other words, the Bedir Khan Brothers made use of the Hamidian notion of Ottoman Pan-Islamism as a primary discursive practice to mitigate the Kurdish nationalist tone of their journal. Pan-Islamism also rendered the Kurdish nationalist discourse more acceptable to the state and the predominantly Sunni Muslim Kurdish community. Thus, the Bedir Khan Brothers frequently cited the hadith and verses from the Qur'an to justify their nationalist arguments and the necessity to modernize the Kurdish community. Accordingly, the modernization of the Kurdish community was necessary for the progress of Islam; literacy was necessary to say the prayers; intertribal disputes were sinful acts because they harmed Islamic unity and solidarity; the progress of Kurdish society in science and technology was a religious duty because an advanced Kurdish society could better serve the Islamic ummah; the Sultan should increase the capacity of the Kurds so that they could protect the Ottoman homeland against the "infidel" Russians; and so forth. Again, it is clear that the Bedir Khan Brother used the strategy of religious allusion to frame their ethno-nationalist claims that were acceptable in the eyes of both the Ottomans and the Kurds.

Since the hegemonic discourses of Pan-Islamism, Islamic Ottomanism, and Kurdish ethnic nationalism were at work in the discourse of the journal, *Kurdistan* became a site of contestation between these ideologies. Subsequently, the editors' arguments fluctuated between ideas of Pan-Islamism and Islamic Ottomanism, on the one hand, and Kurdish ethnic nationalism, on the other. The latter occasionally led the editor Abdurrahman Bedir Khan to entertain secessionism and the formation of an independent Kurdish nation-state at the expense of Ottomanism and Pan-Islamism. This secessionist attitude should not be interpreted as a coherent and widespread discursive act throughout the corpus of *Kurdistan*. However, this should not detract from the fact that Kurdish intellectuals of the period did entertain ideas of Kurdish national independence at the expense of the Pan-Islamist ideals, the Caliphate, and Ottomanism. Most of the literature on this period would have us believe that these ideas never crossed the minds of Kurdish intellectuals during the late Ottoman period.

As far as *Kürd Teavün ve Terakki Gazetesi (KTTG)*, or *The Kurdish Gazette for Mutual Aid and Progress*, is concerned, Ottoman politics changed drastically under the Young Turks and the CUP after the July Revolution of 1908. The new constitutional regime replaced Sultan Abdulhamid's Pan-Islamism policy with a more secular form of Ottomanism to incorporate the non-Muslim elements of the empire into the Ottoman political community and inspire loyalty to the Ottoman state. After this significant paradigmatic shift in Ottoman politics, Kurdish intellectuals and political leaders, this time organized around the *KTTC* and *KTTG*, opted for CUP's secular Ottomanism because Kurds—and other non-Turkish elements of the empire—were convinced that a decentralized constitutional state would allow them to realize their social, cultural, and political goal.

From that point onwards, *KTTG* embraced a rigorous Ottomanist policy. It pledged allegiance to the constitutional state, frequently propagated Ottomanism, and underlined the compatibility of the new regime's modern values with Islamic principles. What is more, the Young Turks, who turned Ottomanism into the new uncompromising hegemonic identity, were wary of those who did not uphold Ottoman identity and saw them as a threat to the Ottoman state. In response, *KTTG* authors developed complex types of discursive strategies to convey their seemingly intense devotion to this new Ottoman identity. The discursive manifestation of *KTTG*'s extreme form of Ottomanism can be observed in (1) the journal's predominant use of the Turkish language, the *lingua franca* of the empire, rather than Kurdish; (2) the journal's desire to communicate its ideas to other Ottomans, Turks in particular; (3) the articulation of Kurdish history as an extension of Ottoman history at the expense of anachronisms; (4) constructing Kurdish culture as a part of the Ottoman culture; (5) constructing the Kurdish homeland as an extension of the Ottoman homeland; and (6) the abundance of articles that dealt with issues which were not directly the concern of the Kurds but of all Ottomans; and so forth. Taking this Ottomanist rhetoric at face value inevitably leads to the erroneous conclusion that Kurdish intellectuals were "Ottoman nationalists with Kurdish colours". The truth of the matter is that this "more royalist than the king" strategy of *KTTG* toward Ottomanism was based more on pragmatism than a sincere ideological adherence to Ottomanism.

Reasons for this pragmatic approach were manifold because Kurdish nationalist intellectuals' reactions to Ottomanism were complex. First and foremost, Ottomanism was the hegemonic narrative of the period. The nationalist Kurdish intelligentsia was convinced that espousing Ottomanism was a means to secure cultural and political autonomy for Kurds without openly opposing the state's hegemonic Ottomanism or the office of the Caliphate. They believed this could be achieved by convincing the Young Turks that the Kurds were committed to the state and the ideals of Ottomanism. Second, in a context in which the Young Turks and the CUP repressed and intimidated non-Turkish nationalist movements, a discursive Ottomanism was instrumental for disguising the journals' nationalist ambitions. It generated a Kurdish nationalism that was more acceptable to the Young Turks and the CUP. In so doing, *KTTG* authors hoped to avoid state sanctions while also having the opportunity to participate in Ottoman politics and possibly steer state policies in a direction that would benefit Kurdish national interests. The Kurdish leadership was also wary of the colonialist ambitions of the Great Powers of Europe,[2] who seemed to be encouraging the Armenians to lay claim to the eastern provinces of the empire concurrently inhabited by both Kurds and Armenians. Because Kurdish nationalists were sceptical that they could confront the Western powers on their own, they found it wiser to have recourse to Ottomanism to oppose this "plot." Arab nationalists expressed a similar concern as most Arab intellectuals regarded the Ottoman state as the ultimate bulwark against European imperialism. In any case, both Sultan Abdulhamid II and the CUP also reinforced this view by presenting themselves as the Muslims' saviors against the threat of the colonialist, Christian West. Fourth, the Kurdish leadership exploited Ottomanism as an effective means to promote a form of civic nationalism while curbing the rising Turkish ethnic nationalism and preventing it from turning into an oppressive chauvinist state ideology. Kurds had good reasons to feel that way because the Young Turks and the CUP had long ago equated Ottomanism or Ottoman nationalism with Turkism and Turkish nationalism, similar to their Young Ottoman predecessors. In short, *KTTG* adopted this pragmatic approach as the circumstances were not conducive to a straightforward expression of Kurdish nationalist aspirations.

Despite its strong Ottomanist rhetoric, when compared to *Kurdistan*, *KTTG* produced a more refined Kurdish nationalist discourse that underlined Kurdish political demands. *KTTG* articles advocated administrative decentralization in favor of more robust regional governance in Kurdistan. Besides, the *KTTC* constitution never lent unconditional support to the CUP. On the contrary, Kurdish support for the CUP regime was conditional. The Kurds would continue to uphold the regime as long as the principles of the Ottoman constitution, in particular, the principle of equality between various Ottoman communities, were realized and maintained. It goes without saying that this condition meant to prevent Turkish dominance over the state apparatus at the expense of non-Turks.

By the time *Rojî Kurd* appeared, sociopolitical circumstances in the empire had evolved, with the shifting balance of power both at home and abroad, causing the Turkish nationalist undertones of Ottomanism to become more visible. The political discord within the Young Turks' ranks was exacerbated by rising nationalist movements in the Balkans and elsewhere, which culminated in humiliating defeats and the loss of territories, for example, the Tripolitan War (aka Italo-Ottoman War) (1911–1912) and the First Balkan Wars (1912–1913). Agitated by the outcome of these wars, in the early 1910s, the Young Turks and CUP abandoned the notion of Ottomanism altogether. Instead, they opted for Akçura's policy of Turkism by fostering Turkish nationalism and Turkish racial superiority more openly as the only viable option to keep intact what was left of the empire. As a consequence, in contrast with the ideals of the 1908 Revolution, starting in the 1910s, the state gradually acquired a Turkish rather than an Ottoman color and an autocratic rather than a liberal form. Under these circumstances, the Kurdish intelligentsia, now composed of a new breed of Kurdish nationalists, was convinced that the notions of Ottomanist and Pan-Islamist were no longer of instrumental use but were rather an impediment to the advancement of Kurdish national interests. In the face of growing Turkish nationalism, even those who were previously silent or seemed to be ardent supporters of the Ottoman reforms and the ideals of Ottomanism moved toward opposing rising Turkish nationalism. Therefore, the Kurds abandoned both notions favoring a purer form of Kurdish nationalism accompanied by Islamic modernism.

Under these circumstances, the Turkish nationalist elements in the CUP carried out a military coup on January 23, 1913, ousting the anti-CUP opposition from the government, many of whom were non-Turkish politicians. This critical turn of events marked the Turkish nationalists' assumption of total control over the state apparatus. An ensuing reign of terror was intolerant of any opposition, particularly nationalist tendencies among non-Turkish Ottoman communities. The new phase of overt Turkish nationalism further shattered the myth of Ottomanism in the view of the Kurds and other non-Turkish Ottoman communities. The ever-worsening circumstances set the scene for the rise of a stronger sense of nationalism among Kurdish intellectuals, which resulted in a major discursive shift in *Rojî Kurd*. Given the new political landscape, the authors of *Rojî Kurd* kept the idea of Ottomanism at arm's length while questioning unreciprocated Kurdish service to Pan-Islamism. The authors of *Rojî Kurd* and the *Hêvî Society* members understood that their solidarity for the meta-identities of Ottomanism and Pan-Islamism could not improve Kurdish society or solve its problems. Thus, they came to recognize that the notion of ethnic nationalism and political autonomy were major preconditions for modernization and the motive power behind the political, economic, social, and cultural progress of the Kurdish community.

Now that Turkish nationalism and Turkish racial superiority were openly the dominant characters of the state, *Rojî Kurd*, in stark contrast with *Kurdistan* and *KTTG*, did not find it necessary to justify its nationalist discourse through Ottomanism or Pan-Islamism. Conversely, the Kurdish identity discourse in *Rojî Kurd* revolved around a unique Kurdish language, culture, history, and political future that aimed mainly at disidentifying Kurds from both Ottoman-Turkish and Arabo-Islamic identities. Instead, from an Islamic modernist perspective, *Rojî Kurd* designated Kurds as an essential pillar of Islam, not of Ottomanism. Despite state retaliation, *Rojî Kurd* writers dared to discuss Kurds' political ambitions. For instance, Abdullah Cevdet proposed a Swiss model, where the Ottoman state would be decentralized in favor of republics based on their respective racial, national, linguistic, and cultural peculiarities, with Kurdistan constituting one of these proposed autonomous republics.

Given the variety of different political views expressed, it is not easy to pinpoint in the mapping of the voices in the corpora of the early Kurdish journals what represented a collective ideology and what was a personal standpoint. These dialogues indicate that the early Kurdish journals might not have had clearly defined political goals, but rather functioned as platforms where the nationalist Kurdish intellectual elite negotiated the form of Kurdish nationalism, its demands, and its objectives. These findings are in stark contrast with the prevailing view in the relevant literature. The empirical findings in this book revealed that the hegemonic Pan-Islamist and Ottomanist narratives were convenient practical and theoretical frameworks in the hands of Kurdish nationalists to promote and disseminate Kurdish nationalist discourse. They dropped both ideologies when they no longer served Kurdish national interests. Moreover, owing to the unfavorable sociocultural and political circumstances—including state retaliation, mainly in the form of intimidation and arrests—Kurdish nationalist intellectuals by and large refrained from overt political expressions of Kurdish nationalism and political objectives. Despite the state's coercive measures, the journals' contributors aspired to achieve Kurdish political autonomy. They took up themes that pertained to Kurds' political ambitions generally via a range of subtle, implicit, or semi-explicit discursive strategies and language devices.

CONCEPTUAL AND TERMINOLOGICAL CONFUSION AROUND THE EMERGENCE OF KURDISH NATIONALISM

Besides methodological issues, there have also been theoretical limitations in some of the relevant scholarship. The general literature on concepts of nation and nationalism offers a plethora of definitions that each inevitably leads to different conclusions. Each definition employs different parameters for a community to qualify as a nation or for a discourse to qualify as nationalist.

It is also noteworthy that certain approaches to the concepts of nation and nationalism do not necessarily originate from scholarly concerns but political ones, in that any definition will legitimate some claims and delegitimize others.[3] The same is true of the Kurdish case. Determining whether or not the discourse of early Kurdish journals and their parent organizations were nationalist depends on one's understanding of the notion of nationalism and what theories or criteria they use for assessment.

If, for example, a theory that requires a clear-cut and robust notion of political self-determination in the form of a nation-state is applied, then certain movements and their discourses might fail to qualify as nationalist. However, demand for self-determination or what is called "statism" might not be one of the prerequisites for an individual, a group, a movement, or a discourse to qualify as nationalist. In other words, "statism"—the pursuit of a nation-state—should not be an essential criterion or prerequisite for a movement to be considered nationalist.[4] Nationalism is "essentially conscious or organized ethno-cultural solidarity which may or may not then be directed outside of its initial sphere toward political, economic and religious goals."[5] Smith argues that not all nationalists make claims to statehood. Accordingly, "the close link between ideology and movement in no way limits the concept of nationalism only to movements seeking independence; a distinction must be made between 'national autonomy' and 'state sovereignty.' "[6] Similarly, due to the terminological confusion in the field, Fishman distinguishes between *nationism* and *nationalism*. While *nationism* signifies the set of behaviors, beliefs, and values pertaining to the acquisition, maintenance, and development of a politically independent nation-state, *nationalism* denotes ethno-cultural solidarity around a collective identity protected by the *polity*, which does not necessarily mean a sovereign-state.[7] Consequently, just because Kurdish intellectuals of the late Ottoman period sought a political solution within the Ottoman political framework—for practical purposes due to local and global circumstances—does not make them non-nationalist or "Ottoman nationalists." In any case, all three Kurdish journals, their editors, and their contributors expressed Kurdish aspirations to national autonomy in various forms, including the formation of a Kurdish nation-state at the expense of the "Holy" Ottoman Empire and the Sultan Caliph.

THE LIMITED SOCIOPOLITICAL IMPACT OF KURDISH JOURNALISTIC DISCOURSE

Anderson asserts that the genres of novels and newspapers were two forms of imagining that contributed to the formation of nations in Europe in the eighteenth century. These fundamental novelties led to one of the earliest forms of capitalist enterprise: *print-capitalism*. Publication activities in

Europe started as a modern mass-produced industrial commodity for which an unsaturated market already existed. Once the small Latin market of the elite was exhausted, entrepreneurs, motivated by the profit-making logic of capitalism, turned to the monoglot masses that spoke vernaculars. Publishing, as a profitable industrial commodity, eventually created unified fields of mass consumption, communication, and exchange in vernacularized languages. This process led to the formation of *standardized, mass civilizations* around national languages, making speakers of the same language aware of their fellow-readers with whom they had something in common, that is, language, and aware of those with whom they did not share this national commodity.[8] In Anderson's theory, newspapers as cultural products are capable of playing the same role as novels. A periodical provides an imagined link when readers of the same language consume it simultaneously on a massive scale during a specific time as a mass ceremony.[9] "The very existence and regularity of newspapers caused readers or the citizens-in-the-making, to imagine themselves residing in a common time and place, united by a print language with a league of anonymous equals."[10] Mass consumption in the same print language *inadvertently* paved the way for the formation of unified fields of mass communication, making the imagining of nations around vernaculars possible. Hence one can surmise that the role of print in imagining the nation was largely an *unselfconscious* activity that resulted from the interplay between print-capitalism, technology, and linguistic diversity. In other words, vernacularization was not a conscious effort to form nations but rather the result of industrial society's necessities.[11]

The process that led to print-capitalism in Europe was reversed in the Kurdish case. In Europe, the printing press was not only a self-sustaining but also a lucrative enterprise, which *unintentionally* contributed to the formation of national communities. In the Kurdish case, however, the publishers of Kurdish journals, and later books, could not have been motivated by the merits of print-capitalism, that is, the profit-making capacity of publishing, because publishing was not a profitable business in the Ottoman Empire, let alone Kurdistan, due to the lack of necessary preconditions, most notably the absence of a mass reading public. As a consequence, Kurdish printing did not start as a lucrative industrial commodity or as an entrepreneurial activity. Instead, it started with Kurdish intellectuals' *deliberate attempt* to imitate the social and political consequences of publication activities in the eighteenth-century Europe. That is, Kurdish nationalist intellectuals pursued print media—particularly newspaper publication—to construct and disseminate a nationalist discourse and ultimately create an imagined Kurdish community around their periodicals. It thus can be argued that in Europe, publishing, which was a self-sustaining as well as a profitable business in the hands of capitalist entrepreneurs, *unintentionally* contributed to the formation of national identities. However, in the Kurdish case, mass publication was an *intentional* and *a self-conscious* activity pursued by the Kurdish *political and ideological entrepreneurs* to bring about an imagined Kurdish national community. What was the *result* in the European case was the *cause* in the Kurdish case. This reality once again confirms the fact that the Kurdish transition to print culture had its origins in the dynamics of Kurdish nationalist activities. Nevertheless, the nation-making power of the printing press required the confluence of modern forces, including a sizable reading public, free press, urbanization, print-capitalism, and so forth, which provide an infrastructural base for the dissemination of the nationalist narratives and the formation of imagined national communities.[12]

Almost none of these modern forces were in place in the late Ottoman and Kurdish contexts. Also, the production and circulation of journals, as well as their owners, editors, contributors, and even readership, were subject to state retaliation, as is evident from several articles published in the journals.[13] Equally important was the high rate of illiteracy exacerbated by the dialectal variations in Kurdish society.[14] The Kurdish press of the pre-World War I period managed to create a nationalist narrative among the Kurdish elite and a small group of literati. Nonetheless, these reading circles remained tiny literate reefs atop a vast ocean of illiteracy, thus preventing the formation of a larger Kurdish reading public. As a result, Kurdish journalistic discourse did not achieve its potential power and remained inconsequential in making an impact on a larger Kurdish community. This situation was not unique to the Kurds, as in most nationalist movements, including Turkish nationalism, the urban elite, equipped with intellectual, political, and technical capacity, became nationalist well before the rest of the population and promulgated their nationalist ideas.[15]

Despite all odds, several reader letters published in the Kurdish journals indicate that the journals were read by commoners, especially at gatherings, perhaps in coffeehouses, medreses, and guest-house settings, which constituted effective agents for disseminating nationalist ideology and feelings. A reader's letter sent to the journal *Kurdistan* from Adana indicated that the paper was read aloud to those present.[16] Moreover, the following extract from an article by Lutfi Fikri gives an idea about the reception of Kurdish language publications among Kurdish commoners. Recounting his visit to a remote Kurdish village, Fikri wrote:

I saw a small booklet [risale] that was carefully placed on a wooden drawer in a niche . . . It was written in Kurdish probably a couple of years back in Istanbul. The villagers venerated it as if it was a religious book. They talked about it with passionate love. "Sir, this is a Kurdish book!" they said, "we had never seen such a thing before. So, there could be books in Kurdish too! We had the village imam read it [to us] several times . . . we cried tears of joy . . ." Then and there, I said to myself that all attempts are of no avail! No one can prevent this national current. The time and place are very favourable [too]. See! How nationalism has yielded such a heavy harvest, even here in this village of 10 households in a remote part of the world away from all civilized centres with no roads and could only be reached with great difficulty.[17]

Fikri presented this encounter as direct evidence of an unstoppable and ubiquitous feeling of nationalism among all members of the Kurdish community, even those living in distant villages. It also proves that "the bond between the written language, perhaps used only by the few, with the oral language forms used by everyone, can ensure that a linguistically based nationalism quickly gains support even in largely non-literate communities."[18]

TÜRKİYELİLİK IS NEO-OTTOMANISM

The founders of the new Turkish Republic, spearheaded by the remaining CUP ideologues, opted for a similar form of Turkish nationalism, laying the foundation for a new state based on the denial of minority identities and their forced assimilation into the dominant and oppressive Hanafi/Sunni Turkish identity. Since then, Turkey has allocated extensive resources to suppress dissent, particularly the Kurds who have struggled for cultural and political rights. Several years after coming to power, the Justice and Development Party (AKP) government under Recep Tayyip Erdogan came to realize that the Kurdish question was a major impediment to Turkish state ambitions to become a regional superpower. Starting in 2008, the AKP government developed a new political solution called *Türkiyelilik* ("Turkeyan" or "begin from Turkey") in an attempt to allegedly come to terms with its culturally, ethnically, and religiously heterogeneous population.

To that end, senior Turkish politicians, particularly those in the ruling AKP government, scholars, journalists, and commentators began to discuss the concept of *Türkiyelilik* as a supra-identity that could embrace and incorporate marginalized non-Turkish and non-Hanafi Muslim communities in Turkey. Ostensibly the term signified the state of "being a citizen of Turkey" or "being from Turkey" to avoid the official and constitutional concept of Turkish identity that defines all citizens of Turkey as *Turkish* or *ethnic Turks*. In this sense, it bore striking similarities to the policy of Ottoman official nationalism known as *Osmanlılık* (Ottomanism) discussed throughout this book. Much like *Osmanlılık*, *Türkiyelilik* denoted a particular brand of civic nationalism that attempted to provide a widely accepted collective identity for Turkey's ethnically and religiously heterogeneous society to garner a universal sense of belonging and loyalty to the Turkish state. Later, the concept of *Türkiyelilik* as a supra-identity was seen as contributing to the ensuing "peace process" between the Turkish state and the PKK.[19]

Turkiyelilik and the peace process initially caused excitement among all segments of Kurdish society. As a gesture of goodwill in support of the process, the PKK announced a unilateral ceasefire. Ahmet Turk, a senior Kurdish politician, suggested in 2008 that *Türkiyelilik* should be designated as the supra-identity in the Turkish constitution.[20] However, it soon transpired that the driving force behind this new Turkish state initiative had arisen not from the Turkish state's genuine concern about past wrongs committed against the Kurds and other minority identities. Instead, it was motivated by the state's desire to appease discontent, keep the existing power structure intact, and build a platform to project regional power. Having "solved" its internal problems, the Turkish state could then commit its resources fully to its quest for a greater role in regional and international politics. Given their resemblances, scholars and political commentators have referred to *Turkiyelilik* as neo-Ottomanism, a claim often refuted by ruling Ottoman-nostalgic AKP politicians.[21] Notably, in the face of Kurdish political demands, which included constitutional recognition, it became clear that the Turkish state was reluctant to make any substantial compromises that would jeopardize the hegemonic power of the Hanafi/Sunni Turkish elements over the state apparatus. The tension between the Kurds and the Turkish state was exacerbated by Kurdish military and political gains in the Syrian Civil War. The peace process eventually collapsed in 2015 with renewed full-scale warfare. In any case, from the very beginning, Kurds were well aware that the Turkish state had proposed the notion of *Türkiyelilik* as a pragmatic policy to pacify the Kurdish nationalist movement for its own ends. However, Kurds still welcomed and promoted the idea, hoping that the process might turn into an opportunity to end the devastating war and bring a wave of permanent peace. It is noteworthy that the notion of *Türkiyelilik* is still at the center of the pro-Kurdish Peoples' Democratic Party (HDP) political line. Nevertheless, supporting *Türkiyelilik* has not made Kurdish politicians Turkish nationalists or "Turkeyan" nationalists, just as supporting *Osmanlılık* or Ottomanism, due to the circumstances, did not necessarily make Kurdish intellectuals of the late Ottoman period Ottoman nationalists.

A FEW WORDS ON THE ROLE OF NATIONAL LANGUAGES IN THE FORMATION OF "IMAGINED COMMUNITIES"

In Anderson's theory of nationalism, a discrete national language is *not* seen as an "objective" criterion in imagining a national community, because the significance of the language is merely the medium through which nations are imagined. In other words, producing a nationalist discourse does not require a particular language because "[m]uch the most important thing about language is its capacity for generating imagined communities . . . If radical Mozambique speaks Portuguese, the significance of this is that Portuguese is the medium through which Mozambique is imagined . . . Print-language is what invents nationalism, not *a* particular language per se" (emphasis in original).[22] Here, Anderson makes two distinctions: (1) any language—as opposed to *a* particular *national* language—can be employed to imagine a nation, as in the case of Mozambique; and (2) only print-languages have the power and capacity to generate imagined communities in the absence of face-to-face communication. Anderson is warning against the nationalist ideologues' tendency to see languages as *emblems* of nation-ness at the same level as flags, costumes, and folk dances. Instead, he lays emphasis on the "capacity of [any] language for creating imagined communities." For Anderson, *a* particular language is neither an exclusive cultural instrument nor an essential component of national identity. Accordingly, the *emblems* cited above (customs, folk dances, values) should not be considered components of national identity either as anyone can *learn* them. Anderson's second point refers to the power of language—"any language" as he puts it—and discourse to produce meaning, hence knowledge and ideologies. However, it seems that Anderson's first point might not be true of or applicable to each and every case in the sense that the use of *a particular language* with its symbolic value and function has been a powerful emblem of national identity from the inception of the idea of nationalism, evident in numerous nationalisms including German, Italian, Kurdish, Jewish and Arab, to name only a few. More contemporary cases where language is the defining feature of national identity include Catalan, Quebecois, Welsh, and Amazigh nationalisms.

The earliest accounts of the centrality of language in a politico-national sense can be traced back to eighteenth-century German romantics such as Johann Gottfried Herder (1744–1803), Johann Georg Hamman (1730–1788), and Johann Gottlieb Fichte (1762–1814). Herder was one of the earliest philosophers to develop a historicist (primordialist) concept of the nation, in which he placed language at the emotional and intellectual center of modern nationalism's concern for authenticity. He proposed that the *Volk*, or *national spirit*, was reflected in a nations' language, which was its primary identity marker. Fichte also felt that the native language contained the national spirit of a nation and was a major sign of national identity. For him, the sameness of language ensures communal bonds of solidarity because "the speakers of the same language belong together and are by nature one and inseparable whole."[23] The focus of German romantics on language as well as on German thought, cultural traditions, folklore, music, dance, and literature, as manifestations of the German *Volk*, later turned into a nationalist narrative claiming not only historical antiquity but also the supremacy of German culture in Europe.

This particular view of language had a profound influence on subsequent nationalisms. Nationalist historians, ideologues, and social philosophers engaged in the social and historical exploration of their respective communities. They "proved" the naturalness and "perennial existence" of their communities by "rediscovering" their unique values and characteristics such as language, myths, customs, literature, and other ethno-symbolic resources. Similarly, in more contemporary politics, language has become an indispensable part of national identity narratives. For instance, a Finnish slogan reads, "without Finnish we are not Finns," while Catalonian nationalists assert, "our language, the expression of our people, which can never be given up . . . is the spiritual foundation of our existence."[24] In the same vein, a popular motto in contemporary Kurdish nationalist discourse goes, "our language is our existence!" Language is thereby transformed into an existential national element or, in other words, an ontological matter. Billig emphasizes the significance of a discrete national language in imagining a nation and considers a discrete language to be a "strong social psychological dimension" of national consciousness and a rallying point with its powerful symbolism. Referring to Anderson's argument, Billig states that "national languages also have to be imagined, and this lies at the root of today's common-sense belief that discrete languages' naturally' exist."[25] Numerous cases of nationalism have shown where the language of the *self* is distinct from that of the *other(s)*, the symbolic use of national language, at least in certain cases, has turned into an element of self-identification as well as dis-identification and distinction from out-groups. In other words, Anderson overlooked the significance of the symbolic use of a particular national language by putting too much emphasis on the communicative and technological aspects of language. Nevertheless, no essential link can be drawn between language and nation because the universalization of the *existence* of a link between *a* particular language and national identity is a misguided judgment as much as the universalization of the *lack of* such a link.

As this book has shown through extracts taken from the Kurdish journals under consideration, language and identity are intimately related in the Kurdish case. As a matter of fact, since the time of Ahmad Khani, the Kurdish language has been the most salient and inseparable component of Kurdish identity. As he explained in his *Mem û Zîn*, Khani deliberately penned his masterpiece in Kurdish instead of Persian, the lingua franca of literature, to mark the Kurds off from Persians, Arabs, and Turks. As we saw, nationalist Kurdish journals of the late Ottoman period used the Kurdish language deliberately in its full capacity as an element of national *self-identification*, *inclusion*, *exclusion*, and *othering*.

SUGGESTIONS FOR FUTURE RESEARCH

From the perspective of a linguistically informed discourse analysis, this book utilized a multifaceted CDA conceptual framework to examine and explain the ideological function of language in Kurdish national identity narratives produced in Kurdish journalistic discourse from the late Ottoman period. To that end, the book adopted two major CDA approaches, namely Fairclough's *three-dimensional analytical framework* and Wodak and her colleagues' *discourse-historical approach.* This multidimensional CDA conceptual framework proved to be extremely fruitful in yielding an in-depth and exhaustive discourse analysis of empirical data collected from the corpora of pre-World War I Kurdish journals.

Although Kurdish intellectuals published several periodicals and books during the last decades of the Ottoman Empire, the present book could cover only three journals to limit its data to a manageable size and offer an in-depth textual analysis. A similar methodological approach will yield fruitful analysis if applied to other Kurdish periodicals, especially those that came out in the immediate aftermath of World War I, for example, *Jîn.* Such comprehensive studies based on close textual analysis would greatly enrich the body of knowledge in the field of Kurdish studies. They could shed light on the way in which Kurdish intellectuals and political leaders reacted to the new social and political circumstances in the post–World War I period by analyzing how the unique circumstances of the period shaped and were shaped by the nationalist narratives developed in Kurdish periodicals.

NOTES

1. Foucault, *Archaeology of Knowledge.*
2. It is important to note that Western colonial expansion in Africa and Asia was in full swing between 1844 and 1900, *see,* Zeine, *The Emergence of Arab Nationalism,* 68–69.
3. Calhoun, Craig. "Nationalism and Ethnicity," *Annual Review of Sociology,* Vol. 19, (August 1993): 211–239, 215.
4. Fishman, *Language and Nationalism,* 72.
5. Ibid.
6. Smith, *Nationalism: Theory, Ideology, History,* 9–26.
7. Fishman, *Language and Nationalism,* 5.
8. Anderson, *Imagined Communities.*
9. McLuhan was the first to argue for the profound effect of the Gutenberg Revolution, that is, the success of print-languages and mass communication in creating unified fields of communication, *see* McLuhan, *Understanding Media.*

10. Kemper, Steven. *The Presence of the Past: Chronicles, Politics, and Culture in Sinhala Life*. (Ithaca: Cornell UP, 1991), 4.

11. Gellner, *Nations and Nationalism*, 35.

12. For a critique of Anderson's concepts of "imagined communities" and "print-capitalism" in the Kurdish context see, Allison, *From Benedict Anderson*.

13. *See*, a reader's letter in *Kurdistan*, No. 13, April 2, 1899.

14. In the late nineteenth and early twentieth centuries, the small segment of the Kurdish reading public did not exceed 10 percent compared to, for instance, eighteenth-century France where the literacy rate among the male population was 47 percent, *see*, Firro, *Metamorphosis of the Nation (al-Umma)*, 55; Klein, *Claiming the Nation*, 123. According to Hassanpour, the literacy rate in Kurdistan was around 4 percent in the 1920s, *see*, Hassanpour, *The Creation of Kurdish Media Culture*, 66.

15. Kedourie, *Nationalism*; Hobsbawm, *Nations and Nationalism since 1780*.

16. Seyid Tahirê Botî, 'Ji bo Cerîdeya Kurdistanê' [To Kurdistan Newspaper], *Kurdistan*, No. 5, June 17, 1898.

17. Lütfî Fikrî, 'Kürt Milliyeti' [Kurdish Nation], *Rojî Kurd*, No. 4, September 12, 1913.

18. Hastings, *The Construction of Nationhood Ethnicity*, 31.

19. The so-called "Peace Process" aka "Kurdish Opening," "Democratic Opening," and "National Unity and Fraternity Project," was a state initiative launched in 2009 to ostensibly improve democratic standards in Turkey and solve the Kurdish problem.

20. http://www.milliyet.com.tr/Siyaset/HaberDetay.aspx?aType=HaberDetay &Kategori=siyaset&KategoriID=&ArticleID=992160&Date=17.09.2008&b=Turk :Turkiyelilik%20%20ust%20kimlik%20olsun

21. "I am not a neo-Ottoman," Davutoğlu says: http://www.todayszaman.com/ tz-web/news-193944-i-am-not-a-neo-ottoman-davutoglu-says.html. However, ironically, the Turkish National Education Council decided, on December 5, 2014, to make the instruction of Ottoman Turkish compulsory in high schools, in line with the state's overall new-Ottomanist policies, *see*: Why Turkey's president wants to revive the language of the Ottoman Empire http://www.washingtonpost.com/blogs/worl dviews/wp/2014/12/12/why-turkeys-president-wants-to-revive-the-language-of-the-o ttoman-empire/ see also: Ottoman language classes to be introduced "whatever they say," vows Erdoğan: http://www.hurriyetdailynews.com/ottoman-language-classes -to-be-introduced-whatever-they-say-vows-erdogan.aspx?pageID=238&nID=75329 &NewsCatID=338.

22. Anderson, *Imagined Communities*, 134.

23. Miscevic, Nenad. "Philosophy and Nationalism," in *Nations and Nationalism: A Global Historical Overview*, edited by Guntram. Henrik Herb and David. H. Kaplan, Vol. 1. (California: ABC-CLIO, Inc, 2008), 85–98, 91.

24. Catalonian Cultural Committee 1924, cited in Fishman, *Language and Nationalism*, 46.

25. Billig, *Banal Nationalism*, 10.

Bibliography

Akçam, Taner. *From Empire to the Republic: Turkish Nationalism and the Armenian Genocide*. London: Zed Books, 2004.

Akçura, Yusuf. *'Üç Tarzi Siyaset'* [Three Kinds of Policy]. Ankara: Turk Tarih Kurumu Basımevi, 1904[1976]. Accessed May 25, 2012. http://aton.ttu.edu/pdf/U c_Tarzi_Siyaset.pdf.

Akhmajian, Adrian, Demers, Richard A., Farmer, Ann K., and Harnish, Robert M. *Linguistics: An Introduction to Language and Communication*. Massachusetts: MIT Press, 1995.

Akşin, Sina. *Turkey from Empire to Revolutionary Republic: The Emergence of Turkish Nation from 1789 to Present*. London: Hurts & Company, 2007.

Alles, Elisabeth. "Minority Nationalities in China: Internal Orientalism," in *After Orientalism*, edited by François Pouillon and Jean-Claude Vatin, 134–141. Laden: Brill, 2014.

Allison, Christine. "Old and New Oral Traditions in Badinan," in *Kurdish Culture and Identity*, edited by Philip Kreyenbroek and Christine Allison, 29–47. London: Zed Book Ltd., 1996.

———. "Yezidis," in *Encyclopaedia Iranica*, online edition, New York, 1996. Accessed June 28, 2010. http://www.iranicaonline.org/articles/yazidis-i-general-1.

———. *The Yezidi Oral Tradition in Iraqi Kurdistan*. Richmond: Curzon Press, 2001.

———. "From Benedict Anderson to Mustafa Kemal: Reading, Writing and Imagining the Kurdish Nation," in *Joyce Blau: l'eternelle chez les Kurdes*, edited by Hamit Bozarslan, Clemence Scalbert-Yucel, 101–134. Paris: Karthala, 2013.

Anderson, Benedict. *Imagined Communities: Reflections on the Origins and Spread of Nationalism*. London: Verso, 2006.

Ang, Ien. *Desperately Seeking the Audience*. London: Routledge, 1991.

Azarian, Reza. "Nationalism in Turkey: Response to a Historical Necessity," *International Journal of Humanities and Social Science*, Vol. 1, No. 12, (September 2011): 72–82.

Bajalan, Djene Rhys. "Kurds for the Empire 'The Young Kurds' 1898–1914," MA thesis, Istanbul Bilgi University, 2009.

———. *Jön Kürtler: Birinci Dünya Savaşı'ndan Önce Kürt Hareketi (1898–1914)* [Young Kurds: Kurdish Movement before World War I (1898–1914)]. Istanbul: Avesta Yayınları 2010.

———. "Kurdish Responses to Imperial Decline: The Kurdish Movement and the End of Ottoman Rule in the Balkans 1878–1913," *Kurdish Studies*, Vol. 7, No. 1, (2019): 51–71.

Baker, Paul. *Using Corpora in Discourse Analysis*. London: Continuum, 2007.

Barber, Karin. *The Anthropology of Texts, Persons and Publics*. Cambridge: Cambridge University Press, 2007.

Bayir, Derya. *Minorities and Nationalism in Turkish Law*. Farnham: Ashgate Publishing Company, 2013.

Bazerman, Charles. "Intertextuality: How Texts Rely on Other Texts," in *What Writing Does and How It Does It: An Introduction to Analysing Texts and Textual Practices*, edited by Charles Bazerman and Paul Prior, 83–86. New York: LEA, 2004.

Bedir Khan, Celadet. Ali. *Günlük Notlar 1922–1925* [Diary 1922–1925]. Edited by Malmîsanij. Istanbul: Avesta, 1997.

Benwell, Bethan, and Stokoe, Elizabeth. *Discourse and Identity*. Edinburg: Edinburg University Press, 2006.

Bhabha, Homi. "Of Mimicry and Man: The Ambivalence of Colonial Discourse," *October*, Vol. 28, (Spring 1984): 125–133.

Billig, Michael. *Banal Nationalism*. London: Sage Publications, 1995.

———. "Discursive, Rhetorical and Ideological Message," in *Discourse Theory and Practice: A Reader*, edited by Margaret Wetherell, Stephanie Taylor, and Simeon J. Yates, 211–221. London: Sage Publications, 2002.

Binark, Ismet and Eren, Halit. *World Bibliography of Translations of the Meanings of the Holy Qur'an: Printed Translations, 1515–1980*. Istanbul: Research Centre for Islamic History, Art, and Culture, 1986.

Blau, Joyce. "Kurdish Written Literature," in *Kurdish Culture and Identity*, edited by Philip Kreyenbroek and Christine Allison, 20–28. London: Zed Book Ltd, 1996.

Bozarslan, Hamid. "Kürd Milliyetçiliği ve Kürd Hareketi (1898–2000)/Kurdish Nationalism and Kurdish Movement," in *Milliyetçilik*, edited by Tanıl Bora. *Modern Türkiye'de Siyasi Düşünce*, 841–870. Istanbul: İletişim Yayınevi, 2002.

Bozarslan, M. Emin. *Jîn - Kovara Kurdî-Tirkî* [Life Kurdish-Turkish Journal]: 1918–1919. Uppsala: Weşanxana Deng, 1985.

———. *Kurdistan (1898–1902)*. Uppsala: Weşanxana Deng, 1991.

———. *Kürd Teavün ve Terakkî Gazetesi* [The Kurdish Gazette for Mutual Aid and Progress] (1908–1909). Uppsala: Weşanxana Deng, 1998.

Brass, Paul R. "Elite Groups, Symbol Manipulation and Ethnic Identity among the Muslim of South Asia," in *Political Identity in South Asia*, edited by David Taylor and Malcolm Yapp, 35–68. London: Curzon Press, 1979.

Brennan, Timothy. "The National Longing for Form," in *Nation and Narration*, edited by Homi K. Bhabha. Translated by Martin Thom, 44–71, London: Routledge, 1990.

Breuilly, John. *Nationalism and the State*, (2nd ed.). Chicago: The University of Chicago Press, 1993.

———. "Reflections on Nationalism," in *Nationalism in Europe: From 1815 to the Present*, edited by Stuart Woolf, 137–154. London: Routledge, 1996.

Brubaker, Rogers. *Nationalism Reframed: Nationhood and the National Question in the New Europe*. Cambridge: Cambridge University Press, 1996.

———. "Religion and Nationalism: Four Approaches," *Nations and Nationalism*, Vol. 18, No. 1, (November 2012): 2–20.

Calhoun, Craig. "Nationalism and Ethnicity," *Annual Review of Sociology*, Vol. 19, (August 1993): 211–239.

Celîl, Celîlê. *Kürt Aydınlanması* [The Kurdish Enlightenment]. Istanbul: Avesta Yayınları, 2000.

Cemilpaşa, Ekrem. *Muhtasar Hayatim* [A Brief Account of My Life]. Brussels: Kurdish Institute, 1989.

Chabod, Federico. "The Idea of Nation," in *Nationalism in Europe: From 1815 to the Present*, edited by Stuart Woolf, 124–136. London: Routledge, 1996.

Chatterjee, Partha. *The Nation and Its Fragments: Colonial and Postcolonial Histories*. New Jersey: Princeton University Press, 1993.

Chyet, Michael L. "And a Thornbush Sprang up between them: Studies on Mem û Zîn, a Kurdish Romance," PhD diss., University of California, Berkeley, 1991.

———. "Foreword," in *Nationalism and Language in Kurdistan 1918–1985*, edited by Amir Hassanpour, xix–xxi. San Francisco: Mellon Press, 1992.

Deringil, Selim. "They Live in a State of Nomadism and Savagery," *Comparative Studies in Society and History*, Vol. 45, No. 2, (April 2003): 311–342.

Dersimi, Nuri. *Hatıratım* [My Memoire]. Ankara: Öz-Ge Yayınları, 1992.

Duman, Gülseren. "The Formation of the Kurdish Movement(s) 1908–1914: Exploring the Footprints of Kurdish Nationalism," Master's Thesis, Istanbul: Boğaziçi University, 2010.

Ekici, Deniz. *Kurmanji Kurdish Reader*. Maryland: Dunwoody Press, 2007.

Enloe, Cynthia. *Bananas, Beaches, and Bases: Making Feminist Sense of International Politics*. Berkeley: University of California Press, 1990.

Fairclough, Norman. *Language and Power*. London & New York: Longman, 1989.

———. *Discourse and Social Change*. Cambridge: Polity Press, 1992.

———. *Critical Discourse Analysis: The Critical Study of Language*. London: Longman, 1995.

———. *Media Discourse*. London: Hodder Education, 1995.

Fatani, Afnan H. "Translation and the Qur'an," in *The Qur'an: an encyclopaedia*, edited by Oliver Leaman, 657–669. London: Routledge, 2006.

Firro, Kais. M. *Metamorphosis of the Nation (al-Umma): The Rise of Arabism and Minorities in Syria and Lebanon, 1850–1940*. Eastbourne: Sussex Academic Press, 2009.

Fishman, Joshua. *Language and Nationalism*. Massachusetts: Newbury House Publishers, Inc., 1972.

Foucault, Michael. "Nietzsche, Genealogy, History," in *Language, Counter-Memory, Practice: Selected Essays and Interviews by Michael Foucault*, edited by Donald

F. Bouchard, 139–164. Translated by Donald F. Bouchard and Sherry Simon. New York: Cornell University Press, 1977.

———. *Archaeology of Knowledge and the Discourse on Language.* Translated by A. M. Sheridan Smith. London: Routledge, 2002.

Fowler, Roger. *Language in the News: Discourse and Ideology in the Press.* London & New York: Routledge, 1991.

Fowler, Roger, Hodge, Robert, Kress, Gunther, and Trew, Tony. *Language and Control.* London: Routledge & Kegan Paul, 1979.

Fuad, Kamal. *Kurdistan (1898–1902).* Tehran: Bedirxan, 2006.

Gellner, Ernest. *Nations and Nationalism.* London: Weidenfeld & Nicolson, 1994.

———. *Nationalism.* London: Weidenfeld & Nicolson, 1997.

Gelvin, James L. *The Modern Middle East: A History.* New York: Oxford University Press, 2005.

Ghaderi, Farangis. "The Challenges of Writing Kurdish Literary History: Representation, Classification, Periodization," *Kurdish Studies,* Vol. 3, No. 1, (January 2015): 3–25.

Göçek, Fatma Müge. *Rise of Bourgeoisie, Demise of Empire: Ottoman Westernization and Social Change.* New York: Oxford University Press, 1996.

Habermas, Jürgen. *The Structural Transformation of Public Sphere: An Inquiry into a Category of Bourgeois Society.* Translated by T. F. Lawrence. Cambridge: MIT Press, 1989.

Haig, Geoffrey and Opengin, Ergin. "Introduction to Special Issue-Kurdish: A Critical Research Overview," *Kurdish Studies,* Vol. 2, No. 2, (October 2014): 99–122.

Halbwachs, Maurice. *On Collective Memory.* Translated by Lewis A. Coser. Chicago: University of Chicago Press, 1992.

Hall, Stuart and Held, David. "Citizens and Citizenship," in *New Times: The Changing Face of Politics in the 1990s,* edited by Stuart Hall and Martin Jacques, 173–188. London: Lawrence and Wishart, 1989.

Halliday, Michael Alexander Kirkwood. *An Introduction to Functional Grammar.* London: Edward Arnold, 1985.

———. *Spoken and Written Language.* Oxford: Oxford University Press, 1985.

Hanes, Philip J. *The Advantages and Limitations of a Focus on Audience in Media Studies.* Cambridge: MIT Press, 2000.

Hanioğlu, M. Şükrü. *Bir Siyasal Düşünür Olarak Doktor Abdullah Cevdet ve Dönemi* [A Political Thinker Doctor Abdullah Cevdet and His Era]. Istanbul: Üçdal Neşriyat, 1981.

———. *Bir Siyasi Örgüt Olarak Osmanlı İttihad ve Terakki Cemiyeti ve Jön Türklük 1889–1902* [Ottoman Committee of Union and Progress and the Concept of Young Turks as a Political Organization 1889–1902], Vol. 1. Istanbul: İletişm Yayınları, 1989.

———. *The Young Turks in Opposition.* New York: Oxford University Press, 1995.

———. "Turkism and the Young Turks, 1889–1908," in *Turkey Beyond Nationalism: Towards Post-Nationalist Identities,* edited by Hans Lukas Keiser, 3–19. London & New York: I.B. Tauris, 2006.

Harris, Nigel. *National Liberation.* London: I.B. Tauris, 1990.

Hassanpour, Amir. *Nationalism and Language in Kurdistan*. San Francisco: Mellon Press, 1992.

———. The Kurdish Experience, *Middle East Report*, No. 189, (July/August 1994) 2–7+23.

———. "The Creation of Kurdish Media Culture," in *Kurdish Culture and Identity*, edited by Philip Kreyenbroek and Christine Allison, 48–84. London: Zed Book Ltd., 1996.

———. "The Making of Kurdish Identity: Pre-20th Century Historical and Literary Sources," in *Essays on the Origins of Kurdish Nationalism*, edited by Abbas Vali, 107–162. California: Mazda Publishers Inc., 2003.

Hastings, Adrian. *The Construction of Nationhood Ethnicity, Religion and Nationalism*. Cambridge: Cambridge University Press, 1997.

Hayes, Carlton J. H. *Essays on Nationalism*. New York: Russell, 1966.

Hobsbawm, Eric John. "Introduction: Inventing Traditions," in *The Invention of Tradition*, edited by Eric John Hobsbawm and Terence Ranger, 1–14. Cambridge: Cambridge University Press, 1983.

———. *Nations and Nationalism since 1780: Programme, Myth, Reality*, (2nd ed.). Cambridge: Cambridge University Press, 1992.

Hodge, Robert and Kress, Gunter. *Social Semiotics*. New York: Cornell University Press, 1988.

Hourani, Albert. "How Should We Write the History of the Middle East," *International Journal of Middle Eastern Studies*, Vol. 23, (1991): 125–136.

Hudson, Michael. C. *Arab Politics: The Search for Legitimacy*. New Haven: Yale University Press, 1977.

Jabar, Faleh A. "Arab Nationalism Versus Kurdish Nationalism: Reflections on Structural Parallels and Discontinuities," in *The Kurds Nationalism and Politics*, edited by Faleh A. Jabar and Hosham Dawod, 277–306. London: Saqi, 2006.

Jwaideh, Wadie. *The Kurdish National Movement: Its Origins and Development*. New York: Syracuse University Press, 2006.

Karababa, Eminegül and Ger, Güliz. "Early Modern Ottoman Coffeehouse Culture and the Formation of the Consumer Subject," *Journal of Consumer Research*, Vol. 37, No. 5, (February 2011): 737–760.

Kedourie, Elie. *Nationalism*, (4th ed.). Oxford: Blackwell, 1994.

Kemper, Steven. *The Presence of the Past: Chronicles, Politics, and Culture in Sinhala Life*. Ithaca: Cornell UP, 1991.

Kendal. "The Kurds under the Ottoman Empire," in *A People without A Country: The Kurds & Kurdistan*, edited by Gerard Chailand, 11–13. London: Zed, 1980.

Kevorkian, Raymond. *The Armenian Genocide: A Complete History*. New York: I.B. Tauris, 2011.

Khalidi, Rashid. *Palestinian Identity: The Construction of Modern National Consciousness*. New York: Columbia University Press, 1997.

Khani, Ahmad. *Mem û Zîn*. Edited by Mehmet Emin Bozarslan. Uppsala: Weşanxana Deng, 2005.

Khoury, Philips. *Urban Notables and Arab Nationalism: The Politics of Damascus 1880–1920*. New York: Cambridge University Press, 1983.

Klancher, Jon P. *The Making of English Reading Audiences, 1790–1832*. Madison: University of Wisconsin Press, 1987.

Klein, Janet. "Claiming the Nation: The Origins and Nature of Kurdish Nationalist Discourse, A Study of the Kurdish Press in the Ottoman Empire," Master's thesis, Princeton University, 1996.

———. *Power in the Periphery: The Hamidiye Light Cavalry and the Struggle over Ottoman Kurdistan, 1890–1914*. New Jersey: Princeton University, 2002.

———. "Kurdish Nationalists and Non-nationalist Kurds: Rethinking Minority Nationalism and the Dissolution of the Ottoman Empire, 1908–1909," *Journal of the Association for the Study of Ethnicity and Nationalism*, Vol. 13, No. 1, (January 2007): 135–153.

———. *The Margins of Empire: Kurdish Militias in the Ottoman Tribal Zone*. California: Stanford University Press, 2011.

Kloss, Heinz. "Abstand Languages and Ausbau Languages," *Anthropological Linguistic*, Vol. No. 7, (October 1967): 29–41.

Koma Xebatên Kurdolojiyê [Kurdology Study Group]. *Di Sedsaliya Wê De Rojî Kurd 1913* [Rojî Kurd (Kurdish Sun) on Its 100th Anniversary 1913]. Istanbul: Istanbul Kurdish Institute Publication, 2013.

Koyî, Haji Qadir. *Dîwanî Hacî Qadirî Koyî* [Collected Poems of Haji Qadir Koyî]. Edited by Sardar H. Mîran and Karim M. Şareza. Stockholm: Nefel, 2004. http://www.pertwk.com/pdf/haciqadikoye.pdf.

Kress, Gunther. "From Saussure to Critical Sociolinguistics: The Turn Towards a Social View of Language," in *Discourse Theory and Practice: A Reader*, edited by Margaret Wetherell, Stephanie Taylor and Simeon J. Yates, 29–39. London: Sage Publications, 2002.

Kress, Gunther and van Leeuwen, Theo. *Multimodal Discourse: The Modes and Media of Contemporary Communication*. London: Edward Arnold, 2001.

Kreyenbroek, Philip. "Religion and Religions in Kurdistan," in *Kurdish Culture and Identity*, edited by Philip Kreyenbroek and Christine Allison, 85–110. London: Zed Book Ltd., 1996.

Kreyenbroek, Philip and Allison, Christine. "Introduction," in *Kurdish Culture and Identity*, edited by Philip Kreyenbroek and Christine Allison, 1–6, London: Zed Book Ltd., 1996.

Kristeva, Julia. *Strangers to Ourselves*. Translated by Leon S. Roudiez. New York: Columbia University Press, 1991.

Kutlay, Naci. *21. Yüzyıla Girerken Kürtler* [Kurds on the Eve of the 21st Century]. Istanbul: Pêrî Yayınları, 2002.

Lapidus, Ira M. "Between Universalism and Particularism: The Historical Bases of Muslim Communal, National, and Global Identities," *Global Networks*, Vol. 1, No. 1, (December 2001): 37–55.

Lewis, Bernard. *The Emergence of Modern Turkey*, (2nd ed.). New York: Oxford University Press, 1968.

Makdisi, Ussama. "Ottoman Orientalism," *The American Historical Review*, Vol. 107, No. 3, (June 2002): 768–796.

Malmîsanij, Memehed. *Yüzyılımızın Başlarında Kürt Milliyetçiliği ve Abdullah Cevdet* [Kurdish Nationalism and Dr. Abdullah Cevdet at the Turn of the Century]. Uppsala: Jîna Nû Yayınları, 1986.

———. *Kürd Teavün ve Terakkî Cemiyeti ve Gazetesi* [The Kurdish Society and Gazette for Mutual Aid and Progress]. Istanbul: Avesta Yayınları, 1999.

———. *Cizira Botanlı Bedirhaniler* [The Bedirkhans' of Jazira Botan]. Istanbul: Avesta, 2000.

———. *Kürt Talebe-Hêvî Cemiyeti* [The Kurdish Student Hope Society]. Istanbul: Avesta Yayınları, 2002.

———. *Diyarbekirli Cemilpaşazadeler ve Kürt Milliyetçiliği* [Cemilpaşazades of Diyarbekir and Kurdish Nationalism]. Istanbul: Avestam 2004.

———. *İlk Kürt Gazetesi Kurdistan'ı Yayımlayan Abdurrahman Bedirhan: 1868–1936* [Abdurrahman Bedir Khan, the Publisher of the First Kurdish Journal Kurdistan: 1868–1936]. Istanbul: Vate Yayın Dağıtım, 2009.

Malmîsanij, Mehemed and Lewendî, Mahmud. *Li Kurdistana Bakur û Tirkiyê Rojnamegeriya Kurdî (1908–1992)* [Kurdish Journalism in Northern Kurdistan and Turkey (1908–1992)], (2nd ed.). Ankara: Özge, 1992.

Mardin, Şerif. *The Genesis of Young Ottoman Thought*. New York: Syracuse University Press, 2000.

———. *Religion, Society and Modernity in Turkey*. New York: Syracuse University Press, 2006.

McLuhan, Marshall. *Understanding Media: The Extensions of Man*. New York: Mentor Books, 1964.

Meyrowitz, Joshua. "Shifting Worlds of Strangers: Medium Theory and Changes in 'Them' versus 'Us'," *Sociological Inquiry*, Vol. 67, No. 1, (January 1997): 59–71.

Minassian, Gaidz F. and Avagyan, Arsen. *Ermeniler ve Ittihat ve Terakki: Işbirliğinden Çatışmaya* [Armenians and the Union and Progress: From Collaboration to Conflict]. Istanbul: Aras Yayınları, 2005.

Miscevic, Nenad. "Philosophy and Nationalism," in *Nations and Nationalism: A Global Historical Overview*, edited by Guntram. Henrik Herb and David. H. Kaplan, 85–98, Vol. 1. California: ABC-CLIO, Inc, 2008.

Mojab, Shahrzad. "Women and Nationalism in the Kurdish Republic of 1946," in *Women of a Non-State Nation: The Kurds*, edited by Shahrzad Mojab, 71–91. California: Mazda Publishers, Inc., 2001.

Muljačić, Zarko. "Standardization in Romance," in *Trends in Romance Linguistics and Philology*, edited by Rebecca Posner et al., 77–116. Berlin: Walter de Gruyter, 1993.

Najmabadi, Afsaneh. *Women with Mustaches and Men Without Beards: Gender and Sexual Anxieties of Iranian Modernity*. California: University of California Press, 2005.

Nezan, Kendal. "The Current Position and Historical Background," in *Kurdish Culture and Identity*, edited by Philip Kreyenbroek and Christine Allison, 7–19. London: Zed Book Ltd., 1996.

O'Shea, Maria T. *Trapped Between the Map and Reality: Geography and Perception of Kurdistan*. New York: Routledge, 2004.

Olson, Robert. *The Emergence of Kurdish Nationalism and Sheikh Said Rebellion, 1880–1925.* Austin: University of Texas Press, 1989.

Opengin, Ergin. "Tevatür ve Temellük Kıskacında Kürt Kültür Tarihçiliği [Kurdish Cultural Historiography Caught between Hearsay and Appropriation]," *Kürt Tarihi Dergisi* [Journal of Kurdish History], No. 11, (February/March 2014): 17–29.

Özoğlu, Hakan. "Nationalism and Kurdish Notables in the Late Ottoman-Early Republican Era," *International Journal of Middle East Studies*, Vol. 33, (February 2001): 383–409.

————. *Kurdish Notables and the Ottoman State: Evolving Identities, Competing Loyalties, and Shifting Boundaries.* Albany: State University of New York Press, 2004.

Penrose, Jan. "Nations, States and Homelands: Territory and Territoriality in Nationalist Thought," *Nations and Nationalism*, Vol. 8, No. 3, (January 2002): 277–297.

Razi, G. Hossein. "Legitimacy, Religion, and Nationalism in the Middle East," *The American Political Science Review*, Vol. 84, No. 1, (March 1990): 69–91.

Renan, Ernest. "What is a Nation?" in *Nation and Narration*, edited by Homi Bhabha. Translated by Martin Thom, 8–22. London: Routledge, 1990.

Sadoğlu, Hüseyin. *Türkiye'de Ulusçuluk ve Dil Politikaları* [Nationalism and Language Policies in Turkey]. Istanbul: Istanbul Bilgi Üniversitesi Yayınları, 2003.

Şengül Birgül Açıkyıldız. "Ezidîlik Dininde Melek Tavus İnancı ve İkonografisi [The Belief and Iconography of the Peacock Angel in Yezidi Religion]," *Kürt Tarihi Dergisi* [Journal of Kurdish History], No. 5, (October 2014): 7–17.

Seton-Watson, Hugh. *Nations and States: An Inquiry into the Origins of Nations and the Politics of Nationalism.* London: Methuen & Co. Ltd., 1977.

Seton-Watson, Robert William. *The Rise of Nationality in the Balkans.* New York: E. P. Dutton and Company, 1918. Accessed January 6, 2011. http://www.promacedonia.org/en/pdf/setton-watson_the_rise_of_nationality_in_the_balkans_1918.pdf.

Sheyholislami, Jaffer. *Kurdish Identity, Discourse, and New Media.* New York: Palgrave, 2011.

Shryock, Andrew. *Nationalism and the Genealogical Imagination: Oral History and Textual Authority in Tribal Jordan.* Los Angeles: University of California Press, 1997.

Silopî, Zinar. *Doza Kurdistan: Kürt Milletinin 60 Seneden Beri Esaretten Kurtuluş Savaşı* [The Kurdish Cause: Sixty Years of Kurdish Nation's War of Liberation from Bondage]. Diyarbekir: Weşanên Bîr, 2007.

Smith, Anthony. D. *The Ethnic Revival in the Modern World.* Cambridge: Cambridge University Press, 1981.

————. *Nationalism: Theory, Ideology, History.* Cambridge & Malden: Polity Press, 2003.

Soleimani, Kamal. *Islam and Competing Nationalisms in the Middle East: 1876–1926.* New York: Palgrave, 2016.

Sönmez, Banu İşlet. *Ikinci Mesrutiyette Arnavut Muhalefeti* [The Albanian Opposition During the Second Constitutional Period]. Istanbul: YKY Yanyınları, 2007.

Stewart, Garrett. *Dear Reader: The Conscripted Audience in Nineteenth-Century British Fiction*. Maryland: John Hopkins University Pres, 1996.

Stewart, William A. "A Sociolinguistic Typology for Describing National Multilingualism," in *Readings in the Sociology of Language*, edited by Joshua A. Fishman, 531–545. The Hague: De Gruyter Mouton, 1968.

Strohmeier, Martin. *Crucial Images in the Presentation of a Kurdish National Identity: Heroes and Patriots, Traitors and Foes*. Laden: Brill, 2003.

Türesay, Özgür. "The Ottoman Empire Seen through the Lens of Postcolonial Studies: A Recent Historiographical Turn," *Revue d'historie modern et contemporaine*. Translated by Cadenza Academic Translation. No. 60–2, (2013/2): 127–145.

Tütengil, Cavit Orhan. *Yeni Osmanlılar'dan Bu Yana İngiltere'de Türk Gazeteciliği (1867–1967)* [Turkish Journalism in England since the New Ottomans (1867–1967)]. Istanbul: Belge Yayınları, 1969.

Üstel, Füsun. *İmparatorluktan ulus-devlete Türk milliyetçiliği: Türk Ocakları 1912–1931* [Turkish Nationalism from the Empire to the Nation-State: the Turkish Hearths 1912–1931]. Istanbul: İletişim, 1997.

Vali, Abbas. "Introduction: Nationalism and the Question of Origins," in *Essays on the Origins of Kurdish Nationalism*, edited by Abbas Vali, 1–13. California: Mazda Publishers, Inc., 2003.

van Bruinessen, Martin. *Agha, Shaikh and State: On the Social and Political Structure of Kurdistan*. London: Zed Books, 1992.

———. "Kurdish Society, Ethnicity, Nationalism and Refugee Problems," in *The Kurds: A Contemporary Overview*, edited by Philip Kreyenbroek and Stefan Sperl, 26–53. London: Routledge, 1992.

———. "Ehmedî Xanî's Mem û Zîn and Its Role in the Emergence of Kurdish National Awareness," in *Essays on the Origins of Kurdish Nationalism*, edited by Abbas Vali, 41–57. California: Mazda Publishers, Inc., 2003.

———. "Kurdish Paths to Natio," in *The Kurds: Nationalism and Politics*, edited by Falah A. Jabar and D. Hosham Dawood, 21–48. London: Saqi, 2006.

van der Veer, Peter. *Religious Nationalism: Hindus and Muslims in India*. California: University of California Press, 1994.

van Dijk, Teun A. "Principles of Critical Discourse Analysis," in *Discourse Theory and Practice: A Reader*, edited by Margaret Wetherell, Stephanie Taylor and Simeon J. Yates, 300–318. London: Sage Publications, 2002.

van Leeuwen, Theo (2005). "Multimodality, Genre and Design," in *Discourse in Action: Introducing Mediated Discourse Analysis*, edited by Sigrid Norris and Rodney H. Jones, 73–94. London: Routledge, 2005.

Whitmeyer, Joseph M. "Elites and Popular Nationalism," *British Journal of Sociology*, Vol. 53, No. 3, (December 2003): 321–341.

Wodak, Ruth. "What CDA is about—A Summary of Its History, Important Concepts and Its Development," in *Methods of Critical Discourse Analysis*, edited by Ruth Wodak and Michael Meyer, 1–13. London: Sage Publications, 2002.

———. "The Discourse-Historical Approach," in *Methods of Critical Discourse Analysis*, edited by Ruth Wodak and Michael Meyer, 63–94. London: Sage Publications, 2002.

Wodak, Ruth, de Cillia, Rudolf, Reisigl, Martin, and Liebhart, Karin. *The Discursive Construction of National Identity*. Translated by Angelica Hirsch & Richard Mitten. Edinburgh: Edinburgh University Press, 1999.

Zadeh, Travis. *The Vernacular Qur'an: Translation and the Rise of Persian Exegesis*. London: Oxford University Press, 2012.

Zeine, N. Zeine. *The Emergence of Arab Nationalism: With a Background Study of Arab-Turkish Relations in the Near East*, (2nd ed.). Beirut: Khayats, 1966.

Zeki Beg, Mihemed Emin. *Dîroka Kurd û Kurdistanê* [The History of Kurds and Kurdistan]. Istanbul: Weşanên Avesta, 2002.

Zürcher, Eric J. *Turkey: A Modern History*, (3rd ed.). London & New York: I.B. Tauris, 2004.

———. *The Ottoman Empire 1850–1922: Unavoidable Failure*, Turkology Update Leiden Project Working Papers Achieve (Department of Turkish Studies, Leiden University, 2004b. Accessed March 21, 2010. http://www.tulp.leidenuniv.nl/conte nt_docs/wap/ejz20.pdf.

———. *The Young Turk Legacy and Nation Building: From the Ottoman Empire to Ataturk's Turkey*. London: I.B. Tauris, 2010.

Index

About the Author

Deniz Ekici holds a PhD from the Institute of Arab and Islamic Studies, Center for Kurdish Studies at the University of Exeter and an MA degree in Political Science from Brooklyn College, CUNY. He is a former lecturer at UC Berkeley, University of Exeter, and Middle Tennessee State University, where he taught such courses as Introduction to the Middle East, Media in the Middle East, Nationalism in the Middle East, Kurdish Culture and Society, and Kurdish Language Courses. His research interests include cultural studies, sociolinguistics, and critical discourse analysis, media studies, applied linguistics, and second-language acquisition. He is the author of *Kurmanji-Kurdish Reader* and *Beginning Kurmanji Kurdish*.